AMERICAN SHOWCASE VOLUME3

A SYMBOL IS A PROMISE.

A symbol is a promise of pride in achievement. In the world of competitive sport. In the world of photography. And Canon's symbol is a promise that our commitment to photography is as strong as humanly attainable.

We're everywhere great images are happening. At the world's top events in championship sports. Because photographers at these events know they have to get the picture. And they need equipment that won't let them down.

Your professional reputation may not ride on the pictures you take. Yet, each is a once-in-a-lifetime creative opportunity. Give them your best shot, and put your trust in the Canon symbol. We won't let you down.

It's a promise.

Canon USA, Inc., 10 Nevada Drive, Lake Success, New York 11042 · 140 Industrial Drive, Elmhurst, Illinois 60126 · 7000 Peachtree Industrial Blvd., Suite 200, Norcross, Georgia 30071 · 123 Paularino Avenue East, Costa Mesa, California 92626 · Bldg. B-2, 1050 Ala Moana Blvd., Honolulu, Hawaii 96814 · Canon Optics & Business Machines Canada, Ltd., Ontario

AMERICAN SHOWCASE VOLUME 3

American Showcase offers art directors, graphic designers, editors and corporate decision makers a sweeping choice of top talent for assignment and also provides a treasure-trove of visual concepts. Over 1,800 of the best four-color images by 232 artists are tastefully presented on more than 250 pages, creating an invaluable resource for everyone interested in the communication arts.

"This new reference book and directory is so well conceived, designed and reproduced that simply to say, 'It's the best of its kind' is the only comment necessary."

Amil Gargano
President and Chief Executive Officer
Ally & Gargano, Inc.

American Showcase, Inc.
New York

Chairman and Co-Publisher: Tennyson Schad
President and Co-Publisher: Ira Shapiro
Manager of Production, Distribution,
and Advertising Sales: Fiona L'Estrange
Office Administration and
Book Sales Manager: Janet Vallochi
Conscience: Nora Lumley
Sales Representatives:
New York: Barbara Lee, Donna Levinstone
Los Angeles: Susan Peters, Grace Woodard
San Francisco: Barbara Davis

Book Design: Herb Lubalin and Michael Aron
Design Production: Jason Calfo
Herb Lubalin Associates, Inc. New York City

Typesetting: Pastore, DePamphilis, Rampone, Inc.
New York City

Color Separations, Printing, and Binding:
Dai Nippon Printing Co., Ltd.
Tokyo, Japan

U.S. and Canadian Book Trade Distribution:
Mayflower Books
575 Lexington Avenue
New York, New York 10022

American Showcase, Inc.
Suite 1929
30 Rockefeller Plaza
New York, New York 10020
(212) 245-0981

INTRODUCTION

Picture cavefuls of Neanderthals dragging around their provisions on a pair of logs long after the invention of the wheel. Old habits are hard to break.

OLD HABITS ARE HARD TO BREAK

More recently, the old habits syndrome compelled people to resist acceptance of the telephone, the horseless carriage, and for that matter, every other labor-saving innovation.

But cultural laggards do come around.

And so it is that in two brief years, thousands of art buyers in the United States and abroad have come around to AMERICAN SHOWCASE. When Volume 1 appeared, the laggards thought it was a beautiful paperweight. More perceptive creative people saw it as a new and useful resource. Upon Volume 2's arrival, some laggards even remembered our name. But for the people in touch, SHOWCASE was already an indispensable hot line to fresh ideas and talent.

Now you have Volume 3...

AMERICAN SHOWCASE was conceived with your needs and tastes in mind. We know that it's working. Art buyers like yourself made thousands of calls to the talent displayed in Volumes 1 and 2—to see portfolios or to hire at a distance. Many used SHOWCASE'S pictures to generate ideas or help crystallize concepts for clients. That was very gratifying.

But Volume 3 is even better. In addition to even more display pages by photographers, illustrators, and designers, we've added a TV/film and video section and over 1,500 phone listings of production companies. This was suggested by ad agency art directors doing print and TV who wanted quick entrée to both worlds. We thought that made sense.

You also may find valuable our extensive selection of photographers based outside of New York City.

Do you want talent that shoots on location for ads and annual reports in editorial style? Our breadth here is unmatched.

And if you need a graphic designer for an annual report or package creation, our design section and phone listings offer the largest published resource of this kind.

It's important for all of us that SHOWCASE be fully responsive to your needs, and there are two ways that you can be involved and influence our development. First, let us hear about your ideas and suggestions. Just tell us what you'd like to see in Volume 4 or future editions. Secondly, when you call talent in AMERICAN SHOWCASE, please don't be shy. Tell them AMERICAN SHOWCASE sent you. How else will they know that SHOWCASE is working for them and for you?

CONTENTS

STOCK PHOTOGRAPHY

VIEWPOINTS

AWARD-WINNING RADIO SCRIPTS

PHONE LISTINGS OF OVER 6,700 REPRESENTATIVES, PHOTOGRAPHERS, STOCK PHOTOGRAPHY SOURCES, ILLUSTRATORS, GRAPHIC DESIGNERS & TV, FILM AND VIDEO PRODUCTION COMPANIES

REPRESENTATIVES

NEW YORK METROPOLITAN AREA

Ken Abbey & Assoc.	212-758-5259
Abel, Ora	212-751-3282
American Artists/R. Mendelsohn Assoc.	212-682-2462
Andrews, Jim.	212-787-6396
Andrews, Margery E.	212-679-8554
Andriulli, Anthony.	212-682-1490
Anton, Jerry	212-679-4562
Arnold, Peter	212-840-6928
Artists Assoc.	212-755-1365
Arton Assoc.	212-661-0850
Backer, Vic.	212-535-9202
Badini, Andrew	212-734-4533
Bahm, Darwin M.	212-989-7074
Barclay, R. Francis	212-255-3440
Barkentin, George	212-532-2985
Basile, Ron	212-986-6710
Baumann, Barbara.	212-674-4535
Becker, Noel.	212-757-8987
Bell, Barbara J	212-265-4300
Berenis & Jones.	212-243-8843
Bernstein, Sam.	212-697-5252
Bishop, Lynn	212-254-5737
Blatt, Abby	212-924-7010
Blum, Felice S.	212-243-3942
Boghosian, Marty	212-371-4961
Booth, Tom.	212-243-2750
Boyle, Janet M.	212-475-0440
Brackman, Selma	212-777-4210
Brindle, Carolyn	212-249-8883
Broderick, William.	212-242-0930
Brody, Sam	212-758-0640
Brown, Doug	212-288-6630
Pema & Perry Browne Ltd.	212-369-1925
Bush, Nan.	212-751-0996
Cafiero, Charles	212-777-2616
Cahill, Joe	212-751-0529
Camera 5	212-989-2004
Carp, Stanley	212-759-8880
Caruso, Frank	212-260-7203
Charteris, Frances	212-679-1358
Chello, Renee	212-689-1982
Chettle, Kate	212-752-0273
Chevrette, Valerie	212-691-7950
Chie.	212-685-6854
Chislovsky, Carol.	212-758-2222
Clements, John	212-348-6806
Collins, Chuck.	212-765-8812
Collins, Patrick M..	212-688-3228
Crabb, Wendy	212-734-4391

Creed, George L.	212-260-0336
Daniels, Camille.	212-947-5065
Davies, Nora	212-840-2866
Davis, Barbara A.	212-242-4199
Denner, Ann.	212-684-5033
Deverin, Daniele	212-755-4945
DiBartolo, Joseph	212-254-6327
Di Martino, Joseph	212-935-9522
Doll, Mary Ann.	212-533-0719
Du Bane, Jean-Jacques	212-697-6860
Dubner, Logan.	212-533-2970
Dunley, Joyce	212-242-4283
Epstein, Ellen	212-889-2172
Erica	212-777-3232
Feder, Theodore H.	212-697-1136
Feld, Robin	212-249-7231
Feldon, Leah	212-725-1325
Ficalora, Michael	212-679-7700
Flah, Linda	212-472-2500
Flock & Lombardi Assoc. Ltd.	212-689-3902
Flood, Phyllis Rich	212-532-9247
Fonyo, Andrea	212-582-3284
Forsyth, Alfred	212-752-3930
Foster, Peter.	212-593-0793
Frattolillo, Rinaldo	212-486-1901
Fried, Robin.	212-564-9050
Furst, Franz	212-753-3148
Galler, Margot	212-989-9825
Jack Garten Representatives Inc..	212-787-8910
Gazebo Productions	212-489-7423
Gelb, Elizabeth	212-243-4539
Giordano, Maria	212-982-2700
Giraldi, Tina	212-840-8225
Goldman, Larry	212-246-3737
Goldstein, Michael L.	212-873-4634
Goldstein, Russell M.	212-986-1783
Goldstein, Suzanne.	212-758-3420
Goodman, Barbara L.	212-593-3723
Goodwin, Phyllis A.	212-753-2857
Gordon, Barbara	212-686-3514
Gordon, Elliott.	212-686-3514
Gould, Linda	212-684-2974
Gould, Stephen Jay	212-686-1690
Grayson, Jay	212-689-1468
Green, Anita	212-532-5083
Greenblatt, Eunice N.	212-628-3842
Grey, Barbara L.	212-851-0332
Grien, Anita	212-697-6170
Grinell, Kate	212-684-3084
Groves, Michael	212-532-2074
Grunell, Kate.	212-684-3084

Henry, John	212-686-6883
Hollyman, Audrey	212-867-2383
Holt, Rita.	212-777-3910
Hottelet, Mary	212-675-2727
Hovde, Nob & Laurence	212-753-0462
Jodell, Joan	212-861-7861
Johnson, Elizabeth S.	212-929-2224
Johnson, Evelyne	212-532-0928
Kahn, Harvey.	212-752-8490
Kammler, Fred.	212-249-4446
Barney Kane Inc..	212-355-1316
Keating, Peggy	212-691-4654
Kim	212-679-5628
Kimche, Tania	212-679-1358
Kirchoff-Wohlberg Inc..	212-753-5146
Klein, Ellen	212-243-0027
Klein, Leslie D.	212-832-7220
Klein, Linda.	212-873-0041
Kline, Linda	212-431-4178
Kleiner, Goldie	212-799-8050
Kochan, Joan S.	212-684-4058
Kopecky, Beth	212-929-7217
Kopel, Shelly	212-986-3282
Krausman, Robert.	212-686-1897
Kreis, Ursula G.	212-562-8931
Laiho, Irmeli	212-682-2462
Lammeck, Denys.	212-582-5572
Lane, Judy	212-861-7225
Jane Lander Assoc.	212-679-1358
Larkin, Mary	212-688-8884
Lavaty, Frank & Jeff	212-355-0910
Lawson, Robert	212-532-9050
Lee, Alan	212-861-1748
Leff, Jerry	212-697-8525
Leinberger, Cliff	212-473-4999
Lento, Julia	212-233-8989
Leonian, Edith.	212-989-7670
Lerman, Gary.	212-683-5777
Levinstone, Donna	212-348-9664
Lombardi, Benedetta	212-689-3902
Lucas, Yvonne.	212-677-5450
Luppi, Judith.	212-677-1910
Mace, Zelda	212-765-3889
Madris, Stephen	212-744-6668
Mandel, Bette	212-737-5062
Mann, Ken	212-245-3192
Mann, William Thompson	212-595-6260
Marino, Frank	212-563-2730
Marino, Louise	212-677-6310
Mariucci, Marie A.	212-594-4950
Martin, Bruce	212-679-1358

Mautner, Jane	212-777-9024
Melsky, Barney	212-532-3311
Melton, Mary L.	212-596-5663
Mendelsohn, Richard	212-682-2462
Mendola, Joseph	212-986-5680
Mercier, Lou.	212-972-1701
Mersel, Constance V.	212-787-4816
Messeroff, Claire.	212-255-8250
Messing, Patricia F.	212-724-1627
Michalski, Ben	212-683-4025
Miller, Marcia	212-682-2555
Milsop, Frances.	212-794-0922
Moretz, Eileen P.	212-254-3766
Morgan, Vicki	212-475-0440
Morrill, Dick.	212-421-5833
Mosel, Sue.	212-288-9204
Moskowitz, Marion	212-472-9474
Moubrie, Gabrielle	212-265-5301
Mullen, Ron M.	212-751-0529
Mulvey Assoc.	212-246-3660
Napolitano, John.	212-638-4690
Nayer, Jack.	212-989-6650
Neal, Peggy.	212-879-2681
Nelson, George L.	212-679-7538
Newborn, Milton	212-421-0050
Opticalusions	212-688-1080
Palevitz, Bob	212-684-6026
Pasqua, Dominique	212-661-0850
Patterson, Sylvia	212-675-2805
Penny, Barbara	212-867-4640
Photo Artists	212-246-3737
Photo Researchers	212-758-3420
Pollens, Linda	212-861-7745
Popper, Serge	212-682-1527
Quercia, Mat.	212-477-4491
Gerald & Cullen Rapp Inc.	212-751-4656
Ray, Marlys	212-222-7680
Kay Reese & Assoc.	212-924-5151
Remler, Gladys	212-244-4270
Renard, Marc	212-736-3266
Richards, Gary	212-691-7950
Riley, Ted	212-355-2763
Rivelli, Cynthia	212-254-0990
Rubin, Elaine R.	212-725-8313
Rosenberg, Arlene.	212-982-7376
Rothenberg, Judith A.	212-861-7745
Rubin, Mel.	212-582-0404
Rudoff, Stanley	212-679-8780
Russo, Karen.	212-143-6778
Sacramone, Dario D.	212-929-0487
Salomon, Allyn	212-684-5586

REPRESENTATIVES

Samuels, Rosemary S.	212-477-3567
Sander, Vicki	212-674-8161
Saunders, Marvin	212-661-4710
Saunders, Michele	212-580-3845
Scanlon, Henry R.	212-989-0500
Scerra, Peter	212-490-1610
Schickler, Paul	212-355-1044
Schifrin, Joan I.	212-686-0907
Schneider, Amy B.	212-490-0673
Schoenfein, Sandy	212-628-2404
Schon, Herb	212-249-3236
Schub, Peter & Robert Bear	212-246-0679
Shamilzadeh, Sol	212-532-1977
Shepherd, Judith	212-838-3214
Shostal Assoc.	212-687-0696
Sigal, Barry	212-684-3416
Silver, Susan	212-674-1151
Sims, Jennifer	212-722-6043
Slesinger, Simon	212-475-2916
Smith, James Forrest	212-674-5566
Snow, Civia	212-674-0259
Sokolsky, Stanley	212-686-5000
Stermer, Carol Lee	212-686-2770
Stiefel, Frank	212-879-6200
Stockland, Bill	212-242-7693
Stogo & Bernstein Assoc. Inc.	212-697-5252
Stogo, Bernstein & Andriulli	212-682-1490
Studer, Lillian	212-683-2082
Sun, Edward	212-674-7288
Susse, Ed	212-472-0674
Tannenbaum, Dennis	212-279-2838
Terrero, Robert	212-881-7146
Tyson, David	212-686-0761
Umlas, Barbara	212-249-4555
Valdetaire, Anne	212-685-5753
Van Arnam, Lewis	212-541-4787
Walker, Eleanora	212-752-6132
Wasserman, Ted	212-867-5360
Wayne, Tony	212-757-5398
Wein, Gita	212-759-2763
Witt, John	212-679-8620
Wohlberg, Helen	212-688-9366
Woodfin Camp & Assoc.	212-355-1855
Yellin, Bert Assocs.	212-889-4701
York, Jim	212-688-7232
Youngs, Maralee	212-679-8124
Zanetti, Lucy	212-473-4999
Zarember, Sam	212-765-8928

NORTHEAST & SOUTHEAST

Alter, Don G./Warren VT	902-496-3574
Amos, Lisa	914-762-5335
Bancroft, Carol/Weston CT	203-226-7674
Benke, Jill/Boston	617-542-4825
Ben Bonart & Assoc. Inc./Wash. DC	202-965-2218
Bloch, Peggy J/Cliffside Park NJ	201-943-9435
Chandoha, Sam/Annandale NJ	201-782-3666
Creative Services/Atlanta	404-262-7424
Darrow, Whitney/Westport CT	203-227-7806
First National Productions/New Orleans	504-897-1592
Grace, Dede/Weston CT	203-226-7674
Groskinsky, Alma/Port Washington NY	516-883-3294
Guerlain-Talbot, Babette/Avon CT	203-753-9242
Hall, Shari /Wash DC	202-244-7823
Holloway, Tom /Port Washington NY	516-883-3408
Hubbell, Marian /Bedford Hills NY	914-666-5792
Jackson, Kate /Boston	617-536-6600
Kenny, Ella/Boston	617-426-3565
Kocher, John E./Montville NJ	212-489-7744
Landsman, Gary/Wash. DC	202-223-1590
Lensman Photo Ltd./Wash. DC	202-333-3850
Mariucci, Marie/Marlboro NJ	201-594-4950
McNamara, Paul B./Wethersfield CT	203-563-6159
Murphy, Michael/Pittsburgh	412-261-2022
Nichols, Eva/Rochester NY	716-275-9666
Nordlum, Karen/Weston CT	203-226-7674
Olive, Bobbi/Atlanta	404-872-0500
Pastore, J. Daniel/Southport CT	203-255-2487
Savadow, Rick/Baltimore	301-685-5423
Taylor, Cory/Baltimore	301-385-1716
Taylor, John/Hopewell NJ	609-466-3151
Valen Assoc./Westport CT	203-227-7806
Watson, Sharon/Philadelphia	215-546-8355
Woodfin Camp Inc./Wash. DC	202-466-3830

MIDWEST

Aiko/Chicago	312-869-7081
Asad, Susan/Chicago	312-266-7540
Ashley, Susan/Chicago	312-348-5393
Ball, John/Chicago	312-332-6041
Berk, Ida/Chicago	312-944-1339
Bernsten, Jim/Chicago	312-822-0560
Bowman, Ann/Chicago	312-337-5664
Brawar, Wendy/Chicago	312-266-1606
Brenner, Harriett/Chicago	312-751-1470
Burch, Ralph/Chicago	312-751-2977
Chambers, Ron/Chicago	312-642-8715
Christell, Jim/Chicago	312-236-2396
Claussen, Bo/Chicago	312-871-1242
Crawford, Cathy/Chicago	312-787-2915
DeGrado, James/Chicago	312-663-9778
Dorman, Paul/Detroit	313-645-2222
Draheim, Jim/Chicago	312-828-9216
Drewel, Judie/St. Louis	314-533-6665
DuBiel, Karen/Chicago	312-266-8559
Dwyer, Debbie/Chicago	312-644-5233
Eakin, Dana/Chicago	312-782-2703
Engh, Rohn/Osceola WI	715-248-3800
Erdos, Kitty/Chicago	312-787-4976
Ferreri, Rosemary/Chicago	312-644-3187
Hammond, Pamela/Chicago	312-726-5678
Harlib, Joel/Chicago	312-329-1370
Harwood, Tim/Chicago	312-828-9117
Myrna Hogan & Assoc./Chicago	312-372-1616
Howze, Walter/Chicago	312-332-5700
Johnson, Ginger Todd/Chicago	312-772-2292
Kamin, Vince/Chicago	312-787-8834
Kapes, Jack/Chicago	312-664-8282
Kelly, Nick/Chicago	312-280-8212
Kezelis, Elena/Chicago	312-644-7108
Kulfan, Cynthia/Chicago	312-944-5680
Lasko, Pat/Chicago	312-787-1316
McMasters, Deborah/Chicago	312-467-4770
McNaughton, Toni/Chicago	312-929-2505
Miles, Thomas/Minneapolis	612-871-0333
Miller, Richard/Chicago	312-271-6644
Moore, Connie/Chicago	312-787-4422
Moravick, Don/Chicago	312-664-9012
Mosier-Maloney/Chicago	312-943-1668
O'Brien, Jim/Chicago	312-856-0007
O'Brien/DeSantiago/Chicago	312-856-0300
Parker, Tom/Chicago	312-266-2891
Potts, Carolyn/Chicago	312-935-1707
Pride, Max/Chicago	312-337-2138
Pulver, Owen/Chicago	312-332-5325
Putnam, Barbara/Chicago	312-266-8352
Quick, Sue/Chicago	312-644-7557
Rabin, Bill/Chicago	312-944-6655
Schuck, John/Minneapolis	612-338-7829
Schwartz/McCarthy/Chicago	312-236-4135
Sell, Dan/Chicago	312-332-5168
Sharrard, Chuck/Chicago	312-642-8715
Skillicorn, Roy/Chicago	312-787-9408
Thiele, Elizabeth/Chicago	312-944-4477
Clay Timon & Assoc./Chicago	312-641-0934
Tracy, Cathleen/Chicago	312-944-7070
Tuke, Joni/Chicago	312-664-4235
West, Karen/Chicago	312-664-5954
Wilde, Nancy/Chicago	312-528-7711
Witmer, Bob/Chicago	312-642-0242
Wood, Chuck/Chicago	312-944-7070
Zimmerman, Amy/Chicago	312-642-4426

SOUTHWEST & WEST

Aline, France/LA	213-550-4572
Antonioli, Gina/LA	213-930-1144
Azzara, Marilyn/LA	213-876-2551
Barton, Stephanie/Dallas	214-647-4133
Bennett, Dianne/LA	213-388-3142
Bishop, Michael/Inglewood CA	213-674-5911
Bonar, Ellen/LA	213-474-7911
Bosworth, Janna/LA	213-475-5513
Bough, Ellen/Los Angeles	213-474-7911
Ashley Bowler & Assoc./LA	213-467-8200
Bright, Sandy/W. LA	213-479-5853
Brown, Dianne/LA	213-386-3414
Brown, George/SF	415-495-7175
Bunce, Judy/SF	415-421-2778
Burke, Donna/LA	213-655-4012
Burlingham, Tricia/LA	213-651-3212
Calo, Richard/LA	213-855-0383
Campagna, Debra/SF	415-546-6536
Campbell, John/LA	213-385-1938
Marilyn Caplan & Assoc./LA	213-459-3301
Carofano, Cynthia/Gardena CA	213-542-3255
Carroll, J.J./Manhattan Beach CA	213-545-3583
Carson, Valerie/LA	213-273-6768
Chan, Arlo/LA	213-659-7647
Cherpitel, Latifah/Newport Beach CA	714-644-6723
Churchill, Christine/SF	415-495-3556
Cogin, Andrea/LA	213-874-2798
Cooley, Chris/LA	213-465-7193
Cormany, Paul/LA	213-828-9653
Creative Assoc./N. Hollywood CA	213-760-1787
Dale, Julie/LA	213-487-0270
Dilts, Gale/Woodland Hills CA	213-388-5043
Diskin, Donnell/LA	213-383-9157
Drayton, Sherryl/Woodland Hills CA	213-347-2227
Dubow & Hutkin/LA	213-938-5177
DuCane, Alex/Hollywood CA	213-654-4505
Duvall, Lynn/LA	213-937-4472
Earl, Al/LA	213-462-7432
Eisenrauch & Fink/LA	213-652-4183
Elias, Annika/LA	213-655-3527
English, Jacqueline/Hollywood CA	213-466-5111
Feldman, Deborah/LA	213-874-4107
Fellows, Kathleen/LA	213-851-5051
Fenton, Irv/LA	213-937-4472
Fields, Mary/LA	213-874-2798
Fleming, Laird Tyler/LA	213-784-5814
Fox, Ruta/LA	213-476-9102
Fred, Richard/Beverly Hills CA	213-273-1870
Friedman, Todd & Lewis Portnoy Beverly Hills CA	213-550-7005
Gardner, Gail/LA	213-931-1108
Garland, Susan/N. Hollywood CA	213-473-6793
Garvin George/Santa Monica CA	213-395-8267
George, Nancy/Los Angeles	213-935-4696
Tom Gilbert & Assoc./Hollywood CA	213-469-8767
Glesby, Ellen/LA	213-477-4648
Globe Photos/LA	213-654-3350
Richard Goldstone Productions/LA	213-931-1305
Graff, Lisa/Hollywood CA	213-461-4969
Graphic Arts Agency/LA	213-820-3791
Greenwald, Kim/LA	213-932-1241
Hackett, Pat/Seattle	206-623-9459
Hallowell, Wayne/N. Hollywood CA	213-769-5694
Hamik, Peggy/SF	415-421-3422
Hammond, Roger/LA	213-937-4472
Happe, Michele/Pasadena CA	213-933-2249
Hart, Ginger/LA	213-931-9393
Haugen Assoc./LA	213-822-4999
Hawes, Nancy D/LA	213-387-6515
Hayes, Annie/Malibu CA	213-457-7670
Hedge, Joanne/LA	213-874-1661
Henry Assoc. Inc./Denver	303-756-4811
Herman, Donna/LA	213-466-9940
Hewson, Janie/Sherman Oaks CA	213-655-3772
Howard, Linda/LA	213-466-3306
Hyatt, Nadine/SF	415-563-5679
L'Hommedieu, Margaret/Santa Monica CA	213-829-5700
Hynes, Kathryn/LA	213-382-5975
Iwataki, Sandy/LA	213-457-7406
Kaiser, Ruth/LA	213-380-5908
Kaplan, Royce W./Studio City CA	213-763-2541
Knable, Ellen/LA	213-990-8084
Kowal, Tad/LA	213-653-2940
Kowalenko, Zina/LA	213-463-1129
Lagerson, Kitty/LA	213-936-6861
Lancaster, Corelli/Hollywood CA	213-876-2552
Landsman, Elyse/LA	213-388-3142
Larson, Maryanne/LA	213-475-7794
La Verne/LA	213-441-3297
Lawson, Karen/Hollywood CA	213-464-3364
Laycock, Louise/Woodland Hills CA	213-703-6498
Lerwill, Phyllis R/LA	213-461-5540
Joan Lesser Etc./Beverly Hills CA	213-550-7619
Lilie, Jim/San Francisco	415-441-4384
Lippert, Tom/Los Angeles	213-279-1539
List, Gloria/LA	213-651-3015
Lombardi, Pie/LA	213-931-5942
London, Valerie/LA	213-655-4214
Lovejoy, Pamela/LA	213-936-1616
Luck, Donna Lee/Los Angeles	213-380-5099
Luna, Tony/Pasadena CA	213-684-0466
MacArthur, Jim/LA	213-660-1321
Marcuse, Sy/LA	213-487-3860
Marshall, J.P./SF	415-543-0190
Martin, Steve/LA	213-936-3131
Maslansky, Marysa/LA	213-934-1384
Matson, Coleen/LA	213-462-3513
Mattei, Michele/LA	213-656-7407
McCullough, Don & Gavin/LA	213-382-6281
Merillat, Susan/LA	213-477-2409
Miller, Katie/North Hollywood CA	213-766-2806
Mitchell, Donna/Los Angeles	213-820-1397
Morico, Mike/LA	213-382-6281
Nichols, Pam/Hollywood CA	213-467-6797
Nazarian, Lernik/Brentwood CA	213-736-3978
Nedra/Hollywood CA	213-461-2239
O'Hara, Pat/LA	213-851-5051
Parsons, Ralph/SF	415-986-0107
Pentecost, Harry/LA	213-395-8500
Pepper, Don/LA	213-382-6281
Philbrook, Bill/LA	213-937-4472
Photo Artists/LA	213-463-7717
Pierceall, Kelly/LA	213-559-4327
Pone, Bob/Hollywood CA	213-464-6443
Prapas, Christine/Los Angeles	213-476-7940
Putnam & Brookhouse/LA	213-256-0502
Quinlan, Kathleen/LA	213-467-2135
Reed, Dick/LA	213-650-6304
Rezos, Andre/Pacific Palisades CA	213-454-6726
Richard, Marilyn/Malibu CA	213-457-3363
Ritchie, Ann/Caoga Park CA	213-887-0200
Rosenthal, Elise/Los Angeles	213-472-0669
Rothouse, Susan/Pacific Palisades CA	213-459-4591
Roybal, Alec/LA	213-258-6500
Runyon, Kathleen/LA	213-384-9952
Sakai, Steve/Temple City CA	213-283-9940
Salisbury, Sharon/SF	415-285-4770
Sato, Carolyn/LA	213-658-8645
Sauers, Joan/Beverly Hills CA	213-274-9859
Schiff, Anthony/LA	213-556-3033
Scott, Alexiy/LA	213-657-8707
Sebree, Sandie/LA	213-874-6322
Sidore, Sharri/Hermosa Beach CA	213-374-4315
Skow, Carol/LA	213-938-6287
Slobodian, Barbara/LA	213-464-2341
Smith, Linda/Dallas	214-651-9701
Souza, Sandy/LA	213-462-4532
Spelman, Martha/W. LA	213-395-9551
Sprading, David/LA	213-475-7794
Stein, Greg/Torrance CA	213-373-6789
Steinberg, John/LA	213-279-1775
Stern, Gregg/Torrance CA	213-545-0359
Sullivan, Diane/SF	415-673-4044
Sweet, Ron/SF	415-433-1222
Tasca, Sandra/LA	213-798-7036
Terry, Gloria/Pasadena CA	213-681-4115
Torres, Gilbert/LA	213-464-5016
Truax, Sharon/Venice CA	213-396-3162
Vandamme, Vicki/SF	415-433-1292
Wagoner, Joe/Venice CA	213-392-4877
Walsh, Sam/Seattle	206-522-0154
Walton, Al/LA	213-661-8273
Watson, Ailene/LA	213-651-3015
Wielage, M.B./LA	213-651-2878
Wihnyk, Martha/LA	213-655-7734
Williams, George/LA	213-382-6281
Willie/LA	213-464-7734
Wood, Joan/LA	213-463-7717
Zimmerman, Delores H./Beverly Hills CA	213-273-2642

PHOTOGRAPHY

PHOTOGRAPHY

Golden, Caren	212-925-7730
Goldman, A. Bruce	212-666-9143
Goldman, Richard 92	**212-675-3021**
Goldsmith, Lynn	212-593-2677
Golob, Stanford	212-532-7166
Gonzales, Manny	212-684-6026
Good, Jay	212-228-2244
Gordon, Joel 93	**212-989-9207**
Goro, Fritz	212-556-2342
Gotfryd, Bernard	212-350-2505
Gottheil, Philip	212-686-6391
Gould, Steve	212-686-1690
Gove, Geoffrey	212-541-7600
Gray, Dudley	212-929-3181
Gray, Mitchel	212-427-2287
Green, Al	212-486-0725
Green, Beth	212-580-1928
Green-Armytage, Stephen 95	**212-247-6314**
Greenberg, David	212-243-7351
Greene, Sue	212-691-1389
Greenfield, Lee	212-832-0130
Gregory, John	212-691-1797
Grill, Tom	212-989-0500
Griner, Norman	212-246-7600
Gropper, Hank	212-243-5413
Gross, Cy	212-533-2970
Gross, Garry	212-533-2970
Grossberg, Steven	212-929-8260
Grossman, Eugene	212-961-6395
Grossman, Henry	212-580-7751
Grossman, Mildred	212-426-0740
Group Four	212-249-4446
Gscheidle, Gerhard E.	212-666-0748
Gudnason, Torkil	212-929-6680
Guenblatt, Eunice	212-628-3842
Gulardo, John	212-736-2172
Gurovitz, Judy	212-988-8685
Guyaux, Jean-Marie	212-677-1224
Haak, Ken	212-679-6284
Haar, Thomas	212-929-9054
Haas, David	212-877-5003
Haas, Ernst	212-247-4543
Haas, Ken	212-255-0707
Hackett, Gabriel D.	212-265-6842
Hadjolian, Serge E.	212-722-2191
Haggerty, David	212-628-3691
Haling, George 96	**212-683-2558**
Hall, Dick	212-246-7600
Halmi, Robert	212-867-1460
Hamilton, Alexander	212-857-1583
Hamilton, David	212-686-5000
Hammond, Jeanne	212-348-8623
Hammond, Maury	212-564-5508
Hanlon Studios	212-532-8195
Harbutt, Charles	212-541-7570
Hardin, Edward	212-242-2958
Harrington, Phillip	212-284-0212
Harris, Michael	212-255-3377
Harris, Ronald G.	212-861-7861
Hartman, A.J.	212-989-0500
Hartman, Harry	212-675-5454
Hartmann, Erich	212-541-7570
Hashi Studio	212-245-3192
Hausman, George	212-686-4810
Haviland Photography	212-260-3670
Hedrich, David	212-WA4-3324
Hege, Laszlo	212-679-8220
Heisler, Greg 98	**212-580-2712**
Helms, Bill 100	**212-759-2079**
Henry, Diana Mara	212-722-8803
Don Henze Studio	212-989-3576
Heron, Michal	212-787-1272
Herr, Jim	212-371-0076
Hess, Trudee	212-755-0532
Heyman, Abigail	212-982-4595
Heyman, Ken	212-421-4512
Hideoki Studio	212-255-1532
Hine, Skip	212-691-5913
Hiro	212-580-8000
Hirst, Michael	212-982-4062
Hoban, Tana	212-477-6071
Hoebermann, Robert	212-840-2678
Hofer, Evelyn	212-691-0084
Hollyman, Tom	212-867-2383
Holt, Katheryn	212-243-5137
Holt, Tim	212-737-5103
Homan, Bill	212-879-7116
Hopkins, Stephen	212-725-0169
Horn, Steve	212-752-3500
Horowitz, Ryszard	212-243-6440
Horowitz, Ted 102	**212-595-0040**
Horst	212-246-3737
Horvat, Frank	212-675-2805
Houghton, Jim	212-889-3920
Howard, Ken	212-691-3445
Howard, Rosemary	212-473-5552
Huerta, Gerard	212-753-2895
Hugelmeyer, John	212-889-1189
Huntzinger, Bob	212-675-1710
Hutzler, Jacques	212-532-7363
Hyatt, Morton	212-889-2955
Hyde, Dana	212-472-8815
Hyman, Paul	212-255-1532
Iger, Martin	212-755-7226
Ihara, Hiro	212-982-5760
Ikeda, Shig	212-924-4744
Ing, Francis	212-279-5022
Intrater, Roberta	212-941-7246
Ioss, Walter	212-787-8984
Irving, Jay	212-677-8600
Ishimuro, Eisuke	212-255-9198
Izu, Kenro	212-254-1002
Jacobs, Marty	212-475-1160
Jacobs, Raymond	212-777-4779
Jacobsen, Paul	212-243-4732
Jaffe	212-685-5740
Janeart Ltd.	212-765-1121
Jangoux, Jacques	212-840-6928
Jawitz, Louis 105	**212-929-0008**
Jay, Alan	212-673-8370
Jeffery, Richard	212-255-2330
Jeffrey, Lance	212-260-3971
Jeffry, Alix	212-982-1835
Joel, Yale	212-556-2342
Johnson, Doug	212-989-7473
Jones, Wesley	212-269-5700
Jorgensen, Warren D.	212-986-1224
Joseph, Meryl	212-861-5057
Juliano, Vincent T.	212-777-2980
Jurado, Lou	212-889-6524
Juschkus, Raymond	212-552-3716
Kachaturian, Armen	212-533-3550
Kage, Manfred	212-840-6928
Kahn, R.T.	212-988-1423
Kait, Rosemary	212-221-1246
Kalisher, Simpson 106	**212-288-5542**
Kaltman, Len	212-254-4070
Kamsler, Leonard	212-242-4678
Kane, Art	212-679-2016
Kane, Peter T.	212-687-5848
Kaplan, Alan	212-982-9500
Kaplan, Peter B.	212-989-5215
Kaplan, Peter J.	212-222-1193
Karales, James H.	212-799-2483
Karia, Bhupendra	212-595-1047
Karlin, Lynn	212-243-0631
Karlson, Norman	212-753-3155
Karp, Albert	212-683-5055
Katchian, Sonia	212-925-7705
Katz, Paul 107	**212-684-4395**
Katz, Susan	212-362-5120
Kaufman, Curt 108	**212-759-2763**
Kaufman, Irving	212-687-8343
Kazhdan, Naum	212-499-5039
Keaveny, Francis	212-691-1989
Keegan, Marcia	212-682-7486
Keller, John F.	212-989-1587
Kellman, Ray	212-686-5958
Kender, John	212-228-1964
Kennedy, David Michael	212-255-9212
Kennedy, Donald J.	212-877-4583
Kennedy, William	212-874-4200
Kent, Al	212-929-5596
Kernan, Sean	212-724-9552
Kerr, Justin & Barbara	212-391-4955
Kiehl, Stuart	212-260-5466
King, Bill	212-675-7575
King, Kathleen	212-475-2685
Kirk, Barbara E.	212-734-3233
Kirk, Charles	212-677-3770
Kirk, Malcolm	212-541-7999
Kirk, Russell	212-777-3533
Kiss, Bob	212-260-2929
Klein, Matthew 110	**212-255-6400**
Klein, Wolfgang	212-675-2805
Kligge, Robert	212-686-4224
Koenig, Gea	212-243-3248
Koenig, Phil 111	**212-777-8282**
Kolansky, Palma 112	**212-243-4077**
Komar, Greg	212-674-0085
Koner, Marvin	212-751-7734
Korsh, Ken	212-685-8864
Kozan, Dan 113	**212-691-2288**
Kozan, Marvin D.	212-473-5287
Kozlowski, Mark	212-475-7133
Kramer, Barry	212-247-7860
Kramer, Daniel	212-873-7777
Krauss, Lester	212-228-2190
Krementz, Jill	212-688-0480
Kresch, Jerry	212-787-7396
Krieger, Harold	221-686-1690
Krockman, Arnold F.	212-889-1979
Kuhn, Ann	212-685-1774
Kuhn, Werner J.	212-245-0344
Lambray, Maureen	212-879-3960
LaMonica, Chuck	212-986-7163
Lange, Paul	212-362-6105
Langerman, Steven	212-691-9322
Langley, David	212-581-3930
Langley, J. Alex	212-752-3930
Lanne, Judy	212-832-3943
Laredo, Victor	212-874-1975
Larrain, Gilles	212-925-8494
Laszlo Studio	212-575-0314
Lategan, Barry	212-228-6850
Latham, Sid	212-661-9190
Laure, Jason	212-691-7466
Laurence, Bruce	212-889-7140
Laurents, Gene	212-582-2430
Lavine, Arthur	212-522-3716
Lax, Kenneth	212-228-6191
LeBaube, Guy	212-986-6981
Lee, Jim	212-988-7288
Leeds, Karen	212-243-4546
Leiter, Saul	212-243-0664
Leo, Donato	212-989-4200
Leonard Studio	212-581-5323
Leonian, Phillip	212-989-7670
Lerner, Ira	212-242-6696
Lerner, Ken	212-777-2820
Let There Be Neon 114	**212-226-7747**
Levy, Peter	212-691-6600
Lewis, Ross	212-691-6878
Liberman, Alexander	212-246-0679
Lichtman, Bob	212-582-4354
Lieberman, Allen	212-AL5-4646
Lim	212-736-4143
Lindley, Thomas	212-533-6813
Lindner, Steven	212-988-6997
Lipton, Trina	212-533-3148
Lisanti, Vincent	212-226-1126
Little, Christopher	212-691-1024
Litwin, Richard	212-757-2142
Litwin, Wallace	212-925-7357
Lloyd, Harvey	212-533-4498
Lockhart, George	212-355-1313
Lombardi, Frederick	212-568-0740
Lomeo, Angelo	212-663-2122
Londener, Hank	212-354-0293
Long, Joe	212-249-4446
Lonsdale, William J.	212-834-8281
Low, Gerry	212-695-8672
Lucka, Klaus 115	**212-594-5910**
Ludders, Leora	212-929-1462
Lupone, Carl	212-977-3203
Luria, Dick 117	**212-929-7575**
Lusk, Frank	212-679-1441
Mace, Mort	212-765-3889
Macedonia, Carmine	212-255-7910
Mack, Donald	212-755-3536
MacWeeney, Alen	212-473-2500
Maisel, Jay	212-475-6489
Malignon, Jacques	212-682-2462
Malone, Lyn	212-534-5827
Malphettes, Benoit	212-737-6339
Mandarino, Tony	212-686-2866
Manna, Lou	212-683-8689
Manos, Constantine	212-541-7570
Marchand, Nicole	212-362-8943
Marckrey, George	212-489-6090
Marco, Phil 15, 119	**212-929-8082**
Marcus, Helen	212-879-6903
Maresca, Frank	212-683-3034
Margerin, William D.	212-473-7945
Mario, Cal	212-586-3142
Mark, Mary Ellen	212-982-8775
Marks, Don	212-228-2190
Marmaras, John 120	**212-741-0212**
Marshall, Lee 121	**212-799-9717**
Martel, Maria	212-246-1910
Martin, Bard	212-929-6712
Martin, Bill	212-929-2947
Martin, Dennis	212-679-8620
Martin, Miguel	212-564-3677
Marvullo, Joseph F.	212-532-2773
Marx, Richard	212-929-8880
Masca	212-675-2580
Mate, Jon	212-679-1154
Mathews, Marlis	212-777-3800
Matsumoto, Tosh	212-673-8100
Matthews, Cynthia	212-288-7349
Maucher, Arnold	212-982-2090
Mazzurco, Phil	212-989-1220
McCabe, David	212-874-7480
McCabe, Inger	212-535-3030
McCabe, Robert	212-677-1910
McCartney, Susan	212-868-3330
McClean, Cyril H.	212-989-7880
McCurdy, John Chang	212-243-6949
McDarrah, Fred W.	212-777-1236
McElroy, Robert R.	212-866-1877
McFarland, Lowell	212-674-5566
McGinty, Kathy	212-674-1452
McGrath, Norman	212-799-6422
McLaughlin-Gill, Frances	212-369-4460
McQueen, Hamilton	212-924-1393
Melgar, Fabian	212-725-2714
Mellon	212-242-3472
Memo Studio	212-787-1658
Menashe, Abraham	212-254-2754
Menken/Seltzer	212-924-4240
Meola, Eric 124	**212-255-8653**
Merrim, Lewis J.	212-265-6736
Mervar, Louis 126	**212-354-8024**
Mesneys Third Bardo	212-535-0992
Meyerowitz, Joel	212-666-6505
Meyers, Robert	212-741-1050
Michael, Lee	212-683-0651
Michals, Duane	212-473-1563
Miles, Ian	212-688-1360
Mili, Gjon	212-586-1212
Miljakovich, Helen	212-242-0646
Miller, Bert	212-567-7947
Miller, Donald	212-986-9783
Miller, Eileen	212-838-0015
Miller, Josh	212-777-2616
Miller, Myron	212-532-7257
Miller, Wayne F.	212-541-7570
Mills, Steve	212-243-1969
Mistretta, Martin 127	**212-675-1547**
Mitchell, Benn	212-255-8686
Mitchell, Darnell	212-929-8103
Mitchell, Jack	212-737-8940
Moldoff, Stan	212-673-7940

PHOTOGRAPHY

PHOTOGRAPHY

Varnedoe, Samuel	212-986-7862
Venant, Pierre	212-624-5099
Vern, Ike	212-228-9020
Vicari, Jim	212-675-3745
Vickers, Camille	212-580-8649
Victor, Thomas	212-582-1882
Vidal, Bernard	212-582-3284
Vidol, John	212-889-0065
Villegas, Ronald	212-683-7897
Villota, Louis	212-758-5791
Vine, David	212-691-7433
Vlamis, Suzanne	212-879-4587
Vogel, Allen	212-675-7550
Vokeman, Roy	212-889-7067
Von Hassell, Agostino	212-986-4800
Von Wangenheim, Chris	212-787-8910
Vos, Gene	212-685-8384
Wagner, David	212-532-4015
Waine, Michael 156	**212-533-4200**
Wallach, Jack	212-564-3144
Walsh, Bob	212-684-3015
Waltzer, Carl	212-929-7844
Walz, Barbra	212-242-7175
John Wang Studio Inc.	212-982-2765
Warsaw Photographic Assoc.	212-725-1888
Watson, Albert M.	212-628-7886
Weber, Tommy	212-683-6161
Weckler, Chad	212-541-4787
Weckler, Charles	212-683-6161
Weihs, Tony	212-889-5157
Weinberg, Michael	212-691-0713
Weinstein, Todd	212-254-7526
Weinstein, Todd	212-673-5855
Weiser, Barry	212-674-8457
Weiss, Michael	212-929-4073
West, Charles H.	212-242-4894
West, Jerry	212-245-2416
White, Anne B.	212-289-4556
White, Frank	212-581-8338
Whitely, Howard	212-490-3111
Wiesehahn, Charles	212-679-8342
Williams, Larry 158	**212-684-1317**
Wilson, Mike	212-683-3557
Wing Studio	212-535-9202
Witlin, Ray	212-866-7625
Wolf, Bernard	212-427-0220
Wolf, Henry	212-472-2500
Wolff, Werner	212-679-3288
Wolfson, Steve	212-532-2580
Wolters, Richard A.	212-533-8280
Wood, Susan	212-242-2557
Woodward, Herbert	212-685-4385
Woolfe, Ray	212-249-8372
Wormser, Richard L.	212-928-0056
Wunderlich, Gabriele	212-689-6985
Wynn, Dan	212-535-1551
Yaeger, H.	212-777-6225
Yamaoka Studio	212-736-8292
Yamashiro, Tad	212-473-7177
Yee, Tom	212-473-5510
Yulsman, Jerry	212-989-5998
Zack, Patrick	212-758-7030
Zacker, Denis	212-355-6954
Zager, Howard	212-736-1253
Zakarian, Aram	212-674-3680
Zalon, Jules	212-865-8099
Zanetti, Gerry	212-473-4999
Zappa, Tony	212-532-3476
Zedar, Joseph 159	**212-685-5288**
Zipkowitz, Harold	212-685-6150
Zoiner, John 160	**212-972-0357**
Zubrzycki, Paul	212-242-0634
Zuretti, Charles	212-924-9412
Zwiebel, Michael	212-847-0778

NORTHEAST

Adams, Molly/Mendham NJ	201-513-4521
Adams Studio Inc./Wash. DC	202-785-2188
Aks, Lee R./Briarcliff Manor NY	914-941-3833
Alexander, Jules/Rye NY	914-967-8985
Alonso, Manuel/Stamford CT	203-359-2838
Anderson, Pete/Hull MA	617-925-2358
Anderson, Susanne/Wash. DC	202-966-7661
Anderton, David/Ridgewood NJ	201-652-0632
Anyon, Benjamin/Philadelphia	215-644-6422
Ballantyne, Thomas C./Concord MA	617-369-7599
Balz, Wesley/Hartsdale NY	914-949-5962
Barlow, Kurt/Wash. DC	202-543-5506
Barnett, Jim/Colesville MD	301-384-1266
Baskin, Gerry/Boston	617-426-7262
Bates, Ray/Newfane VT	802-365-7770
Bell, Chuck III/Pittsburgh	412-261-2022
Benenate, Joseph/Woburn MA	617-933-2575
Bent, John/N. Kingston RI	401-783-8538
Berg, Hal/New Rochelle NY	914-235-9356
Berman, Mal/Philadelphia	215-928-1061
Bernstein, Daniel/Waltham MA	617-894-0473
Binzen, Bill/Lakeville CT	203-435-2485
Bishop, Edward/Boston	617-536-7465
Blake, Mike/Boston 165	**617-523-3730**
Blevins, Burgess/Baltimore	301-685-0740
Blizzard, William C./Beckley WV	304-252-4652
Bluestein, Jackie/Baldwin NY	516-623-3469
Boatner, E.B./Somerville MA	617-354-7035
Bookbinder, Sigmund/Southbury CT	203-264-5137
Bowker, Bruce A./Milford NJ	201-995-4214
Bragstad, Jeremiah O./Ithaca NY	607-273-4039
Breed, John/Cambridge MA	617-492-6126
Brignolo, Joseph B./Chester NY 56	**914-496-4453**
Broderick, Jim/Tuxedo Park NY	914-351-2725
Brooks, Charlotte/Holmes NY	914-878-9376
Brown, Jim/Marblehead MA	617-631-7444
Burke, John Hamilton/Boston	617-536-4912
Burkhart, Bill/Holyoke MA	413-739-9757
Burnes, Barbara/Westport CT	203-226-0452
Burns, George/Schenectady NY	518-393-3633
Burns, Terry/Philadelphia	215-563-3113
Camp, Don/Philadelphia	215-382-8655
Caravella, Miriam and Wayne/Wash. DC	301-951-0252
Carroll, Hanson/Norwich VT	802-649-1094
Carver, Suzanne/Stonington CT	203-535-3521
Case, H. Robert/Wellesley Hills MA	617-235-6989
Castello, Maggi/Middleburg VA	703-687-6775
Castronovo, John/Montclair NJ	201-227-4646
Chandoha, Walter/Annandale NJ 64	**201-782-3666**
Chapple, Ross/Hume VA	202-332-7708
Chassagne, Claude/Pawling NY	914-955-3286
Cheatham, Edgar J./Charlotte NC	704-536-7257
Chernush, Kay/Wash DC	202-632-8636
Chwatsky, Ann/Rockville Centre NY	516-766-2417
Cleff, Bernie/Philadelphia	215-922-4246
Clemens, Clint/Boston	617-261-3005
Clifford, Geoffrey C./Reading VT	812-484-5047
Cohen, Henry/Philadelphia	215-561-3967
Cohen, Len/Philadelphia	215-568-4120
Cole, Helen/Englishtown NJ	201-446-4726
Collette, Roger/East Providence RI	401-433-2143
Collins, Fred/Boston	617-426-5731
Conboy, John/Schenectady NY	518-346-2346
Condax, John/Philadelphia	215-923-7790
Conklin, Paul S./Wash. DC	202-387-5133
Conte, Margot/Hastings-on-Hudson NY	914-478-0512
Cosindas, Marie/Boston	617-266-3487
Crane, Tom/Philadelphia	215-525-2444
Creighton, William/Germantown, NY	518-537-6513
Cuesta, Mike/Dix Hills NY	516-864-8373
Curtis, Bruce/Roslyn Heights NY	516-484-2570
Curtis, Jackie/Norwalk CT	203-866-9198
D'Arazien, Arthur/New Canaan CT.	203-966-2811
Davidson, Cameron/Bethesda MD	301-657-8894
Davis, Howard/Baltimore	301-288-2133
deCamp, Michael A./Morristown NJ	201-538-1693
DeGast, Robert/Annapolis MD	301-974-4118
deGeorges, Pam/Claremont MA.	413-339-4351
Degginger, Edward R./Convent Station NJ	201-455-2737

DeMunde, Len/Boston	617-522-6666
Deveaney, Joseph/Waldoboro ME	207-549-7693
DeVoe, Marcus/Setauket NY	516-751-1932
Diamond, Joseph/Ridgewood NJ	201-444-7994
Diamondidis, Nick/Philadelphia	215-922-1888
Dickstein, Bob/Roslyn Heights NY.	516-621-2413
Dietz, Donald/Cambridge MA	617-547-1619
DiGiacomo, Melchior/Harrington Park NJ	201-767-0870
Di Maggio, Joe/Centerpoint NY	516-271-6133
DiMarco, Salvatore/Philadelphia	215-789-3239
Doherty, William/Waltham MA	617-899-9466
Dorot, Didier/Mamaroneck NY	914-381-2650
Drake, James A/Philadelphia	215-925-8927
Dreyer, Peter H./Boston.	617-762-8550
Druss, Chuck/Larchmont NY	914-834-3912
Dunlap, D. James/Wash. DC	202-526-5008
Dunn, Paul/Boston.	617-424-1686
Dunn, Phoebe/New Canaan CT 75	**203-966-9791**
Durrance, Dick/Rockport ME 166	**212-355-1855**
Eck, Frank W./Boston	617-266-0896
Eckstein, Ed/Philadelphia.	215-561-0572
Ehrenfeld, Mikki/Lincoln MA	617-259-9581
Eisman, Jamie/Philadelphia 167	**215-922-7652**
Embrey, A. Wilson/Fredericksburg VA	703-373-4023
Endres, Ann/Bernardsville NJ	201-766-3215
Envision Corp./Boston	617-482-3444
Ernst, John/Ringwood NJ	201-962-4114
Eyle, Nicolas/West Edmeston NY	315-824-1780
Ezra, Martin D./Landsdonne PA.	215-622-7792
Faul, Jan/Arlington VA	703-522-0150
Faulkner, Douglas/Summit NJ	201-277-2949
Feinberg, Milton/Boston	617-267-2000
Feininger, Andreas/New Milford CT	203-354-8280
Fernandez, B.J./North Bergen NJ	201-865-6997
Ficalora, Salvatore/Armonk NY	914-273-3990
Fish, Dick/Northampton MA	413-584-6500
Fisher, Al/Boston	617-536-7126
Fishman, Chuck/Roosevelt NY	516-623-6995
Fland, Peter/Deer Park NY	516-667-4436
Foote, James A./Old Greenwich CT.	203-637-3228
Foster, Frank/Boston	617-536-6600
Foster, Nicholas/Gladstone NJ	201-234-1570
Freeman, Roland L./Wash. DC	202-882-7764
Freid, Joel C./Silver Spring MD 168	**301-681-7211**
Furman, Michael/Philadelphia 82	**215-925-4233**
Gaillet, Helen/Bridgehampton NY	516-537-3116
Galella, Ron/Yonkers NY	914-237-2988
Galvin, Kevin/Hanover MA	617-826-4795
Ganton, Brian/Verona NJ	201-221-7318
Garfield, Peter/Wash. DC	202-333-0168
Gates, Ralph/Short Hills NJ	201-379-4456
Germer, Michael/Boston	617-262-6980
Gidley, E. Fenton/Darien CT	203-838-1767
Gilmour, James R./Dumont NJ	201-387-0303
Goell, Jonathan J./Brookline MA	617-731-0936
Goldblatt, Steven/Norristown PA	215-539-7344
Golden, Robert Francis/Monsey NY	914-356-5825
Goldman, Mel/Boston	617-536-0539
Goldsmith, Alan/Newton MA	617-395-9138
Goldstein, Robert/New Milford NJ	201-262-5959
Good, Richard/Philadelphia	215-472-7659
Goodwin, John C./Demarest NJ	201-768-0777
Gorrill, Robert B./Boston	617-328-4012
Grace, Arthur/Wash. DC	202-333-6568
Grehan, Farrell/Piermont NY	914-359-0404
Griffin, Arthur L./Winchester MA	617-729-2690
Griffing, Fred/Upper Grandview NY	914-353-0619
The Steve Grohe Studio/Boston	617-523-6655
Groskinsky, Henry/Port Washington NY	516-883-3294
Haley, Michael/Boston	617-267-7800
Hall, Judson/Putney VT	802-387-6670
Hall, Sam/Boston	617-266-6055
Hamlin, Elizabeth/Cambridge MA	617-547-1619
Hansen, James/Setauket NY	516-941-4179
Hansen, Steve/Boston	617-426-6858
Heayn, Mark/Baltimore	301-235-1608
Heist, Scott/Emmaus PA	215-965-5479
Heller, Brian C./East Stroudsburg PA	717-421-3175
Henis, Marshall C./Great Neck NY	516-466-9098
Herwig, Ellis/Cambridge MA	617-868-6093
Hess, Brad/Grandview NY	914-358-4060

Hires, Charles E./Malvern PA	215-647-3140
Hobermann, L./Chatham MA	617-945-2413
Hocker, John W./Cape May NJ	609-465-4971
Hoffman, Bernard/Freehold NJ	201-780-2578
Hoffman, Lynn/Philadelphia	215-235-0588
Holland, James R./Boston	617-267-9140
Holt, John/Boston 169	**617-426-7262**
Holt, Walter/Bryn Mawr PA	215-525-8040
Hoops, Jay/Southampton NY	516-728-4017
Houser, David/Ridgefield CT	203-438-3441
Howard, Carl/Ballston Lake NY	518-877-7615
Hubbell, William/Bedford Hills NY 104	**914-666-5792**
Hulings, Peter G./Boston	617-426-2565
Hurst, Norman/Cambridge MA	617-868-4869
Jackson, Reggie/New Haven CT	203-787-5191
Joachim, Bruno/Boston 170	**617-266-7552**
Jones, Lou/Boston	617-426-6335
Jongen, Antoinette/East Hampton NY.	516-324-1067
Kalisher, Simpson/Roxbury CT 106	**203-354-8893**
Kaplan, Carol/Boston	617-266-6017
Katz, Alan/West Orange NJ	201-731-8956
Kawalerski, Ted/Rochester NY 109	**716-244-4656**
Kelly, John J./Springfield PA	215-543-1230
King, Ralph/Boston	617-426-3565
Kligman, Fred/Wash. DC	202-234-4622
Knapp, Richard/Edgewater NJ	201-837-6320
Knapp, Stephen/Worcester MA	617-757-2507
Koeniges, Thomas/Islip NY	516-587-8163
Kramer, Erwin/Great Neck NY	516-466-5582
Laab, Ludwig/Woodstown NJ	609-769-3434
Lane, Whitney/Ossining NY	914-762-5335
Lautman, Robert C./Wash. DC	202-966-2800
Lee, Carol/Boston 171	**617-523-5930**
Lee Rue, Leonard III/Blairstown NJ	201-362-6616
Leipzig, Arthur/Sea Cliff NY	516-676-6016
Leney, Julia/Wayland MA	617-358-7229
Lensman Photo Ltd./Wash. DC	202-333-3850
Levart, Herb/Hartsdale NY	914-946-2060
Leveille, David/Rochester NY	716-381-5341
Levy, Rick/Cambridge MA	617-864-4298
Lilley, Weaver/Philadelphia	215-567-2881
Lillibridge, David/Burlington CT	203-673-9786
Limont, Alexander/Philadelphia	215-438-7259
Linck, Anthony/Fort Lee NJ	201-944-5454
Lockwood, Lee/West Newton MA	617-965-6343
Lucas, W. Frederick/Nantucket MA	617-228-9097
Manheim, Michael Philip/Marblehead MA	617-631-3560
Maroon, Fred J./Wash. DC	202-337-0337
Marshall, John/Boston	617-536-2988
Martin, Jack/Pennsauken NJ	609-663-4971
Massie, Kim/Accord NY	914-687-7744
Masters, Hilary/Ancramdale NY	518-329-1522
Matt, Philip/Rochester NY	716-461-5977
McCarthy, Margaret/Harrison NY	914-835-1587
McConnell, Jack/Hartford CT	203-527-7666
McConnell-McNamara/Wethersfield CT	203-563-6154
McCoy, Dan J./Housatonic MA	413-274-6211
McKenna, Rollie/Stonington CT	203-535-0110
McLaren, Lynn/Boston	617-227-7448
Mecca, Pete and Jack/Leonia NJ	201-944-3271
Mednick, Seymour/Philadelphia	215-735-6100
Meek, Richard/Huntington NY	516-271-0072
Mellor, Doug/Philadelphia 122	**215-649-6087**
Menkus, Bob/Philadelphia	215-925-7073
Michaud, Alfred A./Wash. DC	202-554-4032
Miller, Peter M./Waterbury VT	802-244-7887
Miller, Roger/Baltimore	301-566-1222
Millman, Lester Jay/Rye NY	914-967-0486
Minohr, Martha/Wilmington DE	302-762-1250
Mitchell, Mike/Wash. DC	202-347-3223
Mopsik, Eugene/Philadelphia	215-922-3489
Morley, Bob/Boston	617-227-3499
Morrow, Christopher W./Boston	617-482-0710
Morse, Susan W./Glassboro NJ	609-881-3920
Mort, Marvin J./Lafayette Hill PA	215-828-7775
Mroczynsky, Claus/Old Westbury CT	516-333-6319
Munster, Joseph/Phoenicia NY	914-688-5347
Musto, Tom/Wilkes-Barre PA 172	**717-822-5798**
Nalewajk, Jerome/Stratford CT	203-375-0207
Nelder, Oscar/Presque Isle ME	207-769-5911
Nerney, Daniel/Rowayton CT	203-853-2782

PHOTOGRAPHY

Nettis, Joe/Philadelphia 215-563-5444
Neubauer, John/Arlington VA 703-920-5994
Nichols, Don/Rochester NY 173 716-275-9666
Nicotera, Doug and Cindi/Harrisburg PA 717-939-0702
Nocella, Sam/Willow Grove PA 215-659-2171
Nochton, Jack/Bethlehem PA 215-691-2223
Northlight Group/Newark NJ 201-624-3990
Novak, Jack/Alexandria VA 703-836-6464
Olbrys, Anthony/Stamford CT 203-322-9422
O'Mahony, Jack/Boston 617-267-2290
Opus Fotografiks/Bethesda MD 301-986-0161
Orrico, Charles/Syosset NY 516-364-2257
O'Shaughnessy, Bob/Boston 617-542-7122
Palmer/Kane/Weston CT 130 203-227-1477
Parker, Robert B./Corning NY 607-962-4104
Patterson, Roy/Madison CT 203-245-1044
Pease, Greg/Baltimore 301-366-4576
Perry, Robin L./Waterford CT 203-442-3383
Phillips, John/Glen Head NY 516-626-1976
Pickerell, John/Bethesda MD 301-365-1126
Pierce, Michael/Boston 617-267-3984
Pierson, Huntley/Newburyport MA 617-267-5823
Pinney, Doris/Greenwich CT 203-869-0490
Polansky, Allen/Baltimore 301-383-9021
Pollack, Steve/Philadelphia 215-925-7073
Polumbaum, Ted/Lincoln MA 174 617-259-8723
Porcella, Phil/Boston 617-426-3222
Porter, Charles/Poughkeepsie NY 914-454-7033
Profit, Everett R./Boston 617-267-5840
Purring, James/Phoenixville PA 215-933-8393
Randolph, Bob/Wash. DC 202-462-0626
Raycroft, Jim/Boston 175 617-542-7229
Resnick, Stu/Boston 617-734-1998
Richman, Mel/Bala-Cynwyd PA 215-839-6660
Richmond, Jack/Boston 617-482-7158
Riley, Laura/Pittstown NJ 201-735-7707
Roseman, Shelly/Philadelphia 215-922-1430
Ross, Leonard/Bethlehem PA 215-868-8225
Russell, Gail/Darien CT 203-325-0718
Sakmanoff, George/Boston 617-262-7227
Salaff, Fred/Tarrytown NY 914-592-9293
Salgado, Robert/New Hope PA 215-862-2895
Salzbury, Lee/Wash. DC 202-543-5400
Sanford, Eric/Manchester NH 603-624-0122
Sauter, Ron/Rochester NY 716-381-5341
Schill, William/Haddon Heights NJ 609-547-0148
Schlivek, Louis/Ridgewood NJ 201-444-6544
Schmitt, Steve/Boston 617-247-3991
Schwartz, Bunny/Fort Lee NJ 201-886-0268
Schwartz, Robin/Fort Lee NJ 201-886-0268
Schweikardt, Eric/Westport CT 203-227-0371
Seawell, Harry/Parkersburg WVA 18 304-485-4481
Shames, Martin/CT 203-393-0211
Sharpe, David/Wash. DC 176 703-683-3773
Shelton, Sybil/Englewood NJ 201-568-8684
Shroyer, John/Bethlehem PA 215-865-9499
Silk, George/Westport CT 203-227-5757
Silver Image/Wash. DC 202-337-3705
Simmons, Erik Leigh/Boston 177 617-367-6655
Simon, Peter R./Gayhead MA 617-645-9575
Simpson/Flint Baltimore 301-837-9923
Siteman, Frank/Winchester MA 617-729-3747
Smith, Hugh R./Fairfield CT 203-255-1942
Smith, Paul/Roslyn VA 301-530-8916
Smith, Roger B./Avon NY 716-245-5516
Smolan, Rick/Philadelphia 215-799-9570
Smyth, Kevin/Belmar NJ 201-681-2602
Snyder, Clarence/Easton PA 215-252-2109
Solomon, Rosalind/Wash. DC 202-337-0393
Somers, Jo/Boston 617-267-4444
Spiegel, Ted/South Salem NY 914-763-3668
Spivak, I. Howard/Bass River MA 617-394-8334
Stafford, Rick/Allston MA 617-495-1595
Stage, John Lewis/New Milford NY 151 914-986-1620
Stecker, Elinor H./Larchmont NY 914-937-3800
Stein, Geoffrey R./Boston 617-536-8227
Steiner, Lisl/Pound Ridge NY 914-764-5538
Steinhard, Walter/Peekskill NY 914-737-3347
Stoller, Ezra/Rye NY 914-967-3755
Strongin, James W./Huntington NY 516-421-4307
Sullivan, J. Michael/Bethesda MD 178 301-652-7888

Sweet, Ozzie/Francestown NH 603-547-6611
Synchro Photographics Inc.
Mt. Rainier MD 301-699-8142
Tadder, Morton/Baltimore 301-837-7427
Tenin, Barry/Westport, CT 203-226-9396
Tepper, Alan/Hamilton NY 315-824-1000
Tepper, Peter/Fairfield CT 203-367-6172
Tesa, Rudolph J/NJ 201-762-2362
Tessler, Ted/Great Neck NY 516-487-8124
Thomas, Ricardo/Wash. DC 202-265-6568
Thompson, William/Wash. DC 301-599-8876
Tritsch, Joseph J./Cherry Hill NJ 609-667-0974
Trone, Larry P./Wilmington DE 302-328-7172
Tucker, Bill/Boston 617-523-4404
Urban, John/Boston 617-426-8644
Ustinich, Richard/Roanoke VA 703-345-6266
Vaccaro, Michael A./Chichester NY 914-688-5754
Van Arsdale, Nancy/Allendale NJ 201-327-4088
Van Petten, Rob/Boston 617-426-8641
Van-Schalkwyk, John/Boston 617-542-4825
Viertel, Janet/Stamford CT 203-322-2561
Von Koschembohr, Alex/Westport CT 203-226-0452
Von Matthiessen, Maria/Brewster NY 914-279-2663
Wachter, Jerry/Baltimore 301-484-7277
Wahl, Paul/Bogota NJ 201-487-8460
Walch, Robert/Oley PA 716-473-7007
Walker, Terry/Boston 617-283-5200
Warren, Marion E./Annapolis MD 301-974-0444
Wasco, George R./Philadelphia 157 215-922-4662
Watts, C. Moncrief/Larchmont NY 914-834-8079
Weems, Bill/Wash DC 179 202-667-2444
Weisenfeld, Stanley/Painted Post NY 607-962-7314
Weisgrau, Richard/Philadelphia 215-923-3232
Weldon, Mort/North Ardsley NY 914-963-1076
Wendler, Hans/Epsom NH 603-736-9383
Wexler, Ira/McLean VA 804-241-1776
Wheater, Eric/Syracuse NY 315-348-8993
White, Saul/Chappaqua NY 914-769-1933
Wilcox, Elizabeth/Easton CT 203-261-2221
Williams, Lawrence/Upper Darby PA 215-528-6460
Williams, Ron/Feasterville PA 215-322-1166
Wittstein, William H./North Haven CT 203-288-3724
Wohosenko, Ihor/Brookline MA 617-566-1569
Wood, Richard/Boston 617-267-3971
Woujie/Woodstock NY 914-679-7094
Wyman, Ira/West Peabody MA 617-535-2880
Yamashita, Michael/Montclair NJ 201-746-9451
Young, Ellan/Chappaqua NY 914-238-4837

SOUTHEAST

Allard, William A./Barboursville VA 703-832-2037
The Alderman Co./High Point NC 919-883-6121
Alterman, Jack/Charleston SC 803-577-0647
Amberger, Michael/Miami 305-531-4932
Arnold, Harriet/Palm Beach FL 305-582-0606
Baldwin, Frederick/Savannah GA 912-234-0004
Ball, Roger/Charlotte, NC 704-525-2306
Barley, Bill/Cayce SC 803-755-1554
Barton, Paul/Coral Gables FL 305-665-0942
Birdashaw, Bill/Birmingham AL 205-841-2006
Blakeley, Ron/Miami 305-667-9430
Borum, Michael/Nashville 183 615-259-9750
Bullington, Thomas/Durham NC 919-286-4885
Canova, Patricia/Miami 305-221-6731
Carmichael, James H./Sarasota FL 813-922-7372
Cerny, Paul/Tampa FL 813-839-7710
Clayton, Al/Atlanta 404-881-1170
Coleman, Bob/New Orleans 504-866-9001
Cook, Jaimie/Atlanta 404-892-1393
Cromer, Peggo/Coral Gables FL 305-667-3722
David, Alan/Atlanta 404-231-0603
deCasseres, Joseph/Atlanta 404-872-0769
Diamond, Hindi/Miami 305-665-4948
Dinkins, Stephanie/New Orleans 504-866-3337
Edwards, Jack/New Orleans 504-529-2147
Farris, Mark/Arlington VA 703-522-0151
Faustino/Coral Gables FL 184 305-854-4275
Fineman, Michael/N. Miami Beach FL 305-666-1250
Fisher, Ray/Miami 305-665-7659
Forer, Dan/Miami 305-751-5752
Fowley, Douglas/Louisville KY 502-245-1100

Freeman, John/Chapel Hill NC 919-929-3101
Gefter, Judith/Jacksonville FL 904-733-5498
Gelberg, Robert/Miami 305-374-6601
Gleasner, Bill/Denver NC 704-483-9301
Gould, Allan/Miami 305-444-8431
Graham, Fred N./Cocoa Beach FL 305-636-1329
Greenberg, Jerry/Miami 305-667-4051
Greenhaus, Manny/Surfside FL 305-865-0417
Grimes, Bill/Atlanta 404-971-0224
Guravich, Dan/Greenville MS 601-335-2444
Hallinan, Dennis/Winter Haven FL 813-293-7942
Hannau, Michael/Hialeah FL 305-887-1536
Harris, Christopher/New Orleans 504-586-0209
Hazzard, Joseph/Charlotte NC 704-376-6475
Hendley, Arington/Atlanta 404-977-9409
Hines, William/Sarasota FL 813-371-2738
Hoflich, Richard/Atlanta 404-872-3491
Holland, Ralph/High Point NC 919-273-5425
Hunter, Hugh/Birmingham AL 205-879-4773
Hyman, Bill/Atlanta 185 404-355-8069
Image/Tampa FL 813-839-6118
Jamison, Chipp/Atlanta 404-873-3636
Joyner, Louis O./Birmingham AL 205-870-4440
Kaplan, Al/N. Miami FL 305-891-7595
Kennedy, Thomas/Gainesville FL 904-373-3097
Kersh, Viron/New Orleans 504-524-7255
King, J. Brian/Miami 305-856-6534
Kohanim, Parish/Atlanta 186 404-892-0099
Kollar, Robert E./Knoxville TX 615-632-2091
Langone, Peter/Ft. Lauderdale FL 305-467-0654
Lau, Glenn H./Ocala FL 904-237-2129
Leviton, Jay B./Atlanta 404-237-7766
Magruder, Mary & Richard/Decatur GA 404-289-8985
Malles, Ed/Birmingham AL 205-854-3535
May, Clyde/Atlanta 404-873-4329
McCarthy, Tom/Miami 305-233-1703
McGuire, Jim/Nashville TN 615-385-1045
McNeely, Burton/Land O'Lakes FL 813-996-3025
McQuerter, James/Tampa FL 813-872-6383
Medina, Nelson/Tampa FL 813-839-6754
Menzel, Peter J./Charlotte TN 615-789-4335
Miller, Ardean R./Miami 305-661-5688
Miller, Frank J./Hickory NC 704-324-8758
Miller, Frank Lotz/New Orleans 504-899-5688
Miller, Randy/Miami 305-667-5765
Mills, Henry A./Charlotte NC 704-366-3612
Mittleman, Mark/Tampa FL 813-391-5079
Mullen, Edward F./Belair FL 313-585-1763
Myers, Fred/Florence AL 205-766-4802
Nicholson, Nick/Raleigh NC 188 919-787-6076
Olive, Tim/Atlanta 404-872-0500
Osborne, Mitchel L./New Orleans 504-522-1871
Panuska, Robert T./Miami 131 212-752-3930
Parsons, Bill/Little Rock AR 501-372-5892
Pelham, Lynn/Miami 305-371-2013
Poffenberger, Stephen Lee
Sarasota FL 132 813-957-0606
Reetz, Nick/Atlanta 404-874-0822
Roberts, Bruce/Charlotte NC 704-375-3748
Rogers, Chuck/Atlanta 404-872-0062
Sahuc, Louis/New Orleans 504-581-7439
Scheff, Joe/St. Petersburg FL 813-822-3599
Schenck, Gordon H./Charlotte NC 704-332-4078
Schivone, George/Ft. Lauderdale FL 305-643-6976
Schulke, Flip/Miami 305-667-5671
Seitz, Art/Ft. Lauderdale FL 305-391-3136
Sherman, Bob/N. Miami Beach FL 305-944-2111
Sherman, Ron/Atlanta 404-993-7197
Shrout, Bill/Theodore AL 205-973-2417
Siebenthaler, John/Elfers FL 813-848-2927
Smeltzer, Robert/Greenville SC 803-235-2186
Smith, Charles/Jacksonville FL 904-388-6613
Smith, Rick/Greensboro NC 919-275-7691
Steinmetz, Joseph J./Sarasota FL 813-953-7017
Studio III/Atlanta 404-875-0161
Thomas, J. Clark/Nashville TN 615-327-1757
Thompson, Thomas L./Atlanta 404-874-8247
Tilley, Arthur W./Atlanta 404-873-4311
Touchton, Kenneth M., Jr./Atlanta 404-993-6801
Triad Studios/Birmingham AL 189 205-251-0651
Turnau, Jeffrey/Miami 305-685-7636

Uptinick, Richard/Roanoke VA 703-345-6266
Uzzell, Steve/Arlington VA 155 202-522-2320
Van Calsem, Bill/New Orleans 504-522-7346
Vance, David & Assoc./Miami 305-685-2433
Vullo, Phillip/Atlanta 190 404-874-0822
Walters, Tom/Charlotte NC 704-333-6294
Weedman, Brent/Nashville TN 615-254-1324
Whitman, Alan David/Greenville SC 803-271-8238
Williamson, Thomas A./Miami 305-757-3996

MIDWEST

Aleksandrowicz, F.J./Cleveland 216-696-4566
Alfa Studio/Ed Hoppe/Chicago 312-787-2136
Amari, Frank/Chicago 312-787-2240
Arndt & Berthiaume/Minneapolis 193 612-338-1984
Arndt, David M./Chicago 312-664-2879
Arsenault, Bill/Chicago 312-454-0544
Arteaga Photos Ltd./St. Louis 314-352-8345
George Ayala & Assoc./Chicago 312-644-6025
Azuma, Don/Chicago 312-337-2101
B.A.M. Studios/Chicago 312-263-1027
Bachnick, Alex/Chicago 312-280-1201
Baer, Gordon/Cincinnati 513-281-2339
Bailey, Conrad/Chicago 312-337-6951
Bailey, J. Edward/Detroit 313-875-5177
Banner & Burns/Chicago 312-644-4770
Barlow Photography Inc.
Richmond Hgts. MO 314-721-2385
Barrett, Robert J./Kansas City MO 816-276-1506
Basdeka, Peter/Chicago 312-782-4568
Bayles, Dal/Milwaukee 414-464-8917
Bender, Bob/Cleveland 216-861-1525
Bishop, G. Robert/Chesterfield MO 314-532-3698
Block, Stuart/Chicago 312-944-0427
Bosek, Georg/Chicago 312-828-0988
Boyer, Dick/Chicago 312-337-7211
Braddy, Jim/Chicago 312-337-5664
Braun, Marc/Akron OH 216-535-4036
Brimacombe, Gerald/Minneapolis 612-941-5860
Broderson, Fred/Chicago 312-787-1241
Brody, Jerry/Chicago 312-329-0660
Brown, David/Oak Brook IL 312-654-2515
Brown, James F./Cincinnati 513-321-8282
Bruton, Jon/St. Louis 194 314-533-6665
Business Arts/Chicago 312-337-4120
C.M.O. Graphics/Chicago 312-527-0900
Cascarano, John/Chicago 312-266-1606
Chadwick, Taber/Chicago 312-454-0855
Chambers, Tom/Chicago 312-828-9488
Chin, Ruth/Muncie IN 317-284-4582
Clark, Junebug/Detroit 313-399-4480
Clarkson, Rich/Topeka KS 913-295-1196
Cowan, Ralph/Chicago 195 312-787-1316
Curtis, Lucky/Chicago 312-787-4422
DGM Studios/Bloomfield Hills MI 313-645-2222
Damien, Paul/Milwaukee 414-259-1987
Deahl, David/Chicago 312-644-3187
DeBold, Bill/Chicago 312-644-3922
DeNatale, Joe/Chicago 312-329-0234
DeRussy, Myles/Chicago 312-943-3440
Deutsch, Owen/Chicago 312-943-7155
Devenny-Wood Ltd./Chicago 312-944-7070
Ditlove, Michel/Chicago 312-644-5233
DuBiel, Dennis/Chicago 312-266-8559
Dunham, Paul/Chicago 312-649-9554
E.T.M. Studios/Chicago 312-644-2974
Eiler, Terry and Lynthia/Athens OH 614-592-1280
Elliot, Peter/Chicago 312-733-6992
Bob Elmore & Assoc./Chicago 312-236-0233
Epperson, Richard/Chicago 312-337-2138
Ewert, Steve/Chicago 312-440-1197
Faverty, Richard/Chicago 312-943-2648
Feldkamp-Malloy/Chicago 312-263-0633
Floyd, Bill/Chicago 312-321-1770
Foster, Richard/Chicago 312-467-4770
Fotographics/Indianapolis 317-353-6259
Friedman, Bernard/Oak Park IL 312-666-5400
Gabriel/Chicago 312-787-2915
Gale, Bill/Minneapolis 612-827-5858
Getsug-Anderson/Minneapolis 612-332-7007
Gianetti/Hagen/Minneapolis 196 612-339-3172

PHOTOGRAPHY

Gillette, Bill/Ames IA 515-233-3337
Grant-Jacoby/Chicago 312-664-2055
Gray, Walter/Chicago 312-644-2385
Gregory, Gus/Chicago 312-787-7443
Gremmler, Paul/Chicago 312-871-1250
Griffith, Waite/Omaha 402-391-8474
Grippentrag, Dennis/Bloomfield Hills MI 313-645-2222
Grubman, Steve/Chicago 312-787-2272
Haller, Pam/Chicago 312-649-0920
Hamilton, David/Chicago 312-861-1775
Hamilton, David W./Chicago 312-944-6655
Hammarlund, Vern/Troy MI 197 313-588-5533
Handley, Robert E./Bloomington IL 309-828-4661
Harlan, Bruce/South Bend IN 219-283-7350
Harper, Hugo/St. Louis 314-727-4755
Harris, Bart/Chicago 198 312-751-2977
Hart, Bob/Chicago 312-644-3636
Hartig, Geoffrey/Omaha NE 199 402-345-2164
Hauser & D'Orio/Chicago 312-787-8276
Hedrich-Blessing/Chicago 312-321-1151
Hickson Bender/Waldo OH 614-726-2470
Hirschfeld, Corson/Cincinnati 101 513-241-0550
Izokaitis, Kastytis/Chicago 312-321-1388
Izui, Richard/Chicago 200 312-266-8029
Johnson, Jim/Chicago 312-943-8864
Jones, Dawson/Dayton OH 513-435-1121
Jones, Dick/Chicago 312-642-0242
Jordano, Dave/Chicago 312-929-8660
Joseph, Mark/Chicago 312-267-1708
Kaspar, Mel/Chicago 312-528-7711
Kazu/Chicago 312-750-5393
Keeler, Chuck/Minneapolis 612-339-1429
Keeling, Robert/Chicago 312-944-5680
Kelly, Tony/Evanston IL 312-864-0488
Kemper, Susan/Bensenville IL 312-766-0742
Kilkelly, James/Minneapolis 201 612-374-1332
Kolze, Larry/Chicago 312-266-8352
Korab, Balthazar/Troy MI 202 313-641-8881
Kouvatsos, Theo/Cincinnati 513-241-3000
Krantzen Studios/Chicago 312-922-9200
Kroeger-Zieminski/Chicago 312-822-9600
Krueger, Dick/Chicago 312-243-2730
Kulp, Curtis/Chicago 312-266-0477
Kuslich, Lawrence J./St. Paul MN 612-647-0428
Lane, Jack/Chicago 312-337-2326
Lareau, George A./Champaign IL 217-351-8144
LaTona, Tony/Kansas City MO 816-454-7387
Lee, Jared/Lebanon OH 513-932-2154
Lee, Robert F. Jr./St. Louis 314-965-5832
Levey, Don/Chicago 312-329-9040
Lightfoot, Robert/Des Plaines IL 312-297-5447
Lindblade, George R./Sioux City IA 712-277-2345
Lowenthal, Jeff/Chicago 312-861-1180
Malinowski, Stan/Schaumburg IL 312-397-1157
Manarchy, Dennis/Chicago 312-828-9272
Manning Studios Inc./Cleveland 216-861-1525
Marvy, Jim/Hopkins MN 612-935-0307
Maselli Studios/Chicago 312-726-5678
Matz, Fred/Chicago 312-828-9216
McCann, Larry/Chicago 312-329-0370
McMahon, Wm. Franklin/Evanston IL 312-864-2468
McNamara, Norris/Chicago 312-944-4477
Miller, Buck/Milwaukee 203 414-354-9260
Miller, Daniel D./Chicago 312-761-5552
Miller, Edward L./Chicago 312-266-1139
John Mitchell Studios/Elk Grove IL 312-956-8230
Mitchell, Rick/Chicago 312-829-1700
Morrill, Dan/Chicago 312-787-5095
Merle Morris Photographers
Minneapolis 612-338-7829
Moss, Jean/Chicago 312-787-0260
Moy, Willy/Chicago 312-943-1863
Nano, Ed/Cleveland 216-861-0148
Neumer, Koopman/Chicago 312-944-3340
Nicholson, Larry B./Raytown MO 816-356-4505
Niedorf, Steve/St. Paul 204 612-644-7502
Novak, Sam/Chicago 312-664-6733
Nygards, Leif-Erik/Evanston IL 312-869-1257
Jack O'Grady Studios Inc./Chicago 312-726-9833
Olsson, Russ/Chicago 205 312-329-9358
Jack O'Neal Assoc./Mission KS 913-362-4440

O'Rourke, John/Wilmington OH 513-382-3782
Parker, Norm/Chicago 312-644-2248
Parks, Jim/Chicago 312-321-1193
Pazovski, Kazik/Cincinnati 513-281-0030
Perlus & Taxel/Cleveland 216-431-2400
Peterson, Chester N., Jr./Lindsborg KS 913-227-3514
Picture Place/Jim Clarke
St. Louis 206 314-872-7506
Plowden, David/Winnetka IL 312-446-2793
Pokempner, Marc/Chicago 312-525-4567
Poli, Frank/Chicago 312-944-3924
Puffer, David/Chicago 312-266-7540
Raczinski, Walter/Chicago 312-467-0190
Radland, Bud/Madison WI 608-274-0344
Rampy, Thomas/Ann Arbor MI 313-769-4757
Raynor, Dorka/Winnetka IL 312-446-1187
Reichenthal, Martin/Toledo OH 419-475-5102
Warren Reynolds & Assoc./Minneapolis 612-333-4579
Robinson, David/Chicago 312-266-9050
Rocker, Donald/Chicago 312-285-5273
Rogers, Bill Arthur/Oak Park IL 312-848-3900
Rosmis, Bruce/Chicago 312-787-9046
Sacco, Robert T./Chicago 312-663-9778
Sandy, Dick/Hoffman Estates IL 312-359-9580
Saver, Neil/St. Louis 314-241-9300
Schridde, Charles
Madison Heights MI 207 313-589-0111
Schultz, Tim/Chicago 312-871-4488
Scott, Bob/Chicago 312-337-4240
Scott, Denis/Chicago 312-467-5663
Seed, Suzanne/Chicago 312-266-0621
Sevell, Steve/Columbus OH 614-451-9985
Seymour, Frank/Minneapolis 612-338-7829
Seymour, Ronald/Chicago 312-642-4030
Shaffer, Mac/Columbus OH 614-268-2249
Shay, Arthur/Deerfield IL 312-945-4636
Shigeta-Wright Assoc./Chicago 312-642-8715
Shotwell, Chuck/Chicago 312-929-0168
Shoulders, Terry/Chicago 312-644-0616
Silker, Glen/Minneapolis 612-835-1811
Skrebneski, Victor/Chicago 312-944-1339
Sladcik, William/Chicago 312-644-7108
Smetzer, Donald/Chicago 312-327-1716
Smith, C.W./Chicago 312-337-2087
Snook, Allen/Chicago 312-943-7134
Snyder, John/Chicago 312-440-1053
Sohn, Joe/St. Louis, MO 314-965-1811
Soluri, Tony/Chicago 312-243-6580
Sorce, Wayne/Chicago 312-583-6510
Stansfield, Stan/Chicago 312-337-3245
Sterling, Joseph/Chicago 312-348-4333
Stephens Biondi DeCicco Inc./Chicago 312-944-3340
Stierer, Dennis/Ft. Wayne IN 219-483-1313
Straus, Jerry/Chicago 312-787-2628
Studio 400/Ray Mottel/Chicago 312-467-5460
Studio Associates/George Anderson
Chicago 312-372-4013
Studio Due/Chicago 312-981-0880
Styrkowicz, Tom/Chicago 312-528-7114
TRW Inc./Cleveland 216-383-2121
Tatham, Laird/Chicago 312-337-4410
Tenebrini, Paul/Chicago 312-642-0904
Thien, Alex/Milwaukee 414-964-2249
Thomas, Bill/Nashville IN 812-988-7865
Tucker, Bill/Birmingham MI 313-626-4745
Tucker, Paul/Dayton OH 513-435-9866
Tunison, Richard/Chicago 208 312-944-1188
Umland, Steve/Golden Valley, MN 612-546-6768
Upitis, Alvis/Minneapolis 612-374-9375
Urba, Alexis/Chicago 312-644-4466
Vaughan, Jim/Chicago 312-663-0369
Visual Innovations/St. Louis 304-432-4320
Vogue-Wright/Chicago 312-664-5600
Vollan, Michael/Chicago 312-644-1792
Von Photography/Chicago 312-787-9408
Ward, Jack/Indianapolis 317-253-2453
Webb AG Photos/St. Paul MN 612-647-7317
Welzenbach, John/Chicago 312-337-3611
Wenkus, Nugent/Des Plaines IL 312-694-4151
West, Stu/Photogenesis
Minneapolis 612-871-0333

Willett, Mike/Chicago 312-527-2360
Woodcock, Richard/Fenton MO 314-343-5805
Woodward, Greg/Chicago 312-337-5838
Zamiar, Thomas/Chicago 312-787-4976
Zann, Arnold/Oak Park IL 312-386-2864
Zehrt, Jack/St Louis 314-773-2298

SOUTHWEST

Alerdice, Barham/Midlothian TX 214-775-3462
Ashley, Constance/Dallas 211 214-747-2501
Bagshaw, Cradoc/Tesuque NM 505-983-7997
Baker, Bobbe/Dallas 214-748-6346
Baraban, Joe/Houston 713-526-0317
Barnhurst, Noel/Salt Lake City UT 801-532-1725
Bates, Al/Houston 713-466-4977
Bauer, Erwin A./Teton Village WY 307-733-4023
Birnbach, Allen/Denver 303-455-7800
Bouche, Len/Santa Fe NM 505-471-2044
Branner, Phil/Dallas 214-522-1230
Brownlee, Michael V./Denver 303-753-1653
Bruce, A. Dave, Jr./Houston 713-523-6214
Burkhart, John R./Prescott AZ 602-778-0334
Bybee, Gerald/Salt Lake City UT 801-363-1061
Cabluck, Jarrold/Fort Worth TX 817-336-1431
Campbell, Tom/Phoenix 602-252-9746
Carter, Bob/Dallas 214-821-9661
Case, Robert H./Allens Park CO 303-747-2289
Chamberlain, Bob/Telluride CO 303-728-3525
Chavanell, Joe/San Antonio TX 512-222-1167
Chesley, Paul/Aspen CO 303-925-2317
Classon, Norm/Aspen CO 303-925-4418
Collum, Charles/Dallas 214-741-5405
Connolly, Danny F./Houston 713-862-8146
Cupp, David/Denver 303-321-3581
Curtsinger, George/Ft. Worth TX 214-336-9371
Davis, Dave/Phoenix 602-266-9851
DeSciose, Nicholas/Denver 212 303-455-6315
deVore, Nicholas III/Aspen CO 303-925-2317
Eddy, Don/Ft. Collins CO 303-484-8144
Elder, Jim/Jackson Hole WY 307-733-3555
Fahey, Diane D./Denver 303-322-6265
Feulner, Cliff/Phoenix AZ 602-952-0449
Fish, Vinnie/Park City UT 801-649-7373
Forsyth, Mimi/Santa Fe NM 505-982-8891
Francisco & Booth/Dallas 214-688-1855
Freedman, Sue/El Paso TX 915-778-6457
Golden, Frank/Houston 713-524-6620
Gomel, Bob/Houston 713-977-6390
Griffin, John H./Ft. Worth TX 817-923-8666
Hawks, Bob/Tulsa OK 918-584-3351
Haynes, Mike/Dallas 214-522-1230
Haynsworth, John/Dallas 214-748-6346
Hight, George C./Gallup NM 505-863-8922
Hiser, C. David/Aspen CO 303-925-2317
Hoffman, Harold/Richardson TX 214-690-9592
Holdman, Wm. Floyd/Orem UT 801-224-9966
Ivy, Dennis E./Austin TX 512-476-3434
Johnsos, Charles/Vail CO 303-476-4900
Jones, C. Bryan/Houston 713-524-5594
Jones, Don W./Scottsdale AZ 602-948-4591
Jones, Mary Robbins/San Marcos TX 512-392-9561
Karbelnikoff, Mike/Phoenix AZ 213 602-257-9504
Katz, John/Houston 214 713-522-0180
Kehrwald, Richard J./Sheridan WY 307-674-4679
Kenny, Gill C./Tucson AZ 602-743-0963
Kirkley Photography/Dallas 214-651-9701
Klumpp, Don/Houston 215 713-627-1022
Koropp, Robert/Denver 216 303-893-0500
Phil Kretchmar Photography/Dallas 214-744-2039
Lee, Russell/Austin TX 512-452-6174
Lindstrom, Eric/Dallas 214-638-1247
Mayer, Elaine Werner/Phoenix 602-955-5242
McAllister, Bruce/Denver 303-832-7496
McCullough, Bob/Gila NM 505-535-4139
McCullough, Thomas E./Sandia Park NM 505-281-5734
McDowell, Pat/Park City UT 217 801-649-9494
McKee, Mike/Dallas 214-638-1498
McLaughlin, Herb & Dorothy/Phoenix 602-258-6551
Meley, David/Long View TX 214-759-6395
Messineo, John/Ft. Collins CO 303-482-9349
Meyerson, Arthur/Houston 703-526-7972

Mills, Jack R./Oklahoma City OK 405-787-7271
Milmoe, James O./Golden CO 303-279-4364
Moberley, Connie/Houston 713-864-3638
Moore, Terrence/Tucson AZ 602-623-9381
Nelson, Walter/Houston 713-526-5858
Noble, Dee/Lubbock, TX 806-744-2220
The Photographers Inc./Irving TX 214-438-4114
Photographic Illustration/Phoenix 602-252-5654
Ramsey, Steve/El Paso TX 915-532-6491
Running, John/Flagstaff AZ 602-774-2923
Runyan, Peter F./Vail CO 303-476-3142
Russell, John/Aspen CO 303-925-2747
St. Gil, Marc/Houston 713-467-4220
St. John, Charles/Vail CO 303-476-4900
Salas, Michael/Plano TX 214-423-4396
Salomon/Wahlberg & Friends/Dallas 214-823-5851
Schoen, David/Dallas 214-826-8808
Scott, Ron/Houston 218 713-529-5868
Jerry Segrest Photography/Dallas 214-630-8981
Shaw, Robert/Dallas 214-528-8868
The Shooting Gallery Inc./Dallas 214-742-1668
Short, Glenn/Phoenix 602-252-9746
Shupe, John R./Ogden UT 801-392-2523
Stott, Barry/Vail CO 303-476-3334
Stuart, Michael/Dallas 214-826-8449
Sumner, David/Crested Butte CO 303-349-6675
Tatem, Mike/Littleton CO 303-770-6080
Taylor, Marlon/Austin TX 219 512-478-9301
Troxell, William H./Flagstaff AZ 602-779-3626
Untersee, Chuck/Dallas 214-358-2306
Utterback, Michal/Salt Lake City UT 801-531-7767
Walker, Todd/Tucson AZ 602-327-1569
Ward, Sheila/Tucson AZ 602-298-3727
Watkins, J.C./Port Arthur TX 713-982-3666
Whiting, Dennis/Irving TX 214-438-4114
Wilcox, Shorty/Breckenridge CO 303-453-2511
Witt, Lou/Houston 713-944-1603
Wolfhagen, Vilhelm/Houston 713-522-2787
Wollam, Les/Dallas 220 214-521-8038
Wright, Geri/Aspen CO 303-925-2137

WEST

Abecassis, Andree L./Berkeley CA 415-526-5099
Ackroyd, Hugh S./Portland OR 503-227-5694
Ahlberg, Holly/LA 213-462-0731
Ahrend, Jay/LA 213-466-8485
Alexander, David/Hollywood CA 213-464-8690
Alexander, Jesse L./Santa Barbara CA 805-969-3916
Alexander, Michael/SF 415-982-7980
Allan, Larry/San Diego CA 223 714-270-9549
Amer, Tommy/LA 213-469-3305
Anderson, John/Vacaville CA 707-448-4926
Aplin, William/Ventura CA 805-648-4457
Apton, Bill/SF 415-771-9809
Arbogast, Bill/Palo Alto CA 415-323-1336
Armas, Richard 213-464-5016
Arnesen, Eric/SF 224 415-495-5366
Arnold/SF 225 415-621-6161
Arteaga Photos Ltd./Seattle 206-783-0321
Aurness, Craig/LA 213-473-3736
Avery, Sid/LA 213-465-7193
Ayres, Robert Bruce/LA 213-876-1477
Baer, Morley/Monterey CA 408-624-3530
Bailey, Brent P./Costa Mesa CA 714-548-9683
Baker, Jack/Belmont CA 415-592-0292
Ballis, George/Fresno CA 209-237-6516
Barnes, David/Seattle 206-525-1965
Bartone, Tom/LA 213-876-5510
Bartruff, Dave/San Anselmo CA 415-457-1482
Bauer, Karel M./Mill Valley CA 415-863-5155
Bays, Pete/Davis CA 916-756-3640
Becker Bishop Studios/Santa Clara CA 408-244-8484
Beebe, Morton P./SF 415-362-3530
Belknap, Bill/Boulder City NV 702-293-1406
Bergman, Alan/LA 226 213-935-2744
Berman, Steve/LA 213-933-9185
Bernstein, Cal/LA 213-461-3737
Betz, Ted/SF 415-433-0407
Bez, Frank/Los Osos CA 805-528-5500
Biggs, Ken/LA 227 213-462-7739
Blakeley, Jim/SF 228 415-495-5100

PHOTOGRAPHY

Blakeman, Bob/LA	213-479-4327
Blaustein, John/Berkeley CA	415-845-2525
Blodget, Lee/SF	415-495-3995
Boccaccio, Anthony/SF	415-325-7335
Bodnar, Joe/LA	213-838-6587
Bourdet, Al/Olympic Valley CA	916-583-3959
Bourret, Tom/SF	415-777-1736
Braasch, Gary/Vancouver WA	206-695-3844
Bradley, Leverett/Santa Monica CA	213-394-0908
Bragstad, Jeremiah O./SF	415-864-2668
Brascia, Sondra Scott/Beverly Hills CA	213-274-1911
Braun, Ernest/San Anselmo CA	415-454-2791
Brawer, Sid/Beverly Hills CA	213-278-6821
Brenneis, Jon/Berkeley CA	415-845-3377
Britt, Jim/LA 229	**213-936-3131**
Brooks, David B./Nipomo-Mesa CA	213-737-4358
Brown, Richard	213-661-6337
Brown, Delores McCutcheon Canyon Country CA	805-251-2416
George Brown Photography/SF	415-495-7175
Bryan, J.Y./Riverside CA	714-684-8266
Bryson, John/LA	213-456-6170
Buchanan, Craig/F	415-343-5566
Buckman, Rollin/Saratoga CA	408-867-9203
Buelteman, Robert L., Jr./SF	415-566-7670
Burr, Michael/LA	213-399-4767
Bush, Charles/LA	213-937-8248
von dem Bussche, Wolf/ Berkeley CA 62,230	**415-845-2448**
Cahoon, John/LA	213-930-1144
Camozzi, Ieresa/SF	415-421-8898
Capps, Alan/LA	213-276-3724
Carofano, Ray/Gardena CA 231	**213-515-0310**
Carroll, Tom/Malibu CA	213-454-1319
Caswell, Chris/Long Beach CA	714-646-4451
Caulfield, Patricia/Las Vegas NV	702-735-3533
Ralph Chandler Studio, Inc./LA 232	**213-469-6205**
Chen, James/Santa Monica CA 233	**805-965-5849**
Chester, Mark/SF	415-922-7512
Clark, William F./LA	213-486-2564
Claxton, William/Beverly Hills CA	213-276-4228
Clemenz, Bob/Manhattan Beach CA	213-329-0797
Cobb, Vincent/Beverly Hills CA	213-277-5554
Cofrin, John P./Mill Valley CA	415-435-2605
Cogan, Bill/SF	415-391-1350
Coleberd, Frances/Menlo Park CA	415-325-4731
Collison, James/Sherman Oaks CA 235	**213-902-0770**
Colmano, Marino/SF	415-388-4104
Considine, Tim/Beverly Hills CA	213-464-0101
Cornfield, Jim/LA	213-937-5810
Costa, Tony/LA	213-934-3933
Crawford, Del O./Santa Cruz CA	408-475-7511
Crouch, Steve/Carmel CA	408-624-2300
Cummins, Jim/Seattle	206-623-6206
Dain, Martin/Carmel Valley CA	408-659-3259
Dandridge, Frank D./LA	213-233-7304
Daniels, Josephus/Pebble Beach CA	408-372-8812
de Gennaro, George/LA 236	**213-935-5179**
deLancie/Mayer/SF	415-546-1232
deLespinasse, Hank/Las Vegas NV 238	**702-361-6628**
della Grotta, Vivienne/Carpinteria CA	805-684-1339
den Dekker, John/Alhambra CA	213-570-9144
Denman, Frank B./Seattle	206-325-9260
Rick Der Photography/SF	415-433-2055
Derr, Steve/SF	415-641-0550
Desanges, St. Jivago/Westwood CA	213-938-0151
Diaz, Armando/SF	415-495-3552
Doll, Glen L./LA	213-413-2600
Dondero, Donald/Reno NV	702-825-7348
Doty, Tom/Santa Monica CA	805-966-5680
Dow, Larry/LA	213-483-7970
Dubler, Douglas/Malibu CA	213-340-3034
Dudley, Harding & Yang/Seattle	206-623-4100
Dugas, Albert/LA	213-876-7116
Dull, Ed/Portland OR 239	**503-224-3754**
Dumont, Michael P./SF	415-563-1561
Dunbar, Clark M./Mountainview CA 240	**415-964-4225**
Einhouse, Theodore H./LA	213-465-0175
Elich, George/Sacramento CA	916-481-5021
Emanuel, Manny/Hollywood CA	213-465-0259
Emberly, Gordon/SF	415-621-9714
England, Jim/LA	213-413-2575
Engler, Tom/Hollywood CA	213-666-4640
Esgro, Dan/LA	213-655-4012
Evans, Marty/LA	213-466-7279
Eymann, William Charles/Palo Alto CA	415-494-0281
Faulkner, Douglas/Corona Del Mar CA	714-675-5770
Feldman, Marc/LA	213-463-4829
Felt, Jim/Portland OR	503-238-1748
Fenton, Reed/LA	213-651-4646
Fish, Richard/LA	213-986-5190
Fisher, Arthur Vining/SF	415-626-5483
Ford Photography/LA	213-655-7655
Forster, Bruce/Portland OR	503-232-0673
Fousie, Michael Shea/Boise ID	208-345-8635
Fox, Paul/Palm Springs CA	714-325-0386
Freed, Jack/LA	213-931-1015
Freis, Jay/Sausalito CA	415-332-6709
Fries, Janet/SF	415-648-4719
Fruchtman, Jerry/Hollywood CA	213-839-7891
Fukuda, Steve/SF 241	**415-567-1325**
Richard Yutaka Fukuhara Signal Hill CA	213-597-4497
Furuta, Carl/LA 161	**213-655-1911**
Fusco, Paul/SF	415-388-8940
Gage, Rob/Laguna Beach CA	714-494-7265
Gardner, Robert/LA 242	**213-931-1108**
William Garnet Photography/LA	213-931-0367
Garretson, James/Corte Madera CA	415-924-4533
Garrison, Ron/San Diego CA	714-231-1515
Gascon, Enrique/LA	213-383-9157
Gatley, David/Granado Hills CA	213-363-3494
Gechtman, Neal/Beverly Hills CA	213-875-2550
Genter, Ralph/LA	714-754-1164
Gersten, Paul Ben/LA	213-652-6111
Glaubinger, David/San Anselmo CA	415-453-5902
Going, Michael/LA	213-465-6853
Goldstein, Arthur/LA	213-874-6322
Goldstein, Ed/LA 243	**213-663-5800**
Gordon, Charles M./Seattle	206-365-2132
Gordon, Larry Dale/LA	213-874-6318
Gornick, Alan/LA	213-223-8914
Gottlieb, Mark/Palo Alto CA	415-321-8761
Graham, Ellen/Beverly Hills CA	213-275-6195
Gray, Dennis/SF 244	**415-546-6536**
Greene, Herb/SF	415-543-4829
Grimm, Tom/Laguna Beach CA	714-494-1336
Gross, Richard/SF	415-922-6270
Hagyard, Dave/Seattle 245	**206-322-6774**
Hailey, Jason/LA	213-653-7710
Hall, George/SF 246	**415-776-2643**
Hamilton, John R./Gardena CA	213-321-9992
Hampton, Ralph/Manhattan Beach CA	213-429-9678
Harding, C.B./Portland OR	503-281-9907
Harlow, Bruce/Seattle	206-622-4843
Harris, Ron/Hollywood CA	213-937-9900
Harrison, Howard E./SF	415-826-0252
Henman, Graham/LA	213-934-1815
Herrington, Olson/Oakland CA 247	**415-452-0501**
Herron, Matt/Sausalito CA	415-332-7388
Hewett, Richard/LA	213-254-4577
Hicks, Alan/Portland OR	503-226-6741
Hicks, John & Regina/Carmel CA	408-624-7573
Higgins, Donald/Santa Monica CA	213-393-8858
Hishi, James/LA	213-658-8267
Hixson, Richard/SF 248	**415-495-0558**
Hodges, Walter/Seattle	206-935-5649
Hollenbeck, Cliff/Seattle	206-824-7700
Holz, William/LA	213-656-4061
Hooper, H. Lee/Malibu, CA	213-457-3363
Hooper, R. Scott/Las Vegas NV 249	**702-873-5823**
Hopkins, Phil/San Diego CA	714-287-1196
Hough, John David/SF	415-495-5769
Houle, Sue/LA	213-273-1863
Huff, Susan/Tahoe City CA	916-583-3735
Hungerford, Lauren/LA	213-476-8896
Hyman, Milt/LA	213-938-3666
Iri, Carl/LA	213-388-5737
Isaacs, Robert/Sunnyvale CA	408-245-1690
Jacobs, Lou/Studio City CA	213-872-1677
Jensen, John/SF	415-982-0962
Johnson, Lee Baker/LA	213-849-6321
Johnson, Payne B./Del Mar CA	714-223-4567
Jolitz, William R./SF	415-781-8421
Jorgensen, Hans/Seattle	206-622-4269
Kahana, Yoram/Hollywood CA	213-876-8208
Kahn, Steve/Malibu CA	213-459-3058
Kauffman, Mark/Santa Rosa CA	707-528-9466
Kearney, Irene/LA	213-472-2704
Keenan Jr., Larry/Oakland CA	415-339-9733
Kelley, Tom/LA 250	**213-657-1780**
Kemper, Charles/SF 251	**415-495-6468**
Kirkland, Douglas/LA	213-656-8511
Krawczyk, John J./LA	213-768-6888
Kredenser, Peter/Beverly Hills CA	213-278-6356
Krosnick, Alan/SF 252	**415-957-1520**
Kuhn, Chuck/Seattle 253	**206-624-4706**
Kuhn, Robert/LA	213-461-3656
Kwong, Sam/LA	213-931-9393
Lamb & Hall Photography/LA	213-931-1775
Lang, G. Erwin/LA	213-455-1526
Langdon, Harry/LA 254	**213-651-3212**
LaRocca, Jerry/Portland OR	503-223-0300
Laurence, Mary/Santa Monica CA 255	**213-395-1169**
Laurence, Mike/Hollywood CA	213-383-4748
Laxer, Jack/Pacific Palisades CA	213-459-1213
Leatart, Brian/LA	213-386-3003
Lee, C. Robert/Idyllwild CA	714-659-3325
Lee, Larry/Newhall CA 256	**805-259-1226**
Lefferts, Marshall/LA 257	**213-469-6316**
Legname, Rudy/SF	415-777-9569
Lenk, Kurt/Malibu CA	213-457-2621
Lewin, Elyse/LA	213-655-4214
Lewine, Rob/LA	213-654-0830
Liles, Harry/LA	213-466-1612
Linden, Seymour/Santa Monica CA	213-393-5817
Livingston, Jerry P./Long Beach CA	213-434-2777
Livzey, John/LA	213-469-2992
Loeser, Peter/Santa Monica CA	213-393-5576
Lowry, Alexander/Santa Cruz CA	408-475-9683
Lyon, Fred/Sausalito CA 258	**415-332-2056**
Lyons, Marv/LA	213-650-8100
Mackay, Donald/LA	213-776-8250
Maddocks/Allan/LA	213-660-1321
Mahieu, Ted/SF	415-495-3551
Manning, Lawrence/LA	213-472-3351
Marcus, Ken/LA 259	**213-937-7214**
Mareschal, Tom/LA	213-934-7793
Marley, Steve/San Jose CA	408-296-5970
Marshall, Jim/SF	415-931-4555
Marshutz, Roger/LA 260	**213-273-1610**
McAfee, Lynn/Studio City CA	213-761-1317
McCrary, Jim/LA	213-936-5115
McDermott, John/SF	415-668-5622
Medsger, Betty/Berkeley CA	415-849-4445
Meinzinger, George/LA	213-666-4640
Menzie, W. Gordon/San Diego CA	714-234-4431
Merrill, Lee P./Steilacoom WA	206-588-9313
Metzler, Doug/LA	213-876-7320
Miles, Reid/Hollywood CA	213-462-6106
Milkie, Fred/Seattle	206-324-3000
Miller, Bill/LA	213-651-5630
Miller, D.K./Bremerton WA	206-373-1640
Miller, Edward L./Vacaville CA	707-446-8515
Miller, Jim/LA 261	**213-553-8243**
Mitchell, David Paul/Bradbury CA	213-358-3328
Mitchell, Tommy/LA	213-933-7201
Moldvay, Albert/Santa Monica CA	213-393-6587
Monkton, Robert/Laguna Beach CA	714-494-8473
Moore, Charles/SF	415-561-9135
Mougin, Claude/LA	213-465-1071
Mudford, Grant/LA	213-936-9145
Muench, David/Santa Barbara CA 262	**805-967-4488**
Muench, Josef/Santa Barbara CA	805-682-4333
Munroe, Joe/Orinda CA	415-254-5112
Murphy, William/LA	213-651-4800
Myers, Tom/Sacramento CA	916-443-8886
Nadel, Leonard/Hollywood CA	213-465-7405
Nagler, Bernard/LA	213-839-8209
Normark, Don/Seattle	206-284-9393
Nyerges, Suzanne/LA	213-938-0151
O'Brien, Tom/LA 263	**213-938-2008**
Ogilvie, Peter/SF	415-391-1646
Optic Ego/SF	415-285-7215
O'Rear, Charles/Manhattan Beach CA	213-545-2828
Outland, Joe/San Diego CA	714-222-1395
Owens, Bill/Livermore CA	415-447-5943
Painter, Charles/Mountain View CA	415-968-7467
Partipilo, John/LA	213-656-3582
Patterson, Maria/Menlo Park CA	415-323-3482
Pavloff, Nick/SF 264	**415-989-2664**
Payne, Geof/Tarzana CA	213-343-0927
Peak, Robert/LA	213-651-5630
Pearson, Charles R./Leavenworth WA	509-548-7983
Pearson, John/Berkeley CA	415-525-7553
Perkins, Robert/Palm Desert CA	714-568-3871
Perry, Susan Kaye/Sausalito CA	415-332-0232
Pesin, Harry/Rancho Santa Fe CA	714-756-2101
Peterson, Greg/SF	415-543-3484
Peterson, Margaret W./Palo Alto CA	415-327-1184
Peterson, Ragnar M./Sunnyvale CA	408-736-2168
Peterson, Robert/Seattle 265	**206-329-2299**
Pett, Laurence J./Tarzana CA	213-344-9453
Photography Northwest/Seattle	206-682-0824
Pilda, Ave/LA	213-275-2353
Pinder, Robert F./Half Moon Bay CA	415-726-4170
Plehn, Denis/LA	213-876-1477
Porter, James/Newport Beach CA	714-751-7231
Price, Stewart/LA	213-855-0383
Quaranta, Vincent/Santa Monica CA	213-450-4698
Rahn, Steve/SF	415-495-3556
Randlett, Mary/Bainbridge Island WA	206-426-2539
Reiff, Robert/LA	213-466-5706
Riggs, Robin/LA	213-991-1742
Robbins, Bill/LA	213-655-3772
Roberge, Earl/Walla Walla WA	509-525-7385
Rodal, Arney A./Bainbridge Island WA	206-842-4989
Roe, Jeffrey A./San Carlos CA	415-591-1565
Rogers, Kenneth/Beverly Hills CA 266	**213-553-5532**
Rokeach, Barrie/Kensington CA	415-527-5376
Rorke, Lorraine/SF	415-387-2787
Ross, Alan C./Hermosa Beach CA	213-379-2015
Ross, Audrey/Berkeley CA	415-845-5316
Ross, Barry/Sepulveda CA	213-893-5677
Ross, William L./Canoga Park CA	213-884-1083
Rowan, Richard/Monterey CA	408-375-3375
Rozsa, Nick/LA	213-939-4888
Russo, Tom/Maui HI	808-572-0594
Rychetnik, Joseph S./SF	415-563-0851
Sabloff, Steven E./Venice CA	213-938-4961
Sagara, Peter/LA	213-933-7531
Sailors, David/SF	415-398-7454
Saitta, Joseph/San Mateo CA	415-573-7017
Samerjan, Peter/LA	213-653-2940
Sanders, Marilyn/LA	213-828-3445
Sato, Gary/LA	213-658-8645
Satterwhite, Al/Marina Del Rey CA	213-392-4852
Scharf, David/LA	213-666-8657
Scherl, Ron/SF	415-421-1160
Schiller, Lawrence/Beverly Hills CA	213-550-8615
Schneider, Charles/Coronado CA	714-429-3987
Schreib, Larry C./Marina Del Rey CA	213-823-4805
Schroeder, Roxanne/San Jose CA	408-257-1940
Schwartz, George J./Bend OR	503-389-4062
Schwartz, Jon/SF	415-563-1315
Scott, Bill/LA	213-462-1112
Selland, George/SF 269	**415-495-3633**
Shaffer, Bob/SF	415-986-0737
Shortz, Barrie/Santa Monica CA	805-962-2818
Shulman, Julius/LA	213-654-0877
Shuman, Ronald J./Menlo Park CA	415-854-4283
Shuper, Phil & Kay/LA	213-852-0075
Sievert, Jon/SF	415-751-2369
Silverman, Jay/LA 270	**213-931-1169**
Simpson, Craig/SF	415-543-5403
Sjef's Fotographie/Portland 272	**503-223-1089**
Slattery, Chad/LA	213-477-0734
Slaughter, Michael/Glendale CA	213-240-4141
Slaughter, Paul/LA	213-278-7238
Slenzak, Ron/LA	213-934-9088
Slobodian, Scott/LA 273	**213-464-2341**
Smith, Bradley/La Jolla CA	714-454-4321
Smith, Elliott Varner/SF	415-864-1921
Smith, Loren/Oakland CA	415-832-7685

PHOTOGRAPHY

Smith, Philip/Mercer Island WA 206-232-5256
Smith, Robert G./Santa Barbara CA 805-969-2291
Smith, Steve/LA 213-464-8690
Solomon, Marc/LA 213-939-6871
Spitz, Harry/LA 213-385-1705
Springmann, Christopher/SF 274 .... **415-647-5711**
Steinberg, Claire/LA 213-279-1775
Stevens, Bob/LA 213-271-8123
Stewart, Hap/SF 415-863-7975
Strauss, Rick/LA 213-383-2578
Streano, Vince/Laguna Beach CA 714-497-1908
Streshinsky, Ted/Berkeley CA 275 .... **415-526-1976**
Strickland, Steve/San Bernardino CA 714-883-4792
Strock, Douglas/LA 213-479-7477
Stryker, Ray/SF 276 .... **415-285-6526**
Studio 3 Photography/Oakland CA 415-655-4538
Sugasawara, George/LA 213-934-3850
Sugiyama, Ron Y./SF 415-282-3483
Sullivan, Jeremiah/San Diego CA 714-224-0070
Sund, Harald/Seattle 277 .... **206-932-1120**
Sundstrom, John A./Burbank CA 213-846-7613
Sutton, David/Studio City CA 213-654-7979
Swarthout, Walter/SF 278 .... **415-543-2525**
Tachibana, Kenji/LA 213-462-3523
Taggart, Fritz/LA 213-469-8227
Tavel, Jon/LA 213-659-7647
Teke/Studio City CA 213-985-9066
Thompson, Wesley/San Diego CA 714-582-0812
Thornton, Tyler/LA 213-559-1191
Tise, David/SF 415-777-0669
Tolbert, Richard/Anaheim CA 714-533-0333
Tracy, Tom/SF 415-861-2822
Trindl, Gene/West Hollywood CA 213-877-4848
Tropp, Stan/LA 213-352-3169
Tully, Roger/Camarillo CA 805-482-3591
Turner, John Terence/Seattle 279 .... **206-325-9073**
Valentine, Fred/LA 213-651-4646
Van der Poel, J./SF 415-621-4404
Vano, Tom/SF 415-421-8612
Vignes, Michelle/SF 415-285-0910
Wallace, Dan/LA 213-278-3028
Warren, Cameron A./Santa Barbara CA 805-965-0915
Warren, William James/LA 280 .... **213-383-0500**
Waterman, Bob/LA 213-641-9014
Weatherley, Carolyn/San Diego CA 714-826-0533
Weiner, Stuart/Los Alamitos CA 714-554-0216
Werts, Bill/LA 213-386-3414
Wheeler, Nik/LA 213-659-4352
White, Charles William/North Hollywood CA. 213-985-3539
Whitmore, Ken/LA 213-472-4337
Whittington, Robert/SF 415-861-5992
Wieand, Dick/LA 213-769-2113
Wiener, Lee/LA 213-876-0990
Wilder, Mani/LA 213-874-2824
Wilding, Jack S./LA 213-664-9316
Willet, Larry/LA 213-463-7184
Wilson, Burton/Santa Barbara CA 805-687-4408
Wilson, Douglas M./Kirkland WA 206-822-8604
Windham, Dale/Seattle 281 .... **206-622-7474**
Witkowski, Robert J./Renton WA 206-255-7241
Wolfe, Dan E./Pasadena CA 213-684-0466
Wolman, Baron/Mill Valley CA 415-388-0181
Wood, James/LA 213-461-3861
Wortham, Robert/Hollywood CA 213-666-8899
Yavno, Max/LA 213-934-2255
Young, R.W./Pacoima CA 213-767-1945
Zachary, Neil/LA 213-937-1314
Greg Zajack Photography/Santa Ana CA ... 714-545-4022
Zak, Ed/SF 415-781-1611
Zimberoff, Tom/Beverly Hills CA 213-271-5900
Zimmerman, Dick/Hollywood CA 282 ..... **213-204-2911**
Zimmerman, John/Beverly Hills CA 213-273-2642
Zurek, Nikolay/Berkeley CA 415-527-6827

STOCK PHOTOGRAPHY

NEW YORK METROPOLITAN AREA

Air Pixies Co. 212-486-9828
Alpha Photo Assoc. 212-777-4216
American Library Color Slide Co. 212-255-5356
Animals Animals 212-580-9595
Peter Arnold Inc. 288 . . . . **212-840-6928**
Authenticated News Inc. 212-243-6995
Bettmann Archive Inc. 212-758-0362
BIPS-Bernsen's Int'l Press Service. 212-MU5-0464
Black Star Publishing Co. 212-679-3288
Blackstone-Shelburne NY Inc 212-736-9100
Camera Clix Inc. 212-684-3526
Camera MD Studios Inc. 212-628-4331
Camera 5 290 . . . . **212-989-2004**
Bruce Coleman Inc. 291 . . . . **212-683-5227**
College Newsphoto Alliance 212-697-1136
Color Library 212-737-7171
Consolidated Poster Service. 212-581-3105
Contact Press Images 212-799-9570
Jerry Cooke Inc. 212-288-2045
Creative Eye 212-986-1224
Culver Pictures Inc. 212-684-5054
DPI NYC 212-752-3930
Design Photographers Intl. Inc 212-752-3930
DeVaney, George A. 212-682-1017
de Wys, Leo 212-986-3190
Dunningan, John V. 212-889-7594
Eastern Photo Service Inc. 212-986-3190
Eastfoto Agency 212-921-1922
Editorial Photocolor Archives 212-697-1136
European Art Color Slides. 212-877-9654
Fairchild Publications Inc. 212-741-4000
Flying Camera Inc. 212-WH3-5095
Focus on Sports 292 . . . . **212-661-6860**
Ford Foundation Photo Library 212-573-5000
Harrison Forman World Photos 212-697-4165
Four By Five Inc. 212-355-2323
Freelance Photographer's Guild. 212-777-4210
Ewing Galloway 212-986-2910
General Press Features. 212-265-6842
Globe Photos Inc. 212-689-1340
The Granger Collection 212-586-0971
Graphic House Inc. 212-689-1435
Lee Gross Assoc. Inc. 212-682-5240
Group 4 212-249-4446
Heyman, Ken. 212-421-4512
Image Bank 298 . . . . **212-371-3636**
Interpress of London & New York 212-832-2839
Keystone Press Agency Inc. 212-924-8123
Kramer, Joan 212-224-1758
Harold M. Lambert Studios 212-921-2850
Lewis, Frederick 212-921-2850
Liaison Agency 212-355-7310
Long, Joe 212-249-4446
Magnum Photos Inc. 212-541-7570
Maisel, Jay. 212-431-5013
Memory Shop Inc. 212-473-2404
Mercier, Louis 212-972-1701
Monkmeyer Press Photo Agency. 212-755-1715
Movie Star News 212-982-8364
Munsey News Service 212-989-7151
Museum of the City of N.Y. 212-534-1672
Museum of Modern Art 212-956-4209
The N.Y. Historical Soc. 212-TR3-3400
NYT Pictures 212-556-1234
Nancy Palmer Photo Agency. 212-683-9309
Penguin Photo. 212-758-7328
Photo Researchers Inc. 212-758-3420
Photo Trends 212-279-2130
Photo World Inc. 212-777-4214
Photofile Ltd. 212-989-0500
Photography for Industry 212-757-9255
Photoreporters Inc. 212-245-1890
Pictorial Parade Inc. 212-840-2026
Plessner Int'l. 212-686-2444
Press Features Int'l. 212-532-2508
RDR Productions Inc. 212-586-4432
Rebus Photo Library 212-661-8796
Religious News Service 212-688-7094
Retna (Redfern) 212-929-7111
Roberts, H. Armstrong 212-682-6626
Scala Fine Arts Publishers Inc. 212-354-9646
Seidman, Sy 212-982-4318
Shostal Assoc. 212-687-0696
Sovfoto 212-921-1922
Sports Illustrated 212-841-3663
Stock Photos Unlimited Inc. 212-421-8980
Stock Shop 212-687-8080
Sygma Photo News 212-765-1820
Taurus Photos 212-683-4025
Three Lions Inc. 212-691-8640
Time-Life Picture Agency 212-586-1212
Transworld Feature Syndicate 212-997-1880
Underwood & Underwood 212-758-0362
United Press Int'l. News Pictures. 212-682-0400
Wide World Photos Inc. 212-262-6300
Woodfin Camp & Assoc. 296. . . . . **212-355-1855**
Katherine Young Agency 212-684-0999

NORTHEAST & SOUTHEAST

Chandoha, Walter /Annandale NJ 64 201-782-3666
CYR Color Photo Agency /Norwalk CT 203-838-8230
Globe Press Int'l /York PA 717-845-2805
Image Photos /Stockbridge MA 413-298-5500
Lensman Stock Photos Ltd. /Wash. DC 293 . **202-337-8014**
OPUS Fotografiks /Bethesda MD 301-656-7680
Phelps & Thompson Inc. /Atlanta 404-881-1925
Picturemakers Inc. /Succasunna NJ 201-584-3000
Roberts, H. Armstrong /Philadelphia. 215-386-6300
Sickles Photo-Reporting /Maplewood NJ 201-763 6355
Skyviews Survey Inc. /Westbury NY 516-333-3600
Stock Boston /Boston 617-266-2573
Symmes, Ed /Atlanta 404-873-5721
Max Tharpe Photo Library /Ft. Lauderdale. . . 305-763-5449
Trans-World News Service /Wash DC 202-638-7171
Wide World Photos Inc. /Boston 617-357-8104
Woodfin Camp & Assoc. /Wash DC 202-466-3830

MIDWEST

Artstreet /Chicago. 312-664-3049
Branat & Assoc. /Barrington Hills IL 312-428-6363
Campbell Stock Photo Service /Detroit 313-559 6870
Candida Photos Inc. /Chicago 312-736-5544
Collectors Series /Chicago 312-427-5311
Gress-Rupert /Chicago. 312-642-1188
Hedrich-Blessing /Chicago 312-321-1151
Historical Picture Services /Chicago 312-346-0599
Ibid Inc. /Chicago. 312-644-0515
Image Bank /Chicago. 312-944-0424
Lambert, Harold M. /Chicago. 312-332-5350
Piles & Files of Photos /Chicago 312-642-7110
Redman, Lee F. /Chicago 312-973-3441
Webb Photos. /St. Paul MN 612-674-7317
Zehrt, Jack /St. Louis 314-773-2298
TRW Inc /Cleveland 295 . . . . **216-383-2121**

SOUTHWEST & WEST

After Image /LA 287. . . . . **213-467-6033**
American Stock Photos /Los Angeles 213-469-3908
BBM Assoc /Berkeley CA. 415-549-2461
Morton Beebe & Assoc. /San Francisco 415-362-3530
Danpelet Interlinks /San Anselmo CA 415-456-1260
Far West Photography & Assoc. /Albuquerque 505-255-0646
Gemini Smith Inc /La Jolla CA 714-454-4321
Image Bank West /San Francisco. 415-398-2242
McLaughlin, Herb & Dorothy /Phoenix AZ . . . 602-258-6551
Mercury Archives /Hollywood CA 213-463-8000
Photo Unique /Salt Lake City UT. 801-363-5182
Running Productions /Flagstaff AZ 602-774-2923
B P Singer Features Inc. /Anaheim CA 714-527-5650
Visual Media Inc. /Reno NV 702-322-8868
Weckler's World /San Francisco 415-982-1750

ILLUSTRATION

NEW YORK METROPOLITAN AREA

Abraham, D.E.	212-431-7499
Accornero, Franco	212-697-8525
Accurso, Tony.	212-435-1323
Adato, Jacqueline	212-679-8554
Air Stream	212-682-1490
Albahae, Andrea.	212-769-2994
Albano, Chuck.	212-472-9474
Alcorn, John.	212-421-0050
Alcorn, Bob	212-685-2770
Allaux, Jean Francois	212-595-2155
Allegro Studio	212-986-8161
Allen, Mary	212-689-3902
Almquist, Don	212-682-2462
Aloise, Frank	212-869-1150
Alpert, Alan	212-421-8160
Altemus, Robert	212-861-5080
Ameijide, Raymond.	212-832-3214
Amsel, Richard	212-628-5960
Ansado, John.	212-929-0487
Antoni, Volker E.H	212-636-4670
Antonio	212-787-8910
Aplin, Jim	212-989-1797
Applebaum & Curtis	212-752-0679
Arcelle, Joan	212-924-1865
Aristovulos, Nick.	212-725-2454
Arndt, Ursula.	212-647-2718
Aronson, Lynne	212-673-1770
Art Pro Studio	212-532-6844
Aruego, Jose	212-988-5463
Arwin, Melanie	212-924-2020
Asch, Howard	212-352-0256
Ashmead, Hal	212-686-3514
Ayers, Jessie	212-472-3871
BJB Graphics Inc.	212-683-5065
Baldus, Fred	212-757-6300
Barkley, James	212-682-1490
Barr, Ken	212-697-8525
Barrett, Ron.	212-580-0078
Barry, Ron	212-686-3514
Bauer, Carla	212-873-4634
Bazzel, Deborah	212-685-2770
Beaty, Mina	212-243-5267
Becker, Ron.	212-689-3902
Beecham, Tom.	212-697-8525
Bego, Dolores	212-697-6170
Bek-gran, Phyllis	212-689-3902
Bell, Barbara.	212-752-0190
Bergman, Barbra	212-679-4562
Berkey, John.	212-355-0910
Billout, Guy	212-255-2023
Blackwell, Garie	212-752-8490
Blechman, Bob.	212-869-1630
Blumrich, Christoph.	212-684-4508
Bolognese, Raphael	212-228-5219
Bonhomme, Bernard.	212-532-9247
Bornschlegel, Ruth.	212-929-7709
Bossert, Jill	212-838-2560
Bottner, Barbara	212-879-3936
Bozzo, Frank	212-535-9182
Brautigam, Don	212-677-0387
Brickner, Alice	212-549-5909
Bridy, Dan	212-682-2462
Brofsky, Miriam	212-595-8094
Brooks, A.	212-242-3154
Brooks, Lou	212-679-4487
Brown, Judith Gwyn	212-288-1599
Bruck, J.S.	212-247-1130
Brundage, Dick	212-689-3902
Bryan, Diana	212-233-8989
Byrd, David Edward	212-255-5435
Byrd, Robert	212-682-2462
Calogero, Gene	212-873-3297
Cantarella, Virginia Hoyt	212-622-2061
Cardi, Nick	212-688-1080
Cason, Merrill	212-860-2607
Catalano, Sal	212-682-1490
Caulos, Luiz	212-799-8050
Cavanagh, Dorothe.	212-580-7132
Cayard, Bruce	212-697-6170
Charmatz, Bill.	212-595-3907
Chen, Tony	212-699-4813
Chester, Harry	212-752-0570
Chorao, Kay.	212-749-8256
Christensen, David.	212-679-8554
Church, Marilyn	212-242-0324
Chwast, Seymour	212-677-3506
Ciardiello, Joseph	212-351-2289
Clark, Jane	212-685-2770
Clarke, Bob	212-581-4045
Clifton, John	212-464-6746
Cober, Alan E.	212-758-8490
CoConis, Ted	212-856-9055
Coe, Sue	212-734-6698
Collier, John.	212-855-3173
Colton, Keita	212-686-3514
Conover, Chris.	212-852-2986
Continuity Assoc.	212-751-5140
Cooley, D. Gary.	212-695-2426
Cooper, Robert.	212-758-2222
Cornell, Laura	212-534-0596
Crair, Mel.	212-697-8525
Cramer, D.L.	212-799-7138
Crawford, Margery	212-686-6883
Crews, Donald.	212-636-5773
Cross, Peter.	212-687-2272
Crosthwaite, C. Royd	212-355-0910
Cruz, Ray.	212-243-1199
Cuevas, Robert	212-661-7149
Cunningham, Robert M.	212-675-1731
Dacey, Bob.	212-686-3514
Dale, Robert	212-758-2222
Daly, Sean	212-989-5435
Davidson, Everett	212-682-1490
Davis, Jack	212-751-4656
Dawson, Diane	212-362-7819
DeCamps, Craig	212-564-2691
Degen, Paul.	212-638-8247
Deigan, Jim	212-682-2462
De Lattre, Georgette	212-247-6850
Delessert, Etienne.	212-421-0050
Deschamps, Bob.	212-751-4656
Descombes, Roland	212-355-0910
Detrich, Susan	212-237-9174
Deverin, Daniele	212-755-4945
Devlin, Bill.	212-935-9436
Dewey, Kenneth F.	212-755-4945
Diamond, Donna	212-362-3717
Dietz, Jim.	212-686-3514
Difiori, Lawrence.	212-753-4192
Difiori, Mila	212-371-9173
Dillon, Diane	212-624-0023
Dillon, Leo	212-624-0023
Dinnerstein, Harvey	212-783-6879
Domingo, Ray.	212-751-4656
Donner, Carol.	212-751-4773
Doret, Michael.	212-889-0490
Drakides & Assoc.	212-490-0658
Drovetto.	212-787-8910
Drucker, Mort.	212-755-4945
Duarte, Mary	212-674-4513
Durrence, Nancy	212-362-5345
Echevarria, Abe.	212-679-4562
Edwards, Sandie.	212-664-5656
Egielski, Richard	212-255-9328
Ellis, Dean.	212-254-7590
Ellis, Kathy	212-749-6232
Ely, Richard.	212-874-4816
Emmett, Bruce and Lisa.	212-751-6459
Endewelt, Jack	212-877-0575
Engelman, Julie	212-355-1316
Enik, Ted	212-222-9441
Esteves, Jan	212-682-2462
Eutemey, Loring	212-249-8883
Farina, Michael.	212-355-1316
Farley, Eileen M.	212-673-7713
Farmakis, Andrea	212-758-5280
Fasolino, Teresa	212-799-8050
Fassell, Beatrice	212-865-2144
Federico, Helen	212-661-0850
Fennimore, Linda	212-866-0279
Fernandes, Stanislaw 23	**212-533-2648**
Fery, Guy	212-682-2462
Fitzgerald, Frank.	212-722-6793
Forbes, Bart.	212-686-3514
Fox, Barbara	212-752-5846
Francis, Judy	212-866-7204
Fraser, Betty	212-247-1937
Freas, John	212-682-2462
Freeman, Irving.	212-674-6705
Friedland, Lew	212-359-3420
Friscia, Salmon.	212-228-4134
Froom, Georgia	212-944-0330
Fulgoni, Louis.	212-243-2959
G & T Studio	212-687-1684
Gaadt, George.	212-682-2462
Gacci.	212-753-2310
Gadino, Victor.	212-534-7206
Gaetano, Nicholas.	212-674-5749
Gahan, Nancy Lou.	212-674-2644
Gallardo, Gervasio	212-355-0910
Garland, Michael	212-833-3998
Garnett, Joe.	212-688-1080
Gayler, Anne	212-734-7060
Gehm, Charles	212-697-8525
Giglio, Richard	212-675-7642
Geller, Martin.	212-237-1733
Gennard, Jane.	212-289-6710
Genova, Joe	212-682-1490
Gentile, John and Anthony	212-757-1966
George, Andrew.	212-758-2222
Gersten, Gerry	212-928-7957
Geyer, Jackie	212-682-2462
Gignilliat, Elaine.	212-935-1943
Gill, Richard	212-532-4566
Gillott, Carol	212-243-6448
Giovanopoulos, Paul.	212-661-0850
Giusti, Robert	212-752-0179
Gladstein, Renee	212-873-0257
Graber, Norman.	212-682-7932
Graboff, Abner	212-354-5355
Graham, Mariah	212-580-8061
Gray, John	212-447-6466
Gray, Susan.	212-675-2243
Green, Norman	212-679-4562
Grinder, Rainbow	212-682-2462
Gross, Samuel H	212-369-7141
Gross, Steve	212-697-8525
Grossberg, Manuel	212-684-1784
Grossman, Myron	212-751-5125
Grossman, Robert.	212-925-1965
Grote, Rich	212-685-2770
Haas, Arie	212-573-8469
Hall, James J.	212-564-6000
Hall, Joan	212-243-6059
Hamberger, John.	212-679-6573
Hamid, Helen	212-752-2546
Harkins, George	212-964-7210
Harrison, Hugh	212-858-9034
Harrison, Sean	212-369-3831
Henderson, Alan	212-758-2222
Hering, Al	212-986-3282
Hermann, Al	212-752-8490
Hernadez, Raymond	212-221-3460
Hess, Mark	212-421-0050
Hinck, Fred	212-235-0809
Hirschfeld, Al	212-534-6172
Hodges, Mike.	212-794-0922
Hofmann, Ginnie.	212-944-1240
Holland, Brad	212-226-3675
Holt, Katheryn	212-894-2345
Hooks, Mitchell	212-737-1853
Hortens, Walter	212-838-0014
Hour Hands	212-687-0118
Huens, Jean-Leon	212-355-0910
Huffaker, Sandy	212-477-1867
Hull, Cathy	212-683-8559
Hunt, Jim.	212-758-2222
Hunter, Stan	212-677-9510
Hunyady, Brooke	212-254-1506
Huyssen, Roger	212-888-9193
Idelson, Joyce	212-877-6161
Inouye, Carol.	212-787-8535
Ivenbaum, Elliott	212-664-5656
Jampel, Judith.	212-873-5234
Jezierski, Chet.	212-355-0910
Johnson, Doug.	212-260-1880
Johnson, Hedda.	212-737-3236
Johnson, Kristin	212-477-4033
Joseph, Paula	212-242-6137
Juckes, Geoff.	212-567-5676
Juggernaut	212-691-8181
Just, Hal	212-697-6170
Kalish, Lionel	212-751-4656
Kane, Harry	212-486-0180
Kanelous, George	212-688-1080
Kappes, Werner	212-861-1748
Karchin, Steve.	212-689-6928
Karlin, Bernie	212-687-7636
Karlin, Eugene	212-457-5086
Katz, Les 26	**212-625-4741**
Kaufman, Norm	212-427-8361
Kendrick, Dennis.	212-924-3085
Kibbee, Gordon	212-989-7074
King, Jean	212-866-8488
Kingsley, Melinda	212-879-2042
Kirk, Charles	212-677-3770
Klammer, John.	212-837-4424
Klapper, Rhonda	212-490-0673
Kliros, Thea	212-355-1316
Knettell, Sharon	212-751-4656
Knight, Jacob	212-661-0850
Korda, Leslie	212-595-3711
Krakovitz, Harlan	212-689-3902
Kramer, Carveth	212-661-0850
Krieger, Salem.	212-682-2462
Lackow, Andy.	212-685-2770
LaGrone, Roy.	212-975-5420
Landis, Joan	212-989-7074
Lang, Gary.	212-697-8525
Lapsley, Robert	212-689-3902
Laurence, Karen	212-661-0850
Leake, Don.	212-877-8405
Lee, Devorah	212-759-8486
Leffel, David	212-691-1988
Lesser, Ron	212-697-8525
Levin, Arnie	212-472-9474
Levirne, Joel.	212-869-8370
Lewis, Tim	212-986-4072
Lieberman, Ron.	212-947-0653
Lilly, Charles	212-873-3608
Lindlof, Ed.	212-682-2462
Line, Lemuel	212-355-0910
Linn, Warren	212-758-2222
Lloyd, Peter	212-355-1316
Lodigensky, Ted	212-355-1316
Lohne, Garrett.	212-362-3257
Lopez, Antonio.	212-924-2060
Lubey, Dick	212-686-3514
Lyall, Dennis	212-682-2462
Lyons, Ellen	212-794-0922
Maas, Julie	212-646-2764
Maddalone, John.	212-599-1721
Mahoney, Ron	212-682-2462
Mantel, Richard	212-532-9247
Marchesi, Stephen	212-679-8554
Mardon, Allan	212-751-4656
Marich, Felix	212-758-2222
Martin, David	212-242-1450
Mattelson, Marvin.	212-684-2974
Maxwell, Brookie	212-799-8050
McAfee, Mara	212-348-9284
McClelland, John	212-682-2462
McConnell, Gerald	212-475-5466
McCoy, Steve	212-794-0922
McCrady, Lady.	212-532-6317
McDaniel, Jerry	212-697-6170
McLean, Wilson	212-752-8490
McMullan, James	212-683-8530
McNamara Assoc.	212-682-2462
McVicker, Charles	212-697-4451
Mehlman, Elwyn	212-751-4656
Melendez, Robert	212-355-1316

ILLUSTRATION

Metcalf, Roger	212-688-1080
Meyerowitz, Rick	212-989-2446
Michal, Marie	212-348-4668
Michaels, Bob	212-752-1185
Mihaesco, Eugene	212-867-9683
Minor, Wendell	212-691-6925
Mitsuhashi, Yoko	212-686-6631
Miyamoto, Lance R.	212-847-9755
Miyauchi, Haruo	212-532-9247
Morgan, Barry	212-866-8509
Morgan, Jacqui	212-421-0766
Morrison, Don	212-697-6170
Moseley, Marshall	212-499-7045
Moss, Geoffrey	212-472-9474
Myers, Lou	212-751-4656
Nagel, Pat	212-682-2462
Neibart, Wally	212-682-2462
Newcomb, John	212-986-3282
Nessim, Barbara	212-677-8888
Newsom, Tom	212-682-2462
Noonan, Julia	212-879-5916
Nuñez, Carlos	212-935-5942
Ochagavia, Carlos	212-355-0910
Odom, Mel	212-724-9320
Oelbaum, Frances	212-622-8238
Oksenherdler, Marcos	212-625-6175
Orloff, Denis	212-982-8341
Overacre, Gary	212-751-4656
Palladini, David	212-682-1490
Pan, Richard	212-564-9294
Paslavsky, Ivan	212-759-3985
Pepper, Bob	212-355-1316
Pepper, Brenda	212-875-3236
Petragnani, Vincent	212-758-2222
Pimsler, Alvin J.	212-787-4967
Pinkney, Jerry	212-751-4656
Podwil, Jerry	212-255-9464
Pohl, Dennis	212-255 8540
Pomerance, Joseph	212-622-6669
Primavera, Elise	212-689-3902
Punchatz, Don Ivan	212-989-7074
Quartuccio, Dom	212-661-1173
Quay, Mary Jo.	212-249-5288
Quon, Mike	212-226-6024
Radigan, Bob	212-682-2462
Rane, Walter	212-675-7125
Raphael & Bolognese	212-228-5219
Reingold, Alan	212-697-6170
Renfro, Ed	212-691-7344
Rixford, Ellen	212-254-0614
Robinette, John	212-687-2272
Rosenblum, Richard	212-683-4722
Rosenthal, Doug	212-475-9422
Ross, Barry	212-663-7386
Ross, Larry	212-986-3282
Ruffins, Reynold	212-674-8150
Ryan, Terrance J.	212-688-1080
Sandler, Barbara	212-691-2342
Santore, Charles	212-751-4656
Saris, Anthony	212-831-6353
Sauber, Rob	212-679-8554
Schmelzer, John	212-794-0922
Schmidt, Chuck	212-758-2222
Schorr, Todd	212-685-5318
Schongut, Emanuel	212-532-9247
Schwartz, Frank	212-689-3902
Scribner, Joanne L.	212-686-4520
Seaver, Jeffrey	212-925-0369
Seltzer, Isadore	212-666-1561
Shendroff, Kaaren	212-687-2272
Shap, Sandra	212-758-2222
Shea, Mary Anne	212-239-1076
Shilstone, Arthur	212-682-2462
Siegel, Anita	212-697-6170
Silverman, Burt	212-799-3399
Singer, Gloria	212-339-7832
Siracusa, Catherine	212-580-8084
The Sketch Pad Studio	212-989-7074
Skibinski, Ray	212-752-6132
Slackman, Charles	212-758-8233
Slock, Catherine	212-988-6112
Smith, Cornelia	212-689-3902
Smith, Elwood H.	212-982-4882
Soileau, Hodges	212-355-1316
Sorel, Ed	212-421-0050
Spollen, Chris	212-979-9695
Sposato, John	212-477-3909
Stabin, Victor	212-243-7688
Stahl, Nancy	212-865-3665
Staico, Kathy	212-758-2222
Stamaty, Mark Alan	212-475-1626
Star Studios	212-475-0440
Steadman, Barbara	212-684-6326
Sternglass, Arno	212-989-7074
Sterrett, Jane	212-929-2566
Stipelman, Steven	212-689-3902
Barnard Stone Assoc.	212-687-6940
Stone, Gilbert	212-421-0050
Strimban, Robert	212-243-6965
Taback, Simms	212-674-8150
Taylor, Doug	212-674-6346
Taylor, Stan	212-685-4741
Thompson, Arthur	212-685-2770
Thornton, Richard	212-689-3902
Travis, Kathy	212-697-6170
Trossman, Michael	212-691-2312
Trull, John	212-535-5383
Trusilo, Jim	212-682-2462
Tunstull, Glen	212-355-1316
Ungerer, Tomi	212-421-0050
Van Hamersveld, John	212-799-8050
Ventilla, Istvan	212-799-8050
Victor, Joan B.	212-988-2773
Viviano, Sam	212-242-1471
Vizbar, Milda	212-757-2678
Wald, Carol	212-737-4559
Walker, Bob	212-682-2462
Warhol, Andy	212-475-5550
Weaver, Robert	212-254-4289
Weisberg, Glen	212-988-7955
Welkis, Allen	212-686-3514
Weller, Don	212-755-4945
Whistl'n Dixie	212-935-9522
Whitesides, Kim	212-799-4789
Wilcox, David	212-421-0050
Wilkinson, Bill	212-697-6170
Wilkinson, Chuck	212-682-1490
Willardson, Dave	212-475-0440
Wilson, Rowland	212-371-1850
Wohlberg, Ben	212-254-9663
Wolin, Ron	212-682-2462
Wood, Page	212-685-2770
Woodend, James	212-697-8525
Word-Wise	212-246-0430
Young, Bruce	212-688-1080
Zagorski, Stanislaw	212-532-9247
Zick, Brian	212-475-0440
Ziering, Bob	212-873-0034

NORTHEAST

Abel, Roy/Scarsdale NY	914-725-1899
Acuna, Ed/Westport CT	203-227-4090
Amicosante, Vincent/Edgewater NJ	201-224-8195
Andersen, Roy/Ridgefield CT	203-438-6354
Andrew, Joan/Fairfax VA	703-591-8443
Anthony, Carol/Greenwich CT	203-531-7345
Bang, Molly Garrett/Woods Hole MA	617-548-7135
Bangham, Richard/Takoma Park MD	301-270-6986
Bass, Marilyn/Carmel NY	914-225-8611
Berger, Vivian/Yonkers NY	914-237-5914
Boehm, Linda/Weston CT	203-226-7674
Bonner, Lee/Baltimore	301-377-2869
Booth, Carl H./Providence RI	401-274-3919
Bridy, Dan/Pittsburgh	412-343-5549
Brown, Judith Gwyn/Weston CT	203-226-7674
Brown, Michael David/Rockville MD	301-762-4474
Burroughs, Miggs/Westport CT	203-227-9667
Bill Burrows & Assoc./Baltimore	301-752-4615
Butcher, Jim/Baltimore	301-879-6380
Calvin, James/Weston CT	203-226-7674
Carruthers, Roy/Old Greenwich CT	203-637-2957
Cavanagh, Tom/Closter NJ	201-768-2526
Cayea, John/Cornwall-on-Hudson NY	914-534-2942
Chandler, Jean/Wyckoff NJ	201-891-2381
Close, Alex/Greenwich CT	203-869-6440
Cober, Alan/Ossining NY	914-941-8696
Cohen, Gil/Philadelphia	215-247-9007
Colby, Sas/Weston CT	203-226-7674
Collins, Pat/Weston CT	203-226-7674
Colonna, Bernie/Weston CT	203-226-7674
Condak, Cliff/Cold Spring NY	914-265-9420
Corson, Richard/Watchung NJ	201-755-4438
Craft, Kinuko/Weston CT	203-226-7674
Creative Image/Goshen NY	914-294-6743
Cummins, Jim/Weston CT	203-226-7674
Cushman, Doug/Weston CT	203-226-7674
David, Cyril/East Hampton NY	516-324-2802
Davis, Allen/Weston CT	203-226-7674
Davis, Paul/Sag Harbor NY	516-725-2248
Dawson, Diane/Weston CT	203-226-7674
Deigen, Jim/Pittsburgh	412-391-1698
de Kiefte, Kees/Weston CT	203-226-7674
Demarest, Robert/Glen Rock NJ	201-445-4943
Dior, Jerry/Edison NJ	201-561-6536
Downey, William/Red Bank NJ	201-842-5965
Eagle, Mike/Old Saybrook CT	203-388-5654
Ebersole, Patricia/Fishkill NY	914-454-1665
Edwards, William/Waterbury CT	203-754-1298
Einsel, Naiad and Walter/Westport CT	203-226-0709
Ely, Creston/Weston CT	203-226-7674
Enos, Randall/Weston CT	203-227-4785
Epstein, Dave/Irvington-on-Hudson NY	914-591-7470
Etter, Beverly/Poughkeepsie NY	914-471-5126
Eucalyptus Tree Studio/Baltimore	301-243-0211
Farris, Jo/Westport CT	203-227-7806
Felix, Louisa/Hoboken, NJ	201-653-4833
Ford, Pam/Westport CT	203-226-3233
Frazetta, Frank/East Stroudsberg PA	717-424-2945
Frost, Ralph/Wilkes Barre PA	717-472-3600
Fuchs, Bernard/Westport CT	203-227-4644
Garland, Michael/Weston CT	203-226-7674
Gist, Linda E./Ft. Washington PA	215-643-3757
Glanzman, Louis S./Sayville NY	516-589-2613
Glessner, Marc/Somerset NJ	201-249-5038
Michael Gnatek Assoc./Wash DC	202-872-8989
Gnidziejko, Alex/Madison NJ	201-377-2664
Goldman, Marvin/Carmel NY	914-225-8611
Grashow, James/West Redding CT	203-938-9195
Greenhalgh, Robert/New City, NY	914-634-5223
Handville, Robert T./Pleasantville NY	914-969-3582
Hardy, Neil O./Westport CT	203-226-4446
Harris, Sidney/Great Neck NY	516-466-6143
Harsh, Fred/Weston CT	203-226-7674
Harvey, Richard/Ridgefield CT	203-438-0553
Hathaway, Margaret/Weston CT	203-226-7674
Heindel, Robert/Fairfield CT	203-261-4270
Henderson, David/Verona NJ	201-783-5791
Herrick, George W./Hartford CT	203-527-1940
Hess, Richard/Roxbury CT	203-421-7377
Hildebrandt, Greg/West Orange NJ	201-736-1364
Hildebrandt, Tim/Gladstone NJ	201-234-2149
Huehnergarth, John/Princeton NJ	609-921-3211
Hunt, Stan/Westport CT	203-227-7806
Hunter, Allan B./Abington PA	215-657-4614
Jarvis, David/Greenwich CT	203-531-8339
Jean, Carole/Roslyn NY	516-484-4144
Johnson, David A./New Canaan CT	203-966-0245
Jones, George/Wilton CT	203-762-7242
Kalback, Jerry/Glenwood NY	716-592-7767
Kasper, Ed/Wilton CT	203-762-3227
Kidder, Harvey/Pleasantville NY	914-769-6298
Koslow, Howard/East Norwich NY	516-922-7427
Kossin, Sanford/Port Washington NY	516-883-3038
Kuhn, Bob/Roxbury CT	203-354-7607
Lambert, Saul/Princeton NJ	609-924-6518
Lavin, Robert/Huntington NY	516-427-3733
Lazarevich, Mila/Weston CT	203-226-7674
Lee, Robert J./Carmel NY	914-225-4934
Lieberman, Warren/Weston CT	203-226-7674
Lisberger Studios Inc/Boston	617-426-7070
Lonette, Reisie/Weston CT	203-226-7674
Lorenz, Al/Weston Ct	203-226-7674
Lorenz, Lee/Westport CT	203-227-7806
Luber, Mal/Weston CT	203-226-7674
Luzak, Dennis/West Redding CT	203-938-3278
Lynch, Don/Upper Nyack NY	914-358-3939
Mackay, Donald A./Ossining NY	914-941-5036
Maffia, Daniel/Englewood NJ	201-871-0435
Magee, Alan/Camden ME	207-236-2985
Mambach, Alex/Jersey City NJ	201-795-4775
Mardon, Allan/Danbury CT	203-744-5369
Mariano, Mike/Weston CT	203-226-7674
Mariuzza, Pete/Briarcliff Manor NY	914-769-3310
Martinot, Claude/Weston CT	203-226-7674
McCaffery, Janet/Weston CT	203-226-7674
McCollum, Rick/Westport CT	203-255-2275
McGinnis, Robert/Old Greenwich CT	203-537-1259
McIntosh, Jon C./Weston CT	203-226-7674
McQueen, Lucinda Emily/Lyme CT	203-434-8189
Meltzoff, Stanley/Fair Haven NJ	201-747-4415
Mitchell, Ken/Newtown CT	203-426-0388
Modell, Frank/Westport CT	203-227-7806
Moon, Elizia/Weston CT	203-226-7674
Morgaard, Bente/Boston MA	617-426-3565
Myers, Lou/Peekskill NY	914-737-2307
Nelson, Bill/Richmond VA	804-358-9637
Norman, Marty/Glen Head NY	516-671-4482
Oni/Yorktown Heights NY	914-245-5862
O'Sullivan, Tom/Weston CT	203-226-7674
Otnes, Fred/West Redding CT	203-938-2829
Palulian, Dick/Rowayton CT	203-866-3734
Partch, Virgil/Westport CT	203-227 7806
Passalacqua, David/Sayville NY	516-589-1663
Peak, Bob/Greenwich CT	203-869-4404
Pisano, Al/Upper Saddle River NJ	201-327-6716
Pitt Studios/Pittsburgh	412-261-0460
Plotkin, Barnett/Great Neck NY	516-487-7457
Porter, George/West Chester PA	215-692-6618
Provensen, Alice/Staatsburg NY	914-266-3245
Provensen, Martin/Staatsburg NY	914-266-3245
Rabinowitz, Sandy/Weston CT	203-226-7674
Radigan, Bob/Pittsburgh	412-281-9387
Ramus, Michael/Princeton NJ	609-924-4266
Raymo, Anne/West Saugerties NY	914-246-6088
Richter, Mische/Westport CT	203-227-7806
Rogers, Howard/Weston Ct	203-227-2273
Roth, Ferdinand L./Livingston NJ	201-992-1030
Rothacker, George H./Media PA	215-566-8058
Ruggero, Pat/Hicksville NY	516-986-5454
Saldutti, Denise/Colonia NJ	201-381-1931
Sanderson, Ruth/Weston CT	203-226-7674
Santa, Monica/Weston CT	203-226-7674
Saxon, Charles/Westport CT	203-227-7806
Scalera, Ron/Orange NJ	201-674-6266
Schaare, Harry J./Westbury NY	516-333-1526
Schleinkofer, David/Levittown PA	215-946-3464
Schottland, M./Weston CT	203-226-7674
Scrofani, Joseph/Fort Lee NJ	201-461-5123
Seidler, Ned/Wash DC	202-362-2667
Sharpe, Jim/Westport CT	203-226-9984
Sickles, Noel/Stamford CT	203-323-1770
Singer, Arthur/Jericho NY	516-938-8228
Smath, Jerry/Weston CT	203-226-7674
Smith, Douglas/Larchmont NY	914-834-3997
Smith, Joseph/New Fairview CT	203-746-1858
Smith, N.J./Weston CT	203-226-7674
Smith, Phil/Weston CT	203-226-7674
Smollin, Mike/Redding Ridge CT	203-938-2355
Sorel, Ed/Carmel NY	914-225-8086
Sottung, George/Ridgefield CT	203-438-4124
Soyka, Edward/Irvington NY	914-591-7486
Spanfeller, Jim/Katonah NY	914-232-3546
Sparkman, Gene/N. Salem NY	914-669-9443
Sparks, Richard/Norwalk CT	203-866-2002
Spitzmiller, Walter/West Redding CT	203-938-3551
Springer, Sally/Weston CT	203-226-7674
Stahl, Benjamin F./Litchfield Ct	203-567-8005
Stasiak, Krystyna/Weston CT	203-226-7674
Steig, William/Westport CT	203-227-7806
Steinberg, Herb/Roosevelt NJ	609-448-4724
Stevenson, James/Westport CT	203-227-7806
Stirnweis, Shannon/Wilton CT	203-762-7058
Sundgaard, Erik/Weston CT	203-226-7674
Swan, Susan/Westport CT	203-226-9104

ILLUSTRATION

Syverson, Henry /Westport CT	203-227-7806
Taktakajian, Asdur /N. Tarrytown NY	914-631-5553
Tarantal, Stephen /Philadelphia	215-925-2584
Tauss, Herb /Garrison NY	914-424-3765
Tinkelman, Murray /Peekskill NY	914-737-5960
Toulmin-Rothe, Ann /Westport CT	203-226-3505
Troiani, Don /Pound Ridge NY	914-764-5514
Tsui, George /Bellmore NY	516-781-3506
Ulrich, George /Weston CT	203-226-7674
Upshur, Tom /Roslyn Heights NY	516-484-4688
Valla, Victor /Gladstone NJ	201-234-0438
Veno, Joe /Weston CT	203-226-7674
Viskupic, Gary /Center Port NY	516-757-9021
Waldman, Neil /Pearl River NY	914-735-6699
Wallner, John C. /Ossining NY	914-762-5451
Walters, Candace /Weston CT	203-226-7674
Weber, Robert /Westport CT	203-227-7806
Wilson, Gahan /Westport CT	203-227-7806

SOUTHEAST

Berry, Jim /Atlanta	404-262-7424
Boatright, John/Memphis TN	901-683-1856
Boyd, Bob/Atlanta	404-262-7424
Carey, Wayne/Atlanta	404-262-7424
Faure, Renee/Neptune Beach FL	904-246-2781
Gaadt, David M./Atlanta	404-252-7500
Gantt, Carlton/Atlanta	404-262-7424
Graphics Group/Atlanta	404-261-5146
Hamilton, Marcus/Charlotte NC	704-545-3121
Hinojosa, Albino/Ruston LA	318-255-2820
Nunn, J.B./Atlanta	404-262-7424
Overacre, Gary/Marietta GA	404-973-8878
Robinette, John/Memphis TN	901-324-0510
Saffold, Joe/Atlanta	404-231-2168
Turner, Pete/Cary NC	919-467-8466
Wende, Phillip/Atlanta	414-926-6355
Wiley, Ray/Jacksonville FL	904-398-0079
Wilkes, Jean/Atlanta	404-876-1950
Wilson, Meredith/Atlanta	404-262-7424
Wilson, Reagan/Atlanta	404-881-0212
The Workshop/Atlanta	404-575-0141

MIDWEST

Alcorn, John/Chicago	312-944-6655
Altschuler, Franz/Chicago	312-787-8834
Anderson, Bill and Judy/Chicago	312-332-5168
Art Graphics/Chicago	312-236-4955
Biderbost, Bill/Evanston IL	312-787-8834
Billout, Guy/Chicago	312-944-6655
Blechman, R.O./Chicago	312-944-6655
Blick, Al/Chicago	312-332-5168
Bordelon, Melinda/Chicago	312-944-6655
Bridy, Dan/Chicago	312-856-0030
Busch, Lonnie/Fenton MO	314-343-1330
C.M.O. Graphics/Chicago	312-527-0900
Carruthers, Roy/Chicago	312-944-6655
Carugati, Eraldo/Chicago	312-944-3340
Centaur Studios/St. Louis MO	314-421-6485
Clay, Stephen/Chicago	312-664-5954
Cochran, Bobbye/Chicago	312-332-6041
Collins, Koehr, Lund Studios/Clayton MO	314-725-0344
Conahan, Jim/Chicago	312-822-0560
Craft, Kinuko/Chicago	312-372-1616
Crane, Gary/Chicago	312-332-5168
Creative Source/Chicago	312-649-9777
Davis, Paul/Chicago	312-944-6655
Deigen, Jim/Chicago	312-856-0030
DiCianna, Ron/Chicago	312-332-5168
Duggan, Lee/Chicago	312-726-4966
Dyess, John/Fenton MO	314-225-4000
Dypold, Pat/Chicago	312-787-9408
Eaton & Iwen/Chicago	312-332-3256
English, Mark/Fairway KS	913-677-2858
Farrell, Richard/Waterloo IA	319-233-4303
Feldkamp-Malloy/Chicago	312-263-0633
Foley, Mike/Fenton MO	314-225-4000
Fox, James/Chicago	312-856-0030
George, Harry/Cleveland	216-241-5355
Geyer, Jackie/Chicago	312-944-6655
Giancarlo, Jennifer/Chicago	312-822-0560
Giovanopoulous, Paul/Chicago	312-944-6655
Giusti, Robert/Chicago	312-944-6655
Gohman, Lynn/Cincinnati	513-841-6600
Green, Peter/Chicago	312-772-2292
Hagio, Kunio/Chicago	312-664-9012
Handelan-Pederson/Chicago	312-782-6833
Hayes, Phil/Chicago	312-944-6655
Hess, Mark/Chicago	312-944-6655
Hess, Richard/Chicago	312-944-6655
Hoover & Kern Studios/Chicago	312-337-7214
Howe, Robert Charles/Chicago	312-532-7411
Tom Hoyne/Creative Source/Chicago	312-649-9777
Hsi, Kai/Chicago	312-642-9853
Huyssen, Roger/Chicago	312-782-2703
Isom, Joe/Overland Park KS	913-381-1325
Jacobsen, Bill/Chicago	312-321-9558
Johnson, Hedda/Chicago	312-944-6655
Johnson, Indura/Chicago	312-664-5954
Jones, Jan/Chicago	312-751-0033
Kauffman, George/Kansas City MO	816-523-0223
Kelley, Gary/Waterloo IA	319-234-7055
Knight, Jacob/Chicago	312-944-6655
Kock, Carl/Chicago	312-871-1242
Koenig, Rainer/Kansas City MO	816-531-8053
Koopman Neumer/Chicago	312-726-3508
Langeneckert, Donald/St. Louis	314-421-2484
Lee, Jared D./Lebanon OH	513-932-2154
Linoff, Ed/Chicago	312-944-6655
Maffia, Daniel/Chicago	312-944-6655
Magdich, Dennis/Chicago	312-664-4235
Magee, Allen/Chicago	312-944-6655
Mahan, Benton/Chesterville OH	419-768-2204
Mahoney, Ron/Chicago	312-856-0030
Mark, Roger Leyon/Chicago	312-787-8834
McMahon, Mark/Chicago	312-332-5168
Morgan, Mike/Chicago	312-944-6655
Mull, Christy Sheets/Chicago	312-332-6041
Murawski, Alex/Chicago	312-782-2703
Nelson, Fred/Chicago	312-787-8834
Nighthawk/Kent OH	216-673-5032
Nitti, Chuck/Chicago	312-664-7715
Noonan, Julia/Chicago	312-944-6655
Jack O'Grady Graphics Inc./Chicago	312-726-9833
Parker, Hank/Chicago	312-944-6655
Pigalle Studios Inc./St. Louis MO	314-241-4398
Pitt Studios/Cleveland	216-241-6720
Hal Poth Studio/Clayton MO	314-721-7525
Povilaitis, David/Chicago	312-751-1470
Radigan, Bob/Chicago	312-856-0030
Raglin, Kim/Chicago	312-332-5168
Rodriguez, Robert/Chicago	312-944-6655
Rudnak, Theo/Chicago	312-332-5168
Ruffins, Reynold/Chicago	312-944-6655
Saffold, Joe/Chicago	312-332-6041
Sandford, John/Chicago	312-332-5168
Sauber, Rob/Chicago	312-649-9332
Harlan Scheffler/Handelan-Pederson/Chicago	312-782-6833
Schmelzer, J.P./Madison WI	608-244-1937
Schwab, Mike/Chicago	312-944-6655
Sheldon, Steve/Glendale MO	314-961-0713
Simmons, Bob/Chicago	312-787-8834
Simon, William/St. Louis MO	314-421-5544
Sorel, Ed/Chicago	312-944-6655
Star Studios/Chicago	312-944-6655
Stephens Biondi DeCicco Inc./Chicago	312-944-3340
Strosser, Ruth Brunner/Chicago	312-856-0030
Sullivan, Mary Ann/Cincinnati	513-731-6768
Sumichrast, Jozef/Deerfield IL	312-945-6353
Taback, Simms/Chicago	312-944-6655
Taylor, Doug/Chicago	312-664-9012
Thiewes, Sam/Chicago	312-726-5579
Trossman, Michael/Chicago	312-787-8834
Vaccarello, Paul/Chicago	312-822-0560
Bill Vann Studio/St. Louis MO	314-231-2322
Vuksanovich, Bill/Chicago	312-283-2138
Weiss, Barbara/Southfield MI	313-357-5985
Wende, Phillip/Chicago	312-332-5168
Wilcox, David/Chicago	312-944-6655
Wilkes, Jean/Chicago	312-332-5168
Willson Graphics/Chicago	312-642-5328
Wolf, Leslie/Chicago	312-856-0300
Wright, Janie Case/Chicago	312-332-6041
Zingarelli, Louise/Chicago	312-787-8834

SOUTHWEST

Anderson, Jon/Logan UT	801-752-8936
Christensen, James C./American Fork UT	801-224-6237
Durbin, Mike/Houston	713-667-8129
Early, Sean/Arlington TX	817-469-8151
Eubanks, Tony /Grapevine TX	817-481-3792
Forbes, Bart/Dallas	214-526-1430
Goodell, Jon/Tuttle OK	405-348-4183
Katona, Robert/Golden CO	303-279-1302
Lewis, Maurice/Houston	713-664-1807
Lindlof, Ed/Austin TX	512-472-0195
Loveless, Frank/Dallas	214-692-5157
McEntire, Larry/Houston	713-529-9771
Parker, Hank/Frisco CO	303-468-5833
Punchatz, Don Ivan/Arlington TX	817-460-7680
Reynolds, James/Sedona AZ	602-282-7011
Ricks, Thom/San Antonio TX	512-824-7387
Robins, Mike/Houston	713-933-8043
Schorre, Charles/Houston	713-522-8628
Smith, Dennis/Alpine UT	801-756-3635
Strand, David/Dallas	214-745-1210
Toliver, Dale/Austin TX	512-477-4442
Unruh, Jack/Dallas	214-661-5118

WEST COAST

Abrams, Edward/Hermosa Beach CA	213-372-6266
Abrams, Jodell Davidow/Hermosa Beach CA	213-372-6266
Akimoto, George/Monterey Park CA	213-573-3930
Allison, Gene/LA	213-382-6281
Alt, Tim/Beverly Hills CA	213-392-5406
Alvin, John/LA	213-279-1775
Anderson, Jon/Logan UT	801-752-8936
Anderson, Terry/LA	213-645-8469
Ansley, Frank/SF	415-781-6681
Anson, Susan/Beverly Hills CA	213-550-7619
Arens, Barbara/Toluca Lake CA	213-761-1800
Armstrong, Betty/LA	213-660-6251
Asaro, John/Carlsbad CA	714-942-2548
Baine, Vernon/Walnut Creek CA	415-933-5973
Banuelos, Art/Orange CA	714-997-2823
Barbee, Joel/San Clemente CA	714-498-0067
Barrett, Bill/LA	213-822-4999
Barry, Ron/Hollywood CA	213-469-8767
Bartell, George R./LA	213-461-5477
Batcheller, Keith/Covina CA	213-331-0439
Bausch, Robert/SF	415-752-6400
Beach, Lou/Hollywood CA	213-874-1661
Beersworth, Roger/LA	213-392-4877
Beigle, David/Westminster CA	714-893-7749
Bellinger, Cathy/LA	213-938-5177
Bennett, Chuck/LA	213-659-2406
Benson, R.A./Mercer Island WA	206-232-3561
Bernstein, Saul/Hollywood CA	213-467-6832
Berrett, Randy/SF	415-752-4977
Billout, Guy/LA	213-392-7792
Blair, Nancy D./Brentwood CA	213-826-7331
Boisvert, Nick/LA	213-256-0502
Boyle, Neil/LA	213-381-1387
Bradbury, Jack/Sonoma, CA	707-938-2975
Bradley, Barbara/Berkeley CA	415-525-5496
Brenon, Helen/LA	213-462-3513
Broad, David/SF	415-421-2017
Brosio, L.C./San Diego CA	714-232-3433
Buerge, Bill/Long Beach CA	213-597-9991
Burchard, Michelle/LA	213-933-2249
Burnside, John E./LA	213-665-8913
Butte, Annie/Jacksonville OR	503-899-1750
Calver, David/LA	805-255-5166
Campbell, Colin/Hollywood CA	213-851-3630
Camozzi, Teresa/SF	415-421-8898
Candioty, David/LA	213-386-7312
Cann, Nicholas/LA	213-934-8425
Carbojal, Edward/LA	213-221-4878
Carpenter, Mia/LA	213-384-8059
Carr, William W./LA	213-387-3956
Carroll, Justin/Hollywood CA	213-874-1661
Carver, Steve/Beverly Hills CA	213-274-9859
Cavenaugh, Joey/LA	213-467-8200
Chewning, Randy/Huntington Beach CA	714-531-1169
Christensen, David/Long Beach CA	213-439-8947
Cleary, Joe/Orinda CA	415-254-8330
Cockerill, Bruce/Glendale CA	213-240-4026
Cole, Dick/Palo Alto CA	415-322-2007
Conner, Dick/LA	213-382-9834
Coppock, Chuck/LA	213-382-6281
Corey, Christopher/SF	415-421-0637
Coro, Margaret/Beverly Hills CA	213-550-7619
Costelloe, Richard/Sherman Oaks CA	213-995-1035
Criss, Keith/Oakland CA	415-444-4550
Critz, Carl/LA	213-382-6281
Curtis, Art/LA	213-392-4877
Dalton, Patricia/Tustin CA	805-792-2784
Dann, Stan/Oakland CA	415-835-3571
Dean, Donald/Oakland CA	415-451-8330
De Anda, Ruben/LA	213-938-5177
Dearstyne, John/LA	213-789-0743
Deasy, Rosemary/LA	213-874-4552
Deel, Guy/Canoga Park CA	213-346-0048
Densham, Robert S./San Luis Obispo CA	805-543-8394
Desatoff, John J./Gardena CA	213-535-0261
Dietz, James/Seattle WA	206-325-2857
Diffenderfer Ed/Lafayette CA	415-254-8235
Dodig, Lynn/LA	213-651-2878
Doe, Bart/LA	213-383-9707
Donato, Robert/LA	213-384-0884
Drake, Bob/LA	213-931-8690
Drayton, Richard/Woodland Hills CA	213-347-2227
Dubow, Chuck/LA	213-938-5177
Durfee, Tom/SF	415-781-0527
Duffus, Bill/Pasadena CA	213-792-7921
Edwards, Bill/Corona Del Mar CA	714-675-5587
Eichenberger, Dave/LA	213-651-2878
Elgaard, Greta/LA	213-651-3015
Ellefson, Dennis/LA	213-279-1775
Ellenberger, Jack/LA	213-382-6281
Ellescas, Richard/Hollywood CA	213-467-6832
Ellmore, Dennis/Long Beach CA	213-424-9379
Elyea, Jim/LA	213-934-2236
Endicott, James R./Long Beach CA	213-498-2803
Endicott, Jim/Santa Monica CA	213-828-9653
Erickson, Vicki/LA	213-469-0743
Evans, Jim/Santa Monica CA	213-395-8267
Faye, Sandy/Perris CA	714-657-9400
Fedak, Malcom/Alameda CA	415-865-3684
Fell, L. Don/Beverly Hills CA	213-273-8412
Ferrero, Felix/SF	415-981-1164
Fleming, Bill/LA	213-478-6525
Fox, Ronald/Torrance CA	213-325-4970
Francuch, George/Sepulveda CA	213-893-2978
Franklin, Allan/Burbank CA	213-842-2230
Fuchs, Bernie/LA	213-651-3015
Fujisaki, Patrice K./Cypress CA	714-527-2530
Gaetano, Nicholas/LA	213-784-5814
Galli, Stan/Kentfield CA	415-461-5847
Gallon, Dale B./Newport Beach CA	714-646-5550
Galloway, Nixon/LA	213-937-4472
Garbarini, Charlotte/Redondo Beach CA	213-374-4507
Garnett, Joe/Hollywood CA	213-469-8767
Garo, Harry/Downey CA	213-928-2768
Garris, Philip/Santa Monica CA	213-395-8267
Germain, Frank/LA	213-937-4472
Gerrie, Dean /Newport Beach Ca	714-759-9491
Girvin, Tim Seattle 24	**206-623-7918**
Glad, Deanna /Santa Monica CA	213-393-7464
Gleason, Bob /Santa Monica CA	213-828-9653
Goldstein, Howard Van Nuys CA 25	**213-987-2837**
Gomez, Ignacio /LA	213-930-1144
Gorman, Stan /LA	213-937-4472
Graca, Jim/North Hollywood CA	213-980-3284
Green, Peter/LA	213-990-8084
Grim, Elgas/LA	213-382-6281
Group West/LA	213-937-4472
Grove, David/SF	415-433-2100
Guidice, Rick/Los Gatos CA	415-354-7787
Gurvin, Abe/LA	213-826-6879
Hansen, Donald/Tacoma WA	206-582-3208
Hardiman, Miles/Auburn CA	916-823-2653
Harris, Diane Teske/Hollywood CA	213-467-6797
Harris, Ralph/Sun Valley ID	208-726-8077

ILLUSTRATION

Hashimoto, Allan/LA	213-273-6768
Hasselle, Bruce/Santa Ana CA	714-543-2392
Hatzer, Fred/LA	213-937-4472
Heidrich, Tim/Redondo Beach CA	213-535-0405
Heimann, Jim/Santa Monica CA	213-828-9653
Heiner, Joe/LA	213-467-8200
Hendricks, Donald/Riverside CA	714-682-5645
Herrero, Lowell/SF	415-543-6400
Hickson, Ron/LA	213-461-9141
Hinton, Hank/LA	213-279-1775
Hinojosa, Albino/Ruston LA	318-255-2820
Hoburg, Maryanne Regal/SF	415-731-1870
Hodges, Ken/Los Alamitos CA	213-431-4343
Holman, Carol/LA	213-256-0502
Holmstrom, Gralyn/LA	213-937-4472
Hood, Holly/LA	213-652-4183
Hoover, Gary/Pasadena CA	213-681-0516
Hope, Frederic/LA	213-937-4472
Hubbard, Roger/LA	213-938-5177
Hutkin, Elliot/LA	213-938-5177
Hyatt, John/Hollywood CA	213-469-8767
Hyde, Bill/Foster City CA	415-345-6955
Ige, Kim/LA	213-741-4410
Ikkanda, Richard/LA	213-938-5177
Imhoff, Bill/LA	213-383-5125
Ingalls, Betty/Orinda CA	415-254-5036
Ingalls, Ed/Orinda CA	415-254-5036
Irvin, Fred/Santa Barbara CA	805-965-2309
Irvine, Rex John/Agoura CA	213-998-9333
Ivanyi, George/LA	213-381-3977
Jacobi, Kathryn/LA	213-653-1204
Jarvis, David/Chatsworth CA	213-998-7597
Jenott, John/Mill Valley CA	415-383-2330
Johnson, Jack/LA	213-467-8200
Jones, Steve/Venice CA	213-396-9111
Jue, Tommy/South Pasadena, CA	213-388-2111
Juhlin, Don/SF	415-621-1488
Kaufman, Van/LA	213-279-1924
Keefer, Mel/Tarzana CA	213-343-3324
Keeler, Jack/San Leandro CA	415-352-3640
Kelley & Mouse/Santa Monica CA	213-395-8267
Kenyon, Chris/Walnut Creek CA	415-934-5844
Kerr, Ken/Glendale CA	213-240-9430
Kerr, Mollie/LA	213-380-3084
Kincaid, Aron/Hollywood CA	213-874-1661
King, Dale W./LA	213-462-4532
King, Heather/Berkeley CA	415-922-3312
Kinyon, Robert/Orange CA	714-485-5362
Klein, Norman/LA	213-652-4183
Kosh, John/LA	213-461-9141
Kramer, Bertram/Santa Monica CA	213-395-4086
Krieger, E. Salem/Hollywood CA	213-874-1661
Kriss, Ron/LA	213-651-2878
Kroglę, Bob/Santa Monica CA	213-828-9653
Labadie, Ed/Glendale CA	213-240-0802
Lakich, Lili LA 27	**213-413-2404**
Larreco, John/Mill Valley CA	415-982-7771
Laycock, Dick/Woodland Hills CA	213-703-6498
Lee, Jake/LA	213-934-6521
Lee, Warren/Corte Madera CA	415-924-0261
Leedy, Jeff/Mill Valley CA	415-332-9100
Lewis, John/Oakland CA	415-535-1548
Leynnwood, Jack/Woodland Hills CA	213-883-6871
Lichtenwalner, John/Medford OR	503-535-4537
Lieppman, Jeff/Pasadena CA	213-441-9129
Lillard, Jill/Pasadena CA	213-792-5921
Lipking, Ron/Woodland Hills CA	213-703-6498
Lipney, Stephanie Joy/LA	213-388-7611
Lloyd, Peter/LA	213-392-7792
Locke, Margo/Los Altos CA	415-948-3434
Locke, Vance/Los Altos CA	415-948-3434
Loeb, Katherine/Hollywood CA	213-874-1661
Lozano, Henry Jr./LA	213-593-7741
Lum, Darell/Monterey Park CA	213-289-1214
Lyman, Kenvin/Hollywood CA	213-874-1661
Lytle, John/Oakland CA	415-530-0770
Machat, Mike/Long Beach CA	213-433-6221
Mackie, Bob/Pomona CA	714-629-7124
Madrid, Bill/LA	213-380-7223
Manzelman, Judy/Larkspur CA	415-461-9685
Marootian, Dorothy/Pasadena CA	213-462-6131
Marsh, Cynthia/Hollywood CA	213-654-4505
Mattelson, Marvin/LA	213-273-6768
Mazur, Ruby/LA	213-273-6768
McAdams, Larry/Orange CA	714-639-6149
McConnell, Jim/Oakland CA	415-569-0852
McKee, Ron/LA	213-937-4472
McKim, Sam/Glendale CA	213-240-9430
McCarthy, Errol/Woodland Hills CA	213-347-2227
Meagher, Terrence/Palo Alto CA	415-326-5170
Mediate, Frank/LA	213-381-3977
Medoff, Jack/LA	213-784-5814
Meininger, Keith/Reseda CA	213-885-6749
Merritt, Norman/LA	213-937-4472
Messerli, Joseph/Sepulveda CA	213-892-9724
Metcalf, Jim/Baldwin Park CA	213-338-9949
Mikkelson, Linda S./LA	213-937-8360
Mikkelson, R.J./LA	213-938-8631
Miller, Jim/LA	213-388-5043
Miller, Steve/North Hollywood CA	213-985-5610
Millsap, Darrel/LA	213-651-3015
Mode, Nathalee/LA	213-665-8537
Monahan, Leo/LA	213-937-8360
Moreau, Alain/LA	213-651-3015
Morgan, Bob/Danville CA	415-837-6168
Mortimer, Arthur/LA	213-822-4999
Moscoso, Victor/Santa Monica CA	213-395-8267
Mougham, William/LA	213-279-1775
Mueller, Ned/Petaluma CA	707-763-3137
Murphy, James/San Leandro CA	415-278-0369
Naganuma, Tony/SF	415-433-4484
Nagaoka, Shusei/LA	213-939-0683
Naigel, Pat/Hollywood CA	213-469-8767
Neila, Anthony/SF	415-673-6023
Nasser, Christine/Hollywood CA	213-469-8767
Neibauer, Lance/LA	213-382-6281
Nelson, Craig/LA	213-392-4877
Nelson, Mike/Concord CA	415-686-9295
Nethery, Susan/LA	213-392-4877
Nicholson, Norman/SF	415-421-2555
Noble, Larry/LA	213-279-1775
Norman, Gary/Santa Monica CA	213-828-9653
Novinska, Nina/LA	213-653-9718
Nyeland, Paul/SF	415-397-1353
Oden, Richard/Newport Beach CA	714-675-0400
Ohanian, Nancy/Woodland Hills CA	213-884-7088
O'Connor, Margaret/LA	213-380-5908
Pansini, Tom/LA	213-462-4532
Pederson, Sharleen/Hidden Hills CA	213-887-0518
Phillips, Charles/LA	213-741-4410
Platz, Henry III/Bothell WA	206-485-5685
Ponce De Leon, Enrique/Monterey CA	213-268-4111
Porter, Sophie/SF	415-776-6556
Putnam, Donald/LA	213-651-3015
Putnam, Jamie/Berkeley CA	415-549-2500
Pyle, Chuck/SF	415-752-4977
Quilez, Jose/LA	213-652-4183
Ray, Doug/LA	213-933-2249
Rehag, Larry/SF	415-543-7080
Ren, Chuck/LA	213-462-7432
Reynolds, Cathy/LA	213-390-6410
Roberts, Eva/Thousand Oaks CA	805-495-2266
Robertson, Ken/LA	213-382-8081
Robbins, George/Santa Monica CA	213-392-4439
Robles, Bill/LA	213-389-9518
Rodriguez, Bob/LA	213-384-4413
Rodriguez, Manuel Jaramillo/LA	213-643-0850
Rose, David/LA	213-876-0038
Ross, Deborah/Hollywood CA	213-874-1661
Rubin, Marvin/Venice CA	213-392-2226
Rutherford, John/Mill Valley CA	415-383-1788
Salk, Larry/LA	213-934-1975
Sanford, James/SF	415-982-7772
Sano, Kazu/SF	415-641-0713
Sauter, Ron/LA	213-938-5177
Scarisbrick, Ed/Santa Monica CA	213-828-9653
Schaar, Bob/Laguna Niguel CA	714-831-9845
Schorr, Todd/Hollywood CA	213-874-1661
Schwab, Michael/SF	415-391-2217
Schwering, James/Stinson Beach CA	415-868-1062
Seery, John J./LA	213-469-1212
Sessions, Millard F./La Habra Heights CA	213-697-5678
Sharp, Serena/LA	213-825-9441
Shehorn, Gene/Concord CA	415-687-4516
Shenon, Mike/Palo Alto CA	415-494-7198
Shepard, Anne/Hollywood CA	213-874-1661
Sherrod, David V./Hermosa Beach CA	213-376-3173
Shields, Bill/SF	415-543-6599
Sidjakov, Nicholas/Hollywood CA	213-469-8767
Siminger, Suzanne/SF	415-346-7314
Sierra, Frank E./Riverside CA	714-787-1519
Simmons, Bob/LA	213-392-7792
Sims, Norine/LA	213-256-0502
Skeen, Cindy/LA	213-256-0502
Slater, Miriam/Fullerton CA	714-636-7796
Sliffe, Catherine D./Irvine CA	714-581-9068
Smith, Brom/Pasadena CA	213-796-7441
Smith, J. Peter/LA	213-464-1163
Smith, Kenneth/La Crescenta CA	213-248-2531
Smith, Terry/LA	213-937-4472
Snyder, Teresa/Lafayette CA	415-937-1219
Snyder, Wayne/Lafayette CA	415-937-1219
Spencer, Joe/LA	213-392-7792
Spohn, Cliff/Newark CA	415-793-2873
Sprattler, Rob/Glendale CA	213-248-4952
Star Studios/LA	213-467-8200
Stewart, Walt/Sausalito CA	415-332-4823
Stinson, Paul/North Hollywood CA	213-760-1787
Stout, William G./Hollywood CA	213-936-6342
Stow, Dick/Danville CA	415-837-4660
Strand, David/Dallas TX	214-745-1210
Strick, Judith/LA	213-462-3513
Stricker, Carl/LA	213-388-0845
Studio Artists/LA	213-382-6281
Suvityasiri, Sarn/SF	415-922-5916
Tanenbaum, Robert/Tarzana CA	213-345-6741
Taylor, C. Winston/Granada Hills CA	213-363-5761
Taylor, Gerry W./LA	213-659-2406
Terry, Emerson/Pasadena CA	213-681-4115
Timpe, Wil/LA	213-652-9740
Tomita, Tsutomu/SF	415-821-4205
Turner, Nancy/LA	213-256-0502
Tyron-Tatoian, Leslie/LA	213-380-7223
Vaintrub, Elyse/LA	213-655-3772
Valentino, Joseph A./LA	213-386-9444
Vance, Joy/LA	213-382-6281
Vandervoort, Gene/Santa Ana CA	714-549-3194
Vanguard, Wendy/LA	213-661-8273
Van Hammersveld, John/Santa Monica CA	213-395-8267
Van Severen, Joe/Pacifica CA	415-355-7214
Vaughn, Bob/LA	213-651-2345
Vigon-Nahas-Vigon/LA	213-990-8084
Viljamaa, Marty/Palo Alto CA	415-329-0237
Vogelman, Jack H./Glendale CA	213-243-3204
Volquartz, Per/LA	213-474-7911
Waite, Elin/LA	213-741-4410
Ward, Ray/SF	415-989-9078
Watson, O.J./LA	213-651-3015
Watts, Stan/LA	213-382-6281
Webster, Ken/Walnut Creek CA	415-933-6445
Weisman, Joseph/LA	213-667-2662
Weller, Don/LA	213-225-1349
Westlund, Barbara/LA	213-937-4472
Whirl, Walt/Woodland Hills CA	213-703-6498
Wicks, Ren/LA	213-937-4472
Wiencek, J.C./Santa Monica CA	213-450-3085
Willardson, Dave/LA	213-467-8200
Williams, Kim/LA	213-851-5051
Wilson, Becky/SF	415-647-8421
Wilson, Dick/Santa Monica CA	213-828-9653
Wilson, Howard/Santa Monica CA	213-829-7704
Wilson, Reagan/LA	213-392-7792
Winston, Jeannie/Woodland Hills CA	213-347-2227
Wolfe, Bruce/Piedmont CA	415-655-7871
Wolin, Ron/Studio City CA	213-984-0733
Woodcock, Robert G./LA	213-387-1019
Woodward, Teresa/Pacific Palisades CA	213-459-2317
Wootton, Connie/LA	213-256-0502
Wright, Stevens/Long Beach CA	213-593-7741
Wysocki, Harry/Agoura CA	213-889-7855
Yakutis, Tom/Glendale CA	213-242-9819
Yamada, Jane/Sherman Oaks CA	213-663-6264
Yamada, Tony/Sherman Oaks CA	213-663-6264
Yazzolino, Mike/Santa Monica CA	213-393-6731
Yenne, Bill/SF	415-826-6749
Young, George W./Santa Barbara CA	805-966-3178
Zebot, George/Hollywood CA	213-469-8767
Zick, Brian/LA	213-876-0402
Ziemienski, Dennis/Palo Alto CA	415-326-4451
Zito, Andy/LA	213-828-9653

GRAPHIC DESIGN

GRAPHIC DESIGN

Zeitsoff, Elaine 212-580-1282
Zimmerman, Roger 212-674-0259

NORTHEAST

Adler Schwartz Graphics Inc.)/Baltimore 301-433-4400
Amato, John /Wantagh NY 516-785-1521
Milton Anderson Co. /Murray Hill NJ 201-464-9040
Aries Graphics /Londonderry NH 603-668-0811
Aron & Falcone /Chatham NJ 201-635-2900
Art Services /Pittsburgh 412-781-1022
The Artery /Baltimore 301-752-2979
Ashton, Worthington /Baltimore 301-837-4434
BKB Productions Inc. /Boston 617-267-2667
Barton-Gillet /Baltimore 301-685-5411
Baskin & Assoc. /Wash DC 202-331-1098
Jack Bevridge & Assoc. Inc. /Wash DC 202-223-4010
William E. Beyer Assoc. /Boston 617-266-4001
Bogus Assoc. /Melrose MA 617-662-0114
Bookmakers /Westport CT 203-226-4293
Brauer Industrial Design /Bronxville NY 914-337-7660
Bridy, Dan /Pittsburgh 412-288-9362
Brown, Michael David /Rockeville MD 301-762-4474
Bruno-Mease /Philadelphia 215-732-4800
Bill Buckett Assoc. /Rochester NY 716-546-6580
CASE /Wash DC 212-659-3820
Cabot Corp. /Boston 617-423-6000
Harold Cabot & Co. Inc. /Boston 617-426-7600
Cambridge Seven /Stamford CT 617-482-7205
Captain Graphics /Boston 617-262-7575
Carmel, Abraham /Peekskill NY 914-737-1439
Colopy Dale Inc. /Pittsburgh 412-471-0522
Centrum Corp. /Wash DC 202-293-7750
Comite Plus /Boston 617-542-0155
Connecticut Graphics /Stamford CT 203-359-3316
Contis Studios /Boston 617 542-9666
Cook & Shanofsky Assoc. /Princeton NJ 609-921-0200
Creative Communication Center
Pennsauken NJ 609-665-2058
The Creative Group /Baltimore 301-547-1404
Thomas Curran & Assocs /Plainview NY 516-938-3390
Dakota Design /Philadelphia 215-265-1255
D'Art Studio /Natick MA 617-653-2900
Dawson Designers Assoc. /Boston 617-266-5747
Stephen Daye Associates /Everett MA 617-389-1570
Jim Deigin Assoc. /Pittsburgh 412-391-1698
DeMartin-Marona-Cranstoun-Downes
Wilmington DE 302-654-5277
Design Research /Braintree MA 617-848-5210
Design Assoc. /Wash DC 202-467-5550
Design Center Inc. /Boston 617-536-6846
Design Group of Boston /Boston 617-261-2170
The Design Solution /Wash DC 202-837-6663
DiFiore Assoc. /Pittsburgh 412-471-0608
Allan Downing /Advertising Design
Needham MA 617-449-4784
Duffy & Assoc. /Wash DC 202-955-2216
Edigraph Inc. /Katonah NY 914-232-3725
Epstein, Len /Philadelphia 215-664-4700
Eucalyptus Tree Studio /Baltimore 301-243-0211
Evans Garber & Paige /Utica NY 315-733-2313
Fader, Jones & Zarkades /Boston 617-267-7779
Fannell Studio /Boston 617-267-0895
Fletcher-Walker-Gessell Inc.
Midland Park NJ 201-652-7200
Ford /Byrne /Philadelphia 215-564-0500
Gregory Fossella Assoc. /Boston 617-267-4940
Froelich Advertising Services /Mahwah NJ 201-529-1737
Gaadt, George S. /Pittsburgh 412-741-5161
Gasser, Gene /Chatham NJ 201-635-6020
Gateway Studios /Pittsburgh 412-361-7500
Geyer, Jackie /Pittsburgh 412-261-1111
Gianti, Tony /Rockleigh NJ 201-767-9238
Gilliam, Harry /Wash DC 202-857-0331
Gilliam, Williams & Assoc. Inc. /Wash DC 202-857-0331
Frank Glickman Inc. /Cambridge MA 617-354-2700
Peter Good Graphic Design /Chester CT 203-526-9857
Graphic Design /North Babylon NY 516-242-2817
Graphic Studio Inc. /Pittsburgh 412-281-5354
Graphic Supermarket /Boston 617-426-3565
Grinder, Rainbow /Pittsburgh 412-261-1444
Graphics for Industry /Englewood NJ 201-871-3186
Gunn Assoc. /Boston 617-267-0618
Robert Hain Assoc. /Scotch Plains NJ 201-322-1717
Hallock, Robert /Newtown CT 203-426-4757
Harrington-Jackson /Boston 617-536-6164
Harrison Assoc. /Port Washington NY 516-883-3897
Hellmuth, James /Wash DC 202-244-0465
Herbick & Held /Pittsburgh 412-321-7400
Herman & Lees /Cambridge MA 617-876-6463
Jack Hough Inc. /Stamford CT 203-357-7077
Image Consultants /Burlington MA 617-273-1010
Jensen, R.S. /Baltimore 301-225-7900
Johnson & Simpson Graphic Designers
Newark NJ 201-624-7788
Dick Jones Design Inc. /Bridgeport CT 203-334-6912
Just Frank Advertising /Hauppaugue NY 516-231-3216
KBH Graphics /Baltimore 301-539-7916
Henry J. Kaufman & Assoc. Inc. /Wash DC 202-333-0700
King-Casey Inc. /New Canaan CT 203-966-3581
Matt Klim & Assoc. /Avon CT 203-678-1222
Harry Knox & Assoc. /Wash DC 202-833-2305
Kramer /Miller /Lomden /Glossman
Philadelphia 215-545-7077
Krone Art Service /Lemoine PA 717-236-9329
David Lausch Graphics /Baltimore 301-235-7453
The Layout Pad Inc. /Pittsburgh 412-355-0280
Lebowitz, Mo /North Bellmore NY 516-221-8376
Judith K. Leeds Studio /West Caldwell NJ 201-226-3552
Hal Lewis Design /Philadelphia 215-563-4461
Lion Hill Studio /Baltimore 301-728-8571
Matt Lizak Graphic Design
North Smithfield RI 401-766-8885
Kenneth MacKellar Inc. /Boston 617-542-7728
The Magnificent Art Machine /Milford NJ 603-673-5253
Mahoney, Ron /Pittsburgh 412-261-3824
Major Assoc. /Baltimore 301-752-6174
Mandala /Philadelphia 215-923-6020
Marcello Studio /Pittsburgh 412-281-9307
Mariuzza, Pete /Briarcliff Manor NY 914-769-3310
Marini, Climes & Guip /Pittsburgh 412-281-9387
Martucci Studio /Boston 617-266-6960
Donya Melanson Assoc. /Boston 617-482-0421
Micolucci Assoc. 215-265-3320
Mills, Clark /Philadelphia 215-732-3739
Mueller /Wister /Philadelphia 36 215-568-7260
Peter Muller-Munk Assoc. /Pittsburgh 412-261-5161
Munce, Howard /Westport CT 203-227-7362
Gene Myers Assoc. /Pittsburgh 412-661-6314
Nason Design Assoc. /Boston 617-266-7286
Navratil Art Studio /Pittsburgh 412-471-4322
Nimek, Fran Gazze /New Brunswick NJ 201-821-8741
Nolan & Assoc. /Chevy Chase MD 301-652-8600
North Charles Street Design Org. /Baltimore 301-539-4040
Novum Inc. /Boston 617-523-8060
Oei Enterprises Ltd. /Rowayton CT 203-866-2470
Omni Assoc. /Baltimore 301-889-1793
Omnigraphics /Cambridge MA 617-354-7444
Otnes, Fred /West Redding CT 203-938-2829
Ed Parker Assoc. /Boston 617-261-2726
Parks Inc. /Wash. DC 202-452-0096
Paterno Design /Massapequa Park NY 516-541-5839
Paulhus Design Inc. /Providence RI 401-331-8591
Petco Design /Stamford CT 203-348-3734
Philadelphia Creative Workshop
Philadelphia 215-563-3330
Phillips Associates /Natick MA 617-429-1050
The Pilot House /Boston 617-523-2200
Pitt Studios /Pittsburgh 412-261-0460
Paul Planert Design Assoc. /Pittsburgh 412-621-1275
Plataz, George /Pittsburgh 412-322-3177
Plimsoll Productions /Wiscasset MA 207-882-7286
Plus Two Design Assoc. /Nesconset NY 516-265-6441
RSV /Boston 617-262-9450
Rainbow Arts Inc. /Fitchburg MA 617-342-8642
Paul Rand Inc. /Weston CT 203-227-5375
Reinelt-Sundin-Valenti Assoc. /Boston 617-262-9450
Ridgeway, Zaklin & Assoc.
Westwood NJ 38 201-664-4543
Rieb, Robert /Westport CT 203-227-0061
Leonard Lee Ringel Graphic Design
Kendall Park NJ 201-297-9084
Dick Ritter Design /Berwin PA 215-296-0400
Roston, Arnold /Great Neck NY 516-487-8735
Sanders & Noe Inc. /Wash DC 202-657-3700
Schoenfeld, Cal /Parsippany NJ 201-334-6257
Schneider, Ed /Wash DC 202-293-7750
Schneider Design /Baltimore 301-467-2611
James L. Selak Design /Fairport NY 716-223-0150
Selame Design Assoc.
Newton Lower Falls MA 617-969-6690
Smith, Doug /Larchmont NY 914-834-3997
Tyler Smith Art Direction /Providence RI 401-751-1220
Sparkman & Bartholomew /Wash DC 202-785-2414
Stano /Sweeny Design /New Rochelle NY 914-576-1652
Takjian, Asdur /North Tarrytown NY 914-631-5553
Taylor Assoc. /Stratford CT 203-378-3090
Tetrad Inc. /Annapolis MD 301-268-8680
Telesis /Baltimore 301-235-2000
Thompson, Bradbury /Riverside CT 203-637-3614
Thompson, George L. /Reading MA 617-944-6256
Torode, Barbara /Philadelphia 215-665-0265
Fred Troller Assoc. Inc. /Rye NY 914-698-1405
Van Dine, Horton, McNamara Inc. /Pittsburgh 412-261-4280
Victoria Group /Natick MA 617-235-2003
Louisa Viladas Graphics & Design
Greenwich CT 203-661-0053
Visual Research & Design Corp. /Boston 617-536-2111
Wasserman, Myron /Philadelphia 215-922-4545
Weitzman & Assoc. /Bethesda MD 301-652-7035
Weymouth Design /Boston 617-542-2647
Gene Whalen Assoc. /Pittsburgh 412-391-7518
White, E. James /Springfield VA 202-256-7900
Wickham & Assoc. Inc. /Wash DC 202-296-4860
Williams Assoc. /Lynn MA 617-599-1818
Williams, Erni /Wash DC 202-462-1405
The Wills Group /Philadelphia 215-985-1377
Wills /Grant /Philadelphia 215-985-9079
World Wide Agency /Baltimore 301-385-0800
Kent M. Wright Assoc. Inc. /Sudbury MA 617-237-9140
Zeb Graphix /Wash DC 202-293-1687

SOUTHEAST

Ace Art /New Orleans 504-861-2222
The Alderman Company /High Point NC 919-883-6121
Richard Allyn Studio /Miami 305-945-1702
Amberger, Michael /Miami 305-531-4932
And Ink /Sunrise FL 305-731-0551
Art Services /Atlanta 404-892-2105
Artra Inc. /Hollywood FL 305-524-4871
Aurelio & Friends Inc. /Miami 305-661-5369
Barrett & Gaby /Miami 305-661-5369
William S. Bodenhamer Inc. /Miami 305-371-6791
Bonner Advertising Art /New Orleans 504-895-7938
Bornstein Piatti /Coral Gables FL 305-445-0553
Brothers Bogushy /Miami 305-891-3642
Rick Cooper Graphics /Miami 305-358-3170
Corporate Graphics /Ft. Lauderdale FL 305-776-4060
Creative Design Assoc. /Palm Beach FL 305-659-7676
Creative Services Unlimited /Naples FL 813-262-0201
Design Workshop Inc. /N. Miami FL 305-893-2820
Designers Stewart & Winner /Louisville KY 502-636-1423
Erickson Graphics /Largo FL 813-595-9644
First Impressions /Tampa FL 813-224-0454
Kim A. Foster Graphic Design /Miami 305-665-3620
Gerbino Advertising Inc. /Ft. Lauderdale FL 305-776-5050
Graphics 4 /Ft. Lauderdale FL 305-764-1470
Graphics Group /Atlanta 404-261-5146
Graphicstudio /N. Miami FL 305-893-1015
Bill Gregg Advertising Design /Miami 305-854-7657
Hall, Stephen /Miami 305-374-5043
Michael Hannau Enterprises Inc. /Hialeah FL 305-887-1536
James N. Hansen Designer Inc. /Orlando FL 305-896-4240
Hauser Sydney /Sarasota FL 813-388-3021
Idea Factory /Winter Haven FL 813-299-8472
Images /Miami 305-374-5043
Implement Ltd. /Louisville KY 502-459-0804
International Graphics /Hollywood FL 305-945-3441
Kelly & Co. Design Group /St. Petersburg FL 813-346-2226
Howard Kjeldsen Assoc. Inc. /Atlanta 404-266-1897
(Kre • a'tiv) /Miami 305-595-2320
Bruce Lashley Super Graphics /Tampa FL 813-876-6497
Layne & Messina /S. Miami FL 305-661-0682
Leisuregraphics Inc. /Miami 305-620-5525
Leonard Graphics /St. Petersburg FL 813-576-6723
Ross Lewis /Miami 305-443-3620
Lippman, Mogull Advertising
Consultants Inc. /N. Miami FL 305-893-1175
Shelley Lowell Design /Atlanta 404-524-1515
Martin Studio /Miami 305-635-1816
Hugh Miller & Group /Orlando FL 305-293-8220
Morgan-Burchette Assoc. /Alexandria VA 703-548-5106
Bill Mosher Graphics /Clearwater FL 813-447-4996
Multifact Inc. /Orlando FL 305-293-1300
Murray Advertising & PR Inc. /Lakeland FL 813-688-1693
PL&P Advertising Studio /Ft. Lauderdale FL 305-771-7722
Don Platt Advertising Art /Hialeah FL 305-888-3296
Point 6 /Ft. Lauderdale FL 305-563-6939
Arthur Polizos Assoc. /Norfolk VA 804-622-7035
Positively Main St. Graphics /Sarasota FL 813-866-4959
Promotion Graphics Inc. /W. Miami FL 305-891-3941
Rodriguez, Emilio Jr. /Miami 305-235-4700
Ronjo Graphics /Miami 305-446-2006
Sager Assoc. Inc. /Sarasota FL 813-366-4192
Schulwolf, Frank /Coral Gables FL 305-665-2129
Specified Designs /Miami 305-264-7373
Still, Benjamin /Ft. Lauderdale FL 305-462-6184
Swearingen Graphics /Louisville KY 502-459-9960
Dana Thayer: Industrial Design /Monroe VA 804-846-6359
Don Trousdell Design /Atlanta 404-885-1457
Unigraphics Inc. /Ft. Lauderdale FL 305-566-9887
Varisco, Tom /New Orleans 504-581-7086
Visual Graphic Design /Tampa FL 813-877-3804
The Workshop /Atlanta 404-875-0141

MIDWEST

Aarons, Alan /Northfield IL 312-441-5050
Adams, Frank S. /Chicago 312-227-1943
Leonard Ades Graphic Design /Northfield IL 312-441-6737
Album Graphics /Melrose Park IL 312-344-9100
Altschuler, Franz /Chicago 312-664-4876
Ampersand Design /Chicago 312-944-4880
S. Frederick Anderson Studios /Chicago 312-876-0670
Anderson, I.K. /Chicago 312-664-4536
Architectural Graphics Systems /Chicago 312-871-0100
Architectural Signing Inc. /Chicago 312-871-0100
The Art Group /Cincinnati 513-721-1270
Azure Blue /Cleveland Heights OH 216-368-1100
Babcock & Schmid Assoc. /Bath OH 216-666-8826
Bal Graphics Inc. /Chicago 312-337-0325
Terry Barich Graphic Design /Chicago 312-935-3934
Len Beach Assoc. /Toledo 419-535-3151
Burton E. Benjamin Assoc. /Chicago 312-332-0246
Bruce Beck Design Assoc. /Evanston IL 312-869-7100
Belden Liska Design /Chicago 312-787-7095
Hayward Blake & Co. /Evanston IL 312-869-7100
Blau-Bishop & Assoc. /Chicago 312-321-1420
Boller-Coates-Robert /Chicago 312-787-2783
Bradford-Cout Graphic Design /Skokie IL 312-539-5557
Burke, David L. /Chicago 312-648-0566
Center for Advanced Research in Design
Chicago 312-786-5570
Centaur Studios Inc. /St. Louis 314-421-6485
Dave Chapman Design /Chicago 312-782-4050
Chestnut House /Chicago 312-822-9090
Sheila Chin Design /Minneapolis 612-338-4958
Communications Design Group /Evanston IL 312-864-0440
Creative Directions Inc. /Milwaukee 414-466-3910
DeGoede & Others /Chicago 312-828-0056
Design Associates /Indianapolis 317-636-8053
Design Center /Minneapolis 612-835-5999
Design Consultants /Chicago 312-372-4670
Design Group Three /Chicago 312-337-0277
Design North /Racine WI 414-762-1320
The Design Partnership /Minneapolis 612-338-8889
Design Planning Group /Chicago 312-427-3585
Design Two Ltd. /Chicago 312-642-9888
Dickens Design Group /Chicago 312-222-1850
David Doty Design /Chicago 312-348-1200
William Drendel Designs /Chicago 312-944-5411
John Dresser Design /Libertyville IL 312-362-4222
Epstein & Szilagyi /Cleveland 216-421-1600
Robert Falk Design Group /St. Louis 314-531-1410
Feldkamp-Malloy /Chicago 312-263-0633
Ficho & Corley Inc. /Chicago 312-787-1011

GRAPHIC DESIGN

Frank /James Productions /Clayton MO 314-726-4600
Frager, Hob /Cleveland 216-747-2011
Glenbard Graphics Inc. /Wheaton IL 312-653-4550
Goldsholl Assoc. /Northfield IL 312-446-8300
Goldsmith Yamasaki Specht Inc. /Chicago 312-565-1170
M. Gournoe Ltd. /Chicago 312-787-5157
Grant-Jacoby /Chicago 312-664-2055
Graphic Corporation /Des Moines 515-247-8500
Graphic Design Studio /St. Louis 314-991-1820
Graphics Group /Chicago 312-341-9550
John Greiner & Assoc. /Chicago 312-644-2973
The Hanley Partnership /St. Louis 314-621-1400
Hans Design /Northbrook IL 312-272-7890
David Hirsch Design Group /Chicago 312-267-6777
Grant Hoekstra Graphics /Chicago 312-641-6940
Impact Division of FCB /Chicago 312-467-9200
Indiana Design Consortium /Lafayette IN 317-742-5083
Victor Ing Design /Morton Grove IL 312-965-3459
Interdesign Inc. /Minneapolis 612-871-7979
Interface Design Group /Milwaukee 414-276-6688
Richmond Jones Graphics /Chicago 312-935-6500
Juenger, Richard /St. Louis 314-231-4069
Kansas City's Best /Kansas City MO 816-931-4771
Kaulfuss Design /Chicago 312-943-2161
Marilyn Katz, Creative Consultant /Chicago 312-321-0908
Kaleidoscope Art Inc. /Cleveland Heights OH 216-932-4454
Ronald Kovach Assoc. /Evanston IL 312-864-8898
Krudo Design /Chicago 312-764-7669
Merlin Krupp Studios /Minneapolis 612-871-6611
Kuester, Kevin M. /Eden Prairie MN 612-941-3326
Laughing Graphics /Minneapolis 612-929-6400
David Lawrence Design /Chicago 312-944-6620
Kathy Lay Design /Downers Grove IL 312-960-1028
Gerald Lehrfield /Bert Ray Studio /Chicago 312-944-0651
Lesniewicz /Navarre /Toledo OH 419-243-7131
Lawrence Levy Design /Evanston IL 312-869-4410
Lipson-Jacob & Assoc. /Chicago 312-861-0048
Lloydesign /Chicago 312-944-7886
Mabrey Design /Northfield IL 312-446-9595
Charles MacMurray Design Inc. /Chicago 312-822-9636
Manning Studio /Cleveland 216-861-1525
Lynn Martin Design /Chicago 312-737-3717
Massey, John /Chicago 312-786-5500
Mid-America Graphics /Omaha NE 402-554-1416
McMurray, Charles /Chicago 312-664-5885
McNamara Assoc. /Detroit 312-961-9188
Media Loft /Minneapolis 612-831-0226
Meyer Seltzer Design /Illustration /Chicago 312-327-7789
Hal Miller Design /Elgin IL 312-697-5522
Moonink Inc. /Chicago 312-565-0400
Lawrence Muesing Design /Northfield IL 312-446-8326
Multigraphics /Clearwater KS 316-584-6962
Murrie White Drummond Leinhart & Assoc.
Chicago 312-943-5995
Carol Naughton & Assoc. /Chicago 312-782-7589
Newcomb House Inc. /St. Louis 314-569-3750
The Nimi Design Group /Chicago 312-644-8700
Nottingham-Spirk Design Inc. /Cleveland 216-231-7830
Obata Design Inc. /St. Louis 314-241-1710
Jack O'Grady Graphics /Chicago 312-726-9833
Omnigroup /Chicago 312-944-6050
Osborne-Tuttle /Chicago 312-828-9280
Overlock Howe & Co. /St. Louis 37 314-241-8640
P.S. Graphic Design /Des Moines 515-243-3056
Palmer Design Assoc. /Chicago 312-263-1268
Perception Inc. /Chicago 312-782-5019
Perman, Norman /Chicago 312-642-1348
Herbert Pinzke Design /Chicago 312-644-7671
Pitt Studios /Cleveland 216-241-6720
Point 9 Advertising Art /Cleveland 216-523-1827
Porter, Allen E. /Chicago 312-236-5479
Push Pin Studios /Chicago 312-944-6655
R.V.I. Corporation /Chicago 312-787-2220
Barbara & Patrick Redmond Design
Minneapolis 612-341-3910
Michael Reid Design /Chicago 312-337-0556
Robertz Design Company /Chicago 40 312-861-0060
Rotelli Design /Chicago 312-527-9870
Roth, Randall /Chicago 312-467-0140
Rudnak, Theo /Chicago 312-332-5168
Samata Design Group Ltd. /Barrington IL 312-381-9090
Savlin Assoc. /Evanston IL 312-328-3366
Richard Schlatter Design /Battle Creek MI 616-964-0898
E.F. Schmidt Co. /Merromine Falls WI 312-263-0995
Ron Schultz Design /Chicago 312-528-1853
Schumaker Design Inc. /Grand Rapids, MI 616-456-5431
The Shipley Assoc. /Elmhurst IL 312-279-1212
Skolnick, Jerome /Chicago 312-944-4586
Vito Simanis Design /St. Charles IL 312-584-1683
Barry Slavin Design /Chicago 312-944-2920
The Glen Smith Co. /Minneapolis 612-871-1616
H.B. Smith & Assoc. /Chicago 312-787-8920
Stepan Design /Chicago 312-332-3776
Gordon H. Stromberg Visual /Chicago 312-275-9449
Studio One Inc. /Minneapolis 612-831-6313
Gladys Swanson Graphics /Chicago 312-726-3381
Swoger Grafik /Chicago 312-935-0755
Synthesis /Chicago 312-787-1201
TCI Advertising /St. Louis 314-966-6675
Tarpey, Gene /Chicago 312-427-0575
George Tassian Org. /Cincinnati 513-721-5566
Peter Teubner & Assoc. /Chicago 312-467-0021
Thumbnails Inc. /Minneapolis 612-333-6539
Title Design /Chicago 312-477-4667
Underwood, Muriel /Chicago 312-236-8472
Unimark International Corp. /Chicago 312-782-5850
Frederick Vallarta Assoc. Inc. /Chicago 312-944-7300
Bill Vann Studio /St. Louis 314-231-2322
Venture Graphics /Chicago 312-644-0616
Vista Three Design /Minneapolis 612-920-5311
Visual Design Center /Chicago 312-329-1230
Harry B. Voight Graphic Design /Oak Park IL 312-848-0388
Wallner Graphics /Chicago 312-787-6787
Jack Weiss Assoc. /Evanston IL 312-869-7100
Wenzel Studio /Chicago 312-321-0758
Wilkes, Jean /Chicago 312-332-5168
M. Wilson Graphic Design /Columbus OH 614-239-9449
Winbush Design /Chicago 312-527-4478
Wise, Guinotte /Independence MO 816-836-1362

SOUTHWEST

Ad Directors/Dallas 214-634-7337
Advence Design Center/Dallas 214-526-1420
Baxter & Korge/Houston 713-781-5110
Benton, Patrick/Dallas 214-526-1181
CRS/Houston 713-621-9600
Creative Communications/Denver 303-399-4390
Larry Darnell Design/Dallas 214-748-0114
Demlow/Durand Advertising Art/Dallas 214-521-8780
Design & Image Associates/Denver 303-861-4145
Designers & Partners/Dallas 214-630-7504
Eisenberg & Pannell/Dallas 214-528-5990
Envision Art & Design Studio/Houston 713-932-0251
Genesis Inc./Denver 303-825-1230
Freshman, Shelley/Denver 303-759-3541
Graffiti Studios/Boulder CO 303-442-5396
Hendel, Richard/Austin TX 512-345-2578
Herring Design/Houston 713-526-1250
Konig Design Group/San Antonio TX 512-824-7387
Le Vrier, Philip/Welesco TX 512-968-4626
Lidji/Dallas 214-521-6767
Lively/McPhail Studio/Dallas 214-741-5126
Loucks Atelier/Houston 713-528-2945
Lueck, Bob/Dallas 214-521-4291
Morales, Frank/Dallas 214-827-2101
Pierce, Donald/Houston 713-526-8429
Reed, Melnichek, Gentry/Dallas 214-634-7337
Lee Reedy Designer/Denver 303-333-2936
The Richards Group/Dallas 214-231-2500
Roseburg, Pam/Dallas 214-826-0616
Rowley Kahler Assoc./Denver 303-573-6073
Salesvertising Inc./Denver 303-837-1096
Henry Schmidt Design/Boulder CO 303-499-1555
The Sketch Pad/Arlington TX 817-469-8151
Sloves Products/Albuquerque NM 505-255-8661
Smitherman Graphics/Austin TX 512-459-3379
Robert Taylor Design/Denver 303-837-1070
Unit 1/Denver 303-744-1033
Ed Zahra Design/Dallas 214-521-3030

WEST COAST

Abbey, Norman /LA 213-681-6763
Abel, Robert & Assoc. /LA 213-462-8100
Addison & Assoc. /Santa Barbara CA 805-658-8188
A.D.I. /LA 213-254-7131
ADPRO /SF 415-434-1650
Advertizing Designers /LA 213-463-8143
AGI /LA 213-462-0821
Aki, Sharon /LA 213-820-3956
Albers, Hans /LA 213-748-4820
Alcayaga, Rick /LA 213-389-1171
Almquist, David /LA 213-432-5707
Amstutz, Jim /LA 213-477-1583
Andrews, Chris /LA 213-462-7922
Angeli Primo Design /SF 415-989-1830
Anselmo, John Design Assoc.
Santa Monica CA 213-393-9411
Arlt /Stierli Design /Rodondo Beach CA 213-372-1106
Asbury Rome & Assoc. /Long Beach CA 213-595-6481
Baldwin, Nancy /Venice CA 213-392-8474
Carl Ballay & Others /SF 415-421-7278
Berdine, Jan /LA 213-454-2825
Barzman, Allan & Co. /LA 213-462-7261
Saul Bass /Herb Yager Assoc., Inc. /LA 213-466-9701
Beaumont Design Group /LA 213-264-3110
Bennett, Ralph Assoc. /Van Nuys CA 213-782-3224
Better Graphics /LA 213-938-5139
Big Apple Ltd. /LA 213-466-3306
Big Orange Graphics /LA 213-577-1840
Blackwell, Heidi-Marie /LA 213-659-7938
Blumhoff, William Design /Encino CA 213-783-5808
The Boardroom /Santa Monica CA 213-450-8343
Boston,Archie /LA 213-292-2663
Boyd, Douglas Design /Santa Monica CA 213-451-8041
Bright & Agate /LA 213-658-8844
Brinkman, John /LA 213-382-2339
Brookins, Ed /Studio City CA 213-776-7336
Brown, Bill /LA 213-386-2455
Burchard, Joseph Design /Burbank CA 213-762-8775
Burns, Rich /Sausalito CA 415-332-8010
Burridge Design /Santa Barbara CA 805-965-8023
Burridge, Robert /Santa Barbara CA 805-964-9707
Carre Design /Santa Monica CA 213-395-1033
Cato, Bob /LA 213-476-9102
Chapek, Ralph /LA 213-795-4371
Chiang, Philip /LA 213-931-0854
Chorney, Steve /LA 213-665-3464
Cleveland, John /LA 213-826-0948
Coak, Steve & Pamela Designers
Altadena CA 213-797-5477
Collins, Keith /LA 213-667-9326
Comfort, Carole /Woodland Hills CA 213-347-3968
The Committee /LA 213-470-1706
Costelloe Arch. Graphics /Sherman Oaks CA 213-995-1035
Coy, John Design /LA 213-475-9763
Cross, James Design Office /LA 213-484-2525
Crow-Quill Studios /SF 415-989-3334
Cullimore, M. Jack /LA 213-876-5272
D'Addio, Peter Adv. Design /LA 213-386-9938
Dalstrom, Hoeft /Santa Barbara CA 805-962-4849
Danziger, Louis /LA 213-935-1251
Davidow, Jodell /Hermosa Beach CA 213-372-6266
Dawson, Meyerhoff Design /LA 213-278-1760
Dellaportas, Spyros Adv. Design
Santa Monica CA 213-394-0023
DePatie-Freleng Entp., Inc. /Van Nuys CA 213-988-3890
Designall /LA 213-466-7218
Designory /LA 213-432-5707
Designwise, Inc. /LA 213-936-5276
Designworks, Pelly Charles /LA 213-556-2021
Design Projects Corps /LA 213-995-0303
Design SICS /Tarzana CA 213-705-4000
Design Spectrum /LA 213-545-6629
Design Synthesis /LA 213-325-0283
Detanna Adv. Design /LA 213-463-2353
Detiege, David /N. Hollywood CA 213-766-9360
Dillard, Jackson /La Mirada CA 213-921-3443
Deutsch, Laurence /LA 213-937-3521
Dicus, Alexis H. /Santa Monica CA 213-396-3094
Dittman, Tom Design /Beverly Hills CA 213-273-2197
Dinez, Carlos /LA 213-387-1171
Duffus, Bill /LA 213-799-5839
Dyer, Rod Inc. /LA 31 213-937-4100
Eames, Charles Studio /Venice CA 213-396-5991
Earth /Santa Monica CA 213-450-0433
Ellmore, Dennis /Laguna Beach CA 213-424-9379
Emerson /Johnson /Mackay, Inc.
N. Hollywood CA 213-877-0423
Engle, Andy /LA 213-657-2692
Engle, Ray & Assoc. /LA 213-381-5001
Evenson, Stan /LA 213-659-3961
Executive Graphics /LA 213-680-1196
Farber, Rose Graphic Design /Venice CA 213-392-3049
Fifth Street Design /Berkeley CA 415-526-4852
Fine Line Design & Adv. /Santa Monica CA 213-393-0780
Finger, Julie /LA 213-653-0541
Follis, John & Assoc. /LA 32 213-735-1283
Frazier Design Assoc. /LA 213-656-9122
Freeman /Blitzer Assoc. /LA 213-553-3080
Fuhr, Roger /Woodland Hills CA 213-346-9752
Fujimoto, Mitz /LA 213-381-3967
Gaw, George /LA 213-223-4087
Gerds, Donald A. /Manhattan Beach CA 714-546-1934
Georgopoulos Graphics /LA 213-651-2743
Goddell, Ken & Assoc. /Beverly Hills CA 213-274-9095
Goldstein, Gary /Santa Monica CA 213-394-8701
Goldstein, Howard /Van Nuys CA 213-987-2837
Gordon, Jim /Hermosa Beach CA 714-376-4021
Gould & Assoc. /West LA 213-879-1990
Grafx /Inglewood CA 213-674-5911
Graphic Design West /Van Nuys CA 213-346-8139
Graphic Designers, Inc. /LA 213-381-3977
Graphicus /N. Hollywood CA 213-769-5694
Graphic Orb /N. Hollywood CA 213-980-2266
Gresman, April /LA 213-389-4659
Gribbitt ! /LA 34 213-462-7362
The Groot Organization /SF 415-543-9920
Group West /LA 213-937-4472
Group X /Palos Verdes CA 714-557-9960
Haines, Bill /LA 213-387-2197
Hale, Dan Adv. Design /Woodland Hills CA 213-347-4021
Hanson, Boelter /Sherman Oaks CA 213-990-6141
Harte /Yamashita /Harte /LA 213-462-6486
Hauge, Paul /LA 213-658-7113
Hayakawa, Herb & Assoc. /LA 213-385-1681
Hersey, Dale & Assoc. /LA 213-487-0270
Hinsche, Kay & Assoc. /LA 213-387-2111
Hollowell, Wayne /N. Hollywood CA 213-769-5964
Holmes, Richard Design /San Diego CA 213-494-5818
Hood, Brad /LA 213-466-6011
Huerta Design Assoc. /LA 213-381-6641
Huggens, Laurel Design & Consultation /LA 213-277-2424
Hungerford, Lauren /LA 213-476-8896
Hunt, Wayne Graphic Design /LA 213-687-7422
Hunter, Terry /Beverly Hills CA 213-278-7616
Hutkin & Dubow /LA 213-938-5177
Idea Bank, Inc. /LA 213-462-2164
Ikkanda, Richard /LA 213-938-5177
Image Stream /LA 213-933-9196
Inart /Manhattan Beach CA 213-372-7444
Ivanyi, George /LA 213-381-3977
James, Mac /LA 213-874-6622
Jerde Partnership /LA 213-413-0130
JFDO /LA 213-653-0541
Johnson, Jerry & Assoc. /Burbank CA 213-849-1444
Johnson, Rodger Design
Rolling Hills Estates CA 213-377-8860
Jones, Wriston /LA 213-468-3171
Juett, Dennis S. & Assoc. /LA 213-385-4373
Jurdan Design /LA 213-851-5022
Kaiser Design Group, Inc. /LA 213-272-2741
Keating & Keating /SF 415-421-3350
Keck, Craig Sr. /S. Pasadena CA 213-579-1591
Keesher, Jim /LA 213-473-7230
Kehe, John Design /LA 213-275-7161
Kikuchi, Isao /LA 213-278-1703
Kittyhawk Graphics /LA 213-874-1534
Klasky, Earl /LA 213-650-8946
Kleiner, John A. Graphic Design, Inc.
Marina del Rey CA 213-472-7442
Klingensmith, Tom Graphic Design /LA 213-933-1116

GRAPHIC DESIGN

Kracke, Don /Rolling Hills Estates CA 213-541-2448
Krogstad, Yuguchi /LA 213-383-6915
K.O. Productions, Animation /LA 213-664-8545
Kusher Design /Studio City CA 213-872-1824
Lakich, Lili /LA 27 .... **213-413-2404**
Lam, Si /Marina del Rey CA 213-821-9880
Landor, Walter & Assoc. /SF 415-955-1200
Laub, Claudia /LA 213-658-8233
Ledesma & Romero Creative Artists, Inc. /LA 213-269-7316
LeMore, Larry /Pasadena CA 213-794-1446
LeProvost & LeProvost /Malibu CA 213-457-3742
Lipson, Marty & Assoc. /Santa Monica CA ... 213-451-1421
Logan, Carey & Rehag /SF 415-543-7080
Loosen, Ron & Assoc. /Santa Monica CA 213-436-5225
L.A. Design Studio /LA 213-930-1140
L.A. Graphic Arts Group /Canoga Park CA ... 213-368-7059
L.A. Workbook /LA 213-657-8707
Lucas Graphics /Canoga Park CA 213-887-0200
Lum, Darrell /LA 213-613-2538
Macias, Michael /Fullerton CA 714-870-4577
Manoogian, Michael /N. Hollywood CA 213-279-1775
Marcovici, Jalna /LA 213-475-7822
Marshall, Winston Graphics /LA. 213-204-0318
Matrix Design Consultants /LA 213-620-0828
Mediate, Frank /LA 213-381-3977
Mills, Robert /Culver City CA 213-870-7515
Monahan, Leo /LA 213-937-8360
Moore, Roger G. /Laguna Beach CA 714-497-3855
Morley, Christopher /Santa Ana CA 714-547-3964
Morra, Dominick Design /San Marino CA. ... 213-289-5430
Mortense, Gordon /Santa Barbara CA 805-962-5315
McDonald, Max Design Office /LA 213-461-8241
McGee, James /LA 213-385-6287
Murphy, Harry & Friends /Mill Valley. 415-383-8586
Neibauer, Lance /LA 213-382-6281
Nethery, Susan /LA 213-392-4877
Neumeier, Marty Design /Santa Barbara CA . 805-962-8303
New Breath Productions /LA. 213-876-3491
Niehaus, Don /LA 213-279-1559
Nissenbaum, Judith /LA 213-654-2193
Nordenhok, Ove /Newport Beach CA 714-752-8631
Oliver, Jeff /Sherman Oaks CA 213-788-7149
Oliver, Mark /Santa Barbara CA 805-682-7767
Ortega, Orr /LA 213-874-3755
Overby, Robert /Santa Barbara CA 805-966-2359
Parkhurst, Ken /LA 213-653-4301
Pencil Pushers /LA 213-874-7367
Phillips, Charles Dickens /LA. 213-741-4760
Potocki, James /LA 213-380-7281
Price Assoc. Inc. /LA 213-851-4555
Print, Film and Tape /Toluca Lake CA 213-760-3885
Pryor Design Group /LA. 213-650-1324
Quilez, Jose /Granada Hills CA. 213-363-3716
Rado, Jean & Assoc. /Venice CA 213-392-6879
Ramey Communications /LA 213-665-4144
Reid, Scott /Santa Barbara CA. 805-963-8926
Reilly, Charles /Pasadena CA 213-769-7168
Reyes, Gil Graphic Design /LA 213-387-7315
Richter & Carr Communications /LA 213-276-4133
Rinek, Susan /Newport Beach CA 714-631-4200
Rochlin, Leonard /LA. 213-389-1381
Rogow & Bernstein /LA. 213-936-9916
Rosenberg, Barry & Assoc. /Santa Monica CA 213-451-1188
Rosenthal, Herb Assoc. Inc. /LA. 213-655-0214
Rosentsweig, Gerry /LA. 213-655-6739
Ross, Deborah Design /LA 213-654-3395
Rubin, Marvin /Venice CA. 213-392-2226
Rubenstein, Ron Graphic Design /LA. 213-988-0878
Runyan, Robert Miller & Assoc.
    Playa del Rey CA 213-823-0975
Runyan, Richard /LA. 213-879-1999
Sachs-Oehler Studio /N. Hollywood CA 213-769-6656
Salazar, Frank /Alhambra CA. 213-282-0043
Sandvick Studios /LA 213-685-7148
Scarkino, John & Co. /LA. 213-481-2050
Miv Schaaf Assoc. /Pasadena CA 213-681-5353
Scher, Jay & Assoc. /LA. 213-394-2305
Schorer, R. Thomas /Palos Verdes CA 213-377-0207
Schwartz, David Communications
    Santa Monica CA 213-393-0860
Seef, Norman /LA 213-656-7690

Seiniger /Morrison & Assoc. /LA 213-653-8669
Shoji Graphics /LA 213-384-3091
Shook & Co. /Glendale CA. 213-240-7083
Soo Hoo, Patrick Designers /LA. 213-385-1743
Soyster & Ohrenschall /SF 415-956-7575
Specht /Watson Studio /LA 213-651-3015
Spencer, Joe /LA. 213-475-0543
Steinberg, Bruce /SF. 415-648-9037
Strejan, John Design /Encino CA 213-995-4847
Studio Anaconda /Santa Monica CA 213-454-2825
Studio Artists /LA 41 .... **213-382-6281**
The Studio Ink /San Pedro CA. 213-831-3782
Sussman, Deborah & Co. /Santa Monica CA. 213-829-3337
Synapse /LA 213-482-5074
Tartak /Libera Design Inc. /LA 213-477-3571
The Art Bank /TAB /LA 213-838-6108
Thomas, Greg /LA 213-479-2676
Thompson, Kathleen Thorne /LA. 213-385-1511
Todd, Sheryl /LA. 213-559-8737
Tri-Arts, Inc. /LA 213-461-4891
Tribotte, Robert Design /Sherman Oaks CA. . 213-784-6101
TRW /LA 213-645-4198
Unigraphics /SF 42 .... **415-398-8232**
Valentino Graphic Design /LA. 213-386-9444
Van Hamersveld, John /LA 213-656-3815
Vigon /Nahas /Vigon /LA. 213-655-9636
Vinje, Einar /Culver City CA 213-398-2129
Vogelman, Jack /Glendale CA. 213-243-3204
Volquartz, Per /Pasadena CA 213-792-9648
Watchel, Jimmy /LA. 213-656-9110
Weiland, Herb Design /Culver City CA 213-391-0584
Weller, Don Design /LA 213-467-4576
Weston, Joseph /LA 213-385-7910
West End Studios /LA 213-279-1539
West-Towne Studios /LA 213-394-6675
Wheeler, Walt Design & Assoc. /LA. 213-475-5825
Whitbeck /Wolff Design /LA 213-876-1072
White, Charlie III /LA. 213-659-5744
White, Ken /Glendale CA. 213-240-7096
White, Ken Design, Inc. /LA 44 .... **213-467-4681**
Willardson & White, Inc. /LA. 213-659-5744
Williamson /Clave, Inc. /LA 213-836-0143
Wolin, Ron /Studio City CA 213-984-0733
Woodward, Teresa /LA 213-279-1539
Yamashita, Tets /LA 213-462-6486
Yee, Ray Graphics /LA. 213-981-9048
Young, Doyald /LA. 213-933-7963
Yuguchi, Krogstad /LA 213-383-6915
Zamparelli, Mario /Encino CA 213-981-6644
Zubalsky, Don /Studio City CA 213-760-3885

TV, FILM AND VIDEO

NEW YORK METROPOLITAN AREA

A & G Video Inc.	212-288-3883
AIA Productions	212-730-1609
APA	212-929-9436
Martin Abrahams Films Inc.	431-8482-83
Action Productions Inc.	212-391-2747
Ad Film Producers Inc.	212-355-3325
Ad Counseling Productions	212-966-6700
Admaster Inc.	212-679-1134
Aegis Productions	212-684-0810
Agape Films Ltd	212-534-4754
Roger Arles & Assoc Inc.	212-765-3022
Albi Assoc Inc.	212-679-0979
Allegro Film Productions	212-586-3057
Alton Films	212-753-7522
Amberson Assoc.	212-246-0758
American Film Prods Inc.	212-582-1900
American Dream Productions	212-371-2995
American Video-Channels Inc.	212-756-6324
Ampersand Productions Inc.	212-564-9050
Robbie Anderson Prods Inc.	212-737-6815
Gennaro Andreozzi	212-838-6958
Ani-Live Film Service Inc.	212-247-1800
Animated Productions Inc.	212-265-2942
Animation Camera Workshop	212-687-5009
Animation Services Inc.	212-688-6225
Animus Films	212-391-8716
Ansel Productions Inc.	212-674-8221
Apollo & Assoc.	212-489-8433
Hal Marc Arden & Co.	212-765-8366
Arzt Productions Inc	212-753-1050
Atlantis Films	212-989-7489
Audio Graphix Enterprises Inc.	212-787-4200
Audio Prods	212-573-8656
Audioimage Inc.	212-753-8980
Aumont Prods Inc	212-794-2221
Avon Productions	212-581-4460
Bachner Productions	212-354-8760
Bil Baird's Marionettes	212-989-9840
Bajus-Jones	212-752-3856
Fred Baker Films Ltd.	212-757-9845
Bean/Kahn	212-628-0500
Beckerman/Mansfield	212-832-3030
Howard Beckerman Studio	212-869-0595
The Best People Inc.	212-986-0289
Beuth & Co Films Inc.	212-679-8171
Bianchi Films	212-533-3010
Big Apple Cinima	212-873-3295
The Big Orange Productions	212-758-9800
Viviane Bivas-Nathan	212-860-5486
R.O. Blechman Inc.	212-869-1630
Merl Bloom Assoc Inc.	212-935-5866
David Blumenthal Assoc.	212-686-8550
Eric D. Boltax Assoc.	212-687-0963
Barbara Bordnick 55	**212-533-1180**
Mathew Brady Prods Inc. 11	**212-683-6060**
John Bransby Productions	212-688-6225
Bray Studios Inc.	212-245-4582
Brian Film Productions	212-873-8168
Brillig Productions Inc.	212-595-5454
The Broadcast Department Inc.	212-582-1303
Alan Brooks Prods Inc.	212-751-6811
Brumage Productions	212-245-6119
Brut Productions	212-581-3114
Tom Buckholtz Prods.	212-489-9718
Billy Jalius Bud	212-755-3968
Nat Bakar & Assoc.	212-428-5635
Elinor Bunin Productions Inc.	212-688-0759
CDB 111-Kristy	212-244-6187
The CPF Group Inc.	212-986-9329
Cailor/Resnick	212-977-4300
Cammann Productions Inc.	212-369-4511
Steve Campus Productions	914-472-9590
Stan Carp	212-759-8880
Captain Z-RO Prods	212-249-8678
The Cartoon Co Films Inc.	212-935-1440
Bruce Cayard Animation	212-244-5162
Cel-Art Productions	212-751-7517
Cel Specialists	212-490-3728
Centipede Films Inc.	212-532-9050
Centrex Productions Inc.	212-986-8270
Chain Reaction Films Inc.	212-687-3193
Harry Chang Inc.	212-354-8098
Channel Films Inc.	212-586-4311
Charlex Inc.	212-255-9180
Charlie Company	212-924-1432
The Chartmakers Inc.	212-247-7200
Chimera Prods	212-354-1567
Chiasma Productions Inc.	212-582-7095
John Cholakis	212-581-3605
Chrome Yellow Films	212-697-5660
Churchill Films	212-753-9225
Cineffects Visuals Inc.	212-575-5151
Cinema Arts	212-246-2860
Cinemakers	212-765-1168
Cinema 65 Inc.	212-391-2195
Cinetudes Film Prods Inc.	212-966-4600
City Film Center Inc.	212-456-5050
Ian Clark	212-289-0998
Stan Clark Productions	212-725-0555
Jim Coane Productions Inc.	212-687-3554
Comart/Aniforms	212-867-7500
Command Productions Inc.	914-948-6868
Composite Films	212-730-0460
Concepts Unlimited	212-246-9612
Contempo Communications	212-247-4444
Michael Cook Inc.	212-580-0133
Cooper-Dennis & Hirsch	212-751-9450
Corporate Video Systems Inc.	212-888-0208
Raymond Convin & Assoc.	212-371-0877
Robert Crandall Assoc. Inc.	212-661-4710
Thomas Craven Film Corp	212-688-1585
Creative Campaign Analysts	212-245-0666
Creative Productions	212-935-1111
Cullen Assoc.	212-581-2740
DMB Productions Inc.	212-757-7921
D & R Productions Inc.	212-730-1028
Nicholas Dancy Productions	212-684-0376
Darino Films/Copymotion	212-988-6957
Raul DaSilva & Other Film Makers	212-535-5760
Hal Davis Talking Picture Co.	212-831-2791
Gordon Day	212-687-7040
David Dee Productions Inc.	212-486-9364
Ken Delmar Films Inc.	212-869-1440
Demaio Productions	212-354-9381
Depicto Films Corp	212-687-0462
Delvin Prodution Inc.	212-582-5572
Diamond Eye Prods.	212-355-3518
Digital Effects Inc.	212-581-7945
Directors Group Motion Pix Inc.	212-268-1041
The Directors Studio	212-826-6303
Discovery Productions	212-752-7575
Dolphin Productions Inc.	212-628-5930
Jonathon Donald	212-874-6241
Doorbell Productions	212-586-6300
Double HH Productions	212-697-9554
Dozari Marionettes	212-473-6699
Dove Films	212-687-3710
The Dream Stuff Corporation	212-254-1973
Drew Assoc.	212-879-3430
Mark Druck Productions	212-682-5980
Duquet Productions	212-997-0255
Dura-Sell Corp.	212-687-1010
The Dxtrs	212-877-5403
East End Productions	212-421-3967
Arthur Eckstein & Assoc.	212-599-2494
Edstan Group 12	**212-686-3666**
Effective Communication Arts	212-688-6225
Eighth Frame	212-765-0881
Nat Eisenberg	212-685-8913
Electronic Animation-Dolphin	212-628-5930
Ellida Productions Inc.	212-490-2223
Mike Escover Films	212-391-1217
EUE-Screen Gems	212-867-4030
Eye-View Films Inc.	212-838-3329
FPS Productions Inc.	212-682-3877
FRP Productions Inc.	212-421-0074
FWB & Assoc. Inc.	212-682-2013
Fandango Productions	212-986-5676
Doris Faye Prods. Inc.	212-246-0430
Bert Feldman Films	212-371-2330
Dick Feldman Assoc.	212-490-2955
Jose Ferro Films	212-921-7844
Toni Ficalora Productions	212-679-7700
Filmart Communications, Inc.	212-840-6707
Filenco	212-557-9268
Film Enterprises, Inc.	212-840-1966
Film Friends	212-929-7728
Filmfair	212-758-6540
Film Five Associates	212-661-5550
Film Planning Assoc.	212-755-9170
Film Searchers	212-586-3828
Filmstrip & Slide Lab, Inc.	212-684-4700
Filmsounds, Inc.	212-867-0330
Finkinc.	212-595-3604
Imero Fiorentino Assoc.	212-787-3050
Five Seas Prods. Inc.	212-564-4599
Flickers, Inc.	212-753-4840
Franco-American Films SA.	212-355-6486
Edwin Frankel Prods.	212-873-1222
Bob Franz Cinematographer	212-354-1886
Fraser Productions	212-242-8300
Si Fried Productions	212-757-4424
Harold Friedman Consortium	212-697-0858
Marvin Friedman Prods.	212-858-5374
Fucci-Stone Productions	212-688-3410
Bob Gaffney Productions	212-838-1040
George Gage Productions Inc.	212-879-6000
Ganymede Prods. Inc.	212-753-5010
Gregory Tory Prods.	212-759-7806
James Garrett & Partners, Inc.	212-751-7540
Gateway Productions	212-371-8535
Geesink Filmproduktie C.V.	212-972-0717
Gemini Films Inc.	212-757-7997
Mario Ghio Prod. Group Ltd.	212-721-4637
Ormond Gigli Studios	212-758-2860
Bob Giraldi Prods.	212-691-9200
Gittelman Film Assoc. Inc.	212-889-9140
Glen-Warren Prod., Ltd.	212-371-7650
Paul Glickman	212-855-0079
Globus Brothers 91	**212-243-1008**
Gluck Durham Films, Inc. 13	**212-288-6394**
The Glyn Group	212-255-5156
Jeff Gold Productions	212-759-8785
Melvin Gold Enterprises	212-688-0897
Steve Gold Inc.	212-935-1040
Gomes Loew Inc.	212-593-9500
Gotham Film Prods. Inc.	212-697-6020
Goulding-Elliot-Greybar	211-867-9014
Granato Animation	212-869-3231
Gratton Video Service Inc.	212-877-0570
William Greaves Prods.	212-586-7710
R. Greenberg Assoc. Inc.	212-689-7886
Greenberg & Mellon	212-686-0200
Walter Gregg Assoc, Inc.	212-889-7925
Guastella/ZCM Film Productions	212-221-1811
HBO Studio Productions Inc.	212-477-8600
Hankinson Studio Inc.	212-730-0434
Charles Hans Film Prods.	212-867-1107
Harrison Productions	212-683-1850
Harvest Films Inc.	212-684-7950
Haverland Film Productions Ltd.	212-679-0939
Hearst Metrotone News	212-682-5600
William Helburn Prods. Inc.	212-683-4980
Henson Assoc., Inc.	212-794-2400
J.E.G. Hess Prod., Inc.	212-673-6051
Henton-Garrett, Inc.	212-586-4196
Tibor Hirsch Prods.	212-362-1774
Lenny Hirschfield Prods., Inc.	212-686-9320
Tom Hollyman Inc.	212-867-2383
Horizon Studios Inc.	212-421-1441
Steve Horn	212-752-3500
Hubley Studios, Inc.	212-744-8050
Bill Hudson Films	212-679-7199
Huemark Films, Inc.	212-986-5066
Hughes Operation Center	212-765-6600
Hurrah Productions	212-759-6946
ICM Films Ltd.	212-832-0909
I.F. Studios, Inc.	212-697-6805
Illustra Films	212-751-6136
Image Creators, Inc.	212-535-0257
Image Factory, Inc.	212-759-9363
Independent Artists	212-765-4640
Independent Visions Int'l	212-255-4047
In House Producers/Directors	212-697-0550
The Ink Tank	212-869-1630
Intergroup Productions	212-832-8169
International Production Center	212-582-6530
JC Productions	212-575-9611
J.S. Audio-Video Seminars, Inc.	212-575-0296
JSL Video Services	212-575-5082
Jaguar Productions	212-889-9494
Jalbert Productions	212-685-8450
Jefferson Productions	212-532-0922
Jenkins Covington Inc.	212-879-6200
Joel	212-832-0070
Victor Johannes Films Ltd.	212-288-3632
Michael John Assoc.	212-867-1860
Johnston Films Inc.	212-683-7500
L/J Film & Videotape	212-860-5661
Mort Kasman Productions	212-689-9490
Kaspar Productions	212-683-4080
Max Katz Productions, Inc.	212-988-1957
Jerry Kaufmann Prods.	212-593-1670
Victor Kayfetz Productions	212-924-3935
Daniel Kennedy Communications	212-222-8887
Francis Kenny Films	212-472-4231
Key Concepts	212-986-8276
Killiam Shows, Inc.	212-679-8230
Kim & Gifford Productions	212-986-2826
Phil Kimmelman & Assoc., Inc.	212-371-1850
Kinetoscope	212-580-3966
Kingsbury Productions	212-989-6868
Enid Klass Research	212-686-1130
Kleinerman/Kalsar Assoc. Ltd.	212-688-1130
Dan Klugherz Productions	212-595-0058
Frank Kolarek Film Prods.	212-221-1580
Paul Kramer Assoc. Inc.	212-986-6869
L/J Film & Videotape, Inc.	212-860-5661
N. Lee Lacy Assoc. Ltd.	212-758-4242
Lamonte & Cohen Prods.	212-697-3939
Lance Studios	212-586-4233
Philip Landeck Prods.	212-867-1400
Wolf Landis	212-581-8870
Don Lane Pictures	212-682-0045
Langley-Sann	212-581-3930
La Rose Ltd.	212-541-7064
Laszlo Productions	212-679-8220
The Latin Sound	212-787-6763
Leo Animation	212-582-2515
Leodas & Arbusto & Assoc.	212-688-4308
Leroy Motion Picture	212-564-6793
Lear Levin Prods., Inc.	212-595-5526
Irv Levine Assoc.	212-921-8610
Rick Levine Prods. Inc.	212-986-8200
Fred Levinson & Co.	212-472-8888
Liberty Studios Inc.	212-532-1865
Jerry Lieberman Prods.	212-431-3452
Lindberg Productions Inc.	212-582-9060
Lipsin Film Assoc. Inc.	212-628-0774
Locomo Productions	212-222-4833
Loebel Prods., Inc.	212-472-1175
James Love Productions Inc.	212-751-0728
Lovinger, Tardio, Melsky	212-532-3311
Lubliner/Saltz	212-751-2570
Klaus Lucka 115	**212-594-5910**
Lynch Films	212-895-2012
Matrix	212-265-8500
M.C. Productions	212-923-0949
MCK Productions	212-868-0402
MLF Productions	212-581-6772
MPCS Video Center Bldg.	212-586-3690
M & R Productions, Inc.	212-889-7315
MRC	212-989-1754
Madison Films, Inc.	212-838-4856
Madoff, Steve	212-879-5664
Magi Communications Ltd.	212-421-3265
Magic Lantern Prods.	212-873-0486
Mako Oike Productions	212-759-7494
Mallet & Collins	212-245-1395
Max Mambru Films Ltd.	212-247-3190
Manno Productions	516-759-9224
Marathon International	212-688-1130

TV, FILM AND VIDEO

TV, FILM AND VIDEO

Envision Corp./Boston	617-482-3444
Federal Film Productions, Inc./Wash DC	202-628-7089
Filmarts/Boston	617-266-7468
The Film Group, Inc./Cambridge MA	617-354-5695
Film Works/Wash DC	202-833-2666
Stuart Finley, Inc./Falls Church VA	703-820-7700
Fiore Films/Jersey City NJ	201-432-4474
Fiorelli Films, Inc./Darien CT	203-655-8877
Florentine Films/Amherst MA	413-253-9330
Forma Art Assoc./Mamaroneck NY	914-698-2598
Foster & Associates/Gardiner ME	207-582-4607
Frame by Frame Productions Columbia Beach MD	301-596-4868
Frost Media Assocs./Arlington VA	703-356-8457
Gandalf Productions/Wash DC	202-347-1526
Georgetown Productions/Wash DC	202-337-1487
Gordon Films/Wash DC	202-462-5121
Steven Hansen Photography/Boston	617-426-6858
Gallery West Ltd./W. Hartford CT	203-246-7231
Hardley Productions, Inc./Cos Cob CT	203-869-1818
Henry Gregg, Inc./Philadelphia	215-446-8143
Guggenheim Productions/Wash DC	202-337-6900
Hallmark Films & Recording Owings Mills MD	301-363-4500
Hardman Associates, Inc./Pittsburgh	412-281-4450
Hartwick Przyborski Prods./Pittsburgh	412-765-3910
Haycox Photoramic, Inc./Norfolk VA	804-855-1911
Hermes Films, Ltd./Wash DC	202-244-3942
Hills Mfg. Co. Inc./Chalfont PA	215-345-8590
Image-Amation, Inc./Newtown Square PA	215-356-3400
Image Assocs. Inc./Wash DC	202-265-6677
Image Makers, Inc./Baltimore	301-727-8800
Levin Productions/Baltimore	301-366-1450
Insight Into Communication, Inc. Norwalk CT	203-853-1115
Jacoby/Storm Productions., Inc. Westport CT	203-227-2220
Hugh & Suzanne Johnston, Inc. Princeton, NJ	609-924-7505
Hal Kirn & Assoc./Chevy Chase MD	301-986-0616
Ken-Del Productions Inc. Wilmington DE	302-655-7488
Knightsbridge Prod. Inc./Scarsdale NY	914-725-3225
The Latent Image, Inc./Pittsburgh	412-261-5589
Laurence Associates/Boston	617-423-0133
Lisberger Studios, Inc./Boston	617-426-7070
Levin Prods/Baltimore	301-366-1450
Leroy Motion Pictures Prod. Studios Philadelphia	215-925-3769
Lissner & Prindle Inc./ Arlington VA	703-243-6000
Ralph Lopatin Productions Philadelphia	215-568-6400
Masscasting Corporation/Boston	617-247-0400
Master Motion Picture Co./Boston	617-426-3592
W.W. Matthews & Co. Inc./Pittsburgh	412-741-8916
Media Associates/Fairfax VA	703-978-3550
Leo Meister Prods./Nutley NJ	201-667-2323
Merrimack Productions Goffstown NH	603-497-2870
Forney Miller Film Assoc. Philadelphia	215-643-4167
Milner-Fenwick, Inc./Timonium	301-252-1700
Mode-Art Pictures, Inc./Pittsburgh	412-343-8700
Monumental Films Inc./Baltimore	301-462-1550
Motion, Inc./Wash DC	202-363-9450
Owen Murphy Prods., Inc. Westport CT	203-226-4241
National Film Distributors Wilmington DE	302-655-7488
Nicholson-Muir Prods. Inc. Larchmont NY	914-834-3005
Northeast Video & Sound, Inc. Stratford CT	203-377-1444
Walter G. O'Connor Co./Hershey PA	717-534-1000
Parameters Unlimited/Albany NY	518-463-5366
Peter Pastorelle Prods., Inc. Harrison NY	914-835-2930
H.G. Peters & Co., Inc./Primos PA	215-626-6500
Peter M. Piech Assoc./Huntington NY	516-454-6767
Pike Productions of Boston Watertown, MA	617-924-5000
Pilgrim Film Service, Inc. Hyattsville, MD	301-773-7072
John M. Price Films, Inc./Radnor PA	215-687-6699
Joseph Pytka Prods/Pittsburgh	412-391-7919
David Quaid Prod'ns., Inc./Wolfeboro NH	603-569-1817
Queen Village Recording Studios Philadelphia	215-463-2200
Resources/Burlington VT	802-862-0550
SA Films, Inc./Montvale NJ	201-391-4220
Ken Saco-Curt Lowey, Inc./White Plains NY	914-948-6500
Science House/Manchester MA	617-526-1120
Screen Presentations, Inc./Washington DC	202-546-8900
Screenscope, Inc./Arlington VA	703-527-3555
Albert Semels Studio Inc.	203-869-2349
Jamil Simon Productions/Cambridge MA	617-491-4300
Sleeping Giant Films, Inc./Hamden CT	203-248-9323
Snazelle Films/VTR/Washington DC	202-466-2175
Sound Concepts, Inc./Woodbridge CT	203-397-1363
Starbecker, Inc./Silver Spring MD	301-587-8648
E.J. Stewart Video/Broomall PA	215-543-7600
Studio III/Norfolk VA	804-623-0214
Studio 12/Johnston RI	401-943-2333
Symmetry Corp./Upper Marlboro MD	301-627-5050
Tele-Color Productions/Alexandria VA	703-823-2800
Tel-Fax, Inc./Bath PA	215-865-3110
Tel Ra Productions/Wayne PA	215-688-9233
TPC Communications/Pittsburgh	412-682-2300
TR Productions/Boston	617-783-0200
TWII Productions Inc./Washington DC	202-337-7681
Upitn, Inc./Washington DC	202-488-7313
Videoactive, Inc.	203-227-9056
Videocom, Inc./Dedham MA	617-329-4080
Visual Images/Washington DC	202-387-0831
Visual Projects Ltd./Roslyn Heights NY	516-484-1249
Dorian Walker Prods./Washington DC	202-452-1776
Westport Communications Group Westport CT	203-226-3525
Hugh Whittington/Washington DC	202-223-6969
Wildcat Prods./Boston	617-266-5326
Wombat Productions/Ossining NY	914-762-0011
Worldwide Films/Metuchen NJ	201-494-9500
Wren Associates Inc./Princeton NJ	609-924-8085
WUTV-Channel 29/Grand Island NY	716-773-7531

SOUTHEAST

ADCO Prods/Miami	305-751-3118
A&R Films/Miami	305-649-1116
Assoc. Filmmakers, Int'l/Miami	305-856-8541
Advertising & Marketing Assoc., Inc./Miami	305-358-9511
Alpha Productions/Tampa FL	813-689-9649
Don Barton Communications/Jacksonville FL	904-389-4541
Peter J. Barton Prods./Tallahassee FL	904-224-3685
Peter Barton Prods., Inc./Atlanta	404-231-1758
The Big Orange Prods./Miami	305-358-0440
Bluemke Associated Films West Palm Beach FL	305-689-0636
Brooks Read & Associates/Baton Rouge LA	504-343-1715
Burkley Prods./Miami	305-652-8779
Channel One, Inc./Atlanta	404-634-0101
Charbonnet-Stroble/New Orleans	504-949-4040
Chroma Color Corp./Pensacola FL	904-456-2804
Cinematronics, Inc./Ft. Lauderdale FL	305-565-2252
Cinetron Computer Systems, Inc./Atlanta	404-448-9463
Circus People/Atlanta	404-256-2116
Colby, Will/Atlanta	404-876-6676
Colonial Films/Doraville GA	404-458-5775
Com 21/Ted Johnson Prods./Jacksonville FL	904-354-7000
Compro/Atlanta	404-455-1943
Continental Film Productions Corp. Chattanooga TN	615-622-1193
Cook Consultants/Ft. Lauderdale FL	305-525-3355
Coronado Studios/Miami	305-573-7250
Country Television Prods./Nashville TN	615-383-4510
Creative Film & Sound Inc./No. Miami FL	305-891-1800
Daro Prods. Assoc./Savannah GA	912-234-5902
Herb Dietz Enterprises, Inc. Ft. Lauderdale FL	305-463-1270
DMK Films, Inc./Nashville TN	615-383-3044
DuBois Prods./No. Miami FL	305-945-0200
The Editors Center/Atlanta	404-261-3718
The E.O. Corp./Shelby NC	704-482-0611
ETF Productions, Inc./Lexington KY	606-277-8018
Filmakers Group, Inc./Ft. Lauderdale FL	305-763-1555
Filmit Productions, Inc./Savannah GA	912-236-6361
Film Spots/Motion Pictures/Miami	305-358-8129
Filmworks Corp./Miami	305-444-4182
Florida Cypress Gardens Prods. Cypress Gardens FL	813-324-2111
Focus Teleproductions/Metairie LA	504-837-2020
Fotovox, Inc./Memphis TN	901-725-1810
Gordon-Kerckhoff Productions, Inc. of N.Y. Sarasota FL	813-371-0013
Dave Graveline Productions/No. Miami FL	305-940-6999
Great American Cinema Co./Nashville TN	615-256-4982
Image Communications, Inc./Tampa FL	813-872-6828
Jan's Type & Art/Nashville TN	615-833-9622
Jayan Film Prods./Atlanta	404-876-7373
J.B. Productions/Raleigh NC	919-782-6666
Jefferson Productions/Charlotte	704-374-3823
Hamilton Productions, Inc./Miami	305-651-7576
Image 7/Atlanta	404-237-0777
Paul Indianer & Co., Inc./Miami	305-235-6132
Interlock Film Studio, Inc./Birmingham AL	205-785-1461
Key Productions, Inc./Key Biscayne FL	305-361-9567
Walter J. Klein Company, Ltd./Charlotte NC	704-542-1403
LaDel, Inc./New Orleans	504-581-5250
MacDonell & Assoc./N. Miami FL	305-757-9822
Mako Productions/Ocala FL	904-732-2268
Mamre Motion Pictures/Raleigh NC	919-834-7054
Marcus Productions/No. Miami FL	305-944-6646
McLeod Films, Inc./Miami	305-888-2481
Media Design Group/Winterpark FL	305-628-1755
Media Services/Nashville TN	615-367-0851
Metcalfe Films/Birmingham AL	205-591-5310
M & M Photography, Inc./Tampa FL	813-251-3774
Jack Morton Productions/Atlanta	404-758-8400
Multifact Film Productions/Orlando FL	305-298-1300
Multi-National Media Corp./Nashville TN	615-373-2480
Multi Vision Productions/Miami	305-371-3700
Newby's Movies/Miami	305-856-0887
Oglesby-Harden Studios/Atlanta	404-321-7900
Opryland Productions/Nashville	615-889-6840
Jim Owens Productions/Nashville	615-327-4077
Pan American Films/New Orleans	504-522-5364
Preview Plus Productions/No. Miami FL	305-891-2338
Professional Broadcast Prods., Inc. Tampa FL	813-877-7125
Reeder Productions, Inc./Knoxville TN	615-693-1342
Reider Film & TV/Atlanta	404-874-8436
RK Films/Winterhaven FL	813-294-7274
Sandpiper Prods., Inc./Atlanta	404-252-8728
Scene 3/Nashville	615-385-2820
Seawell, Harry / Parkersburg WVA 18	**304-485-4481**
Shelton Productions, Inc./Atlanta	404-355-0091
Spottswood Film Studios/Mobile AL	205-478-9387
Southeastern Films/Atlanta	404-873-5353
Soundlab, Inc./Coral Gables FL	305-448-2673
Hack Swain Productions, Inc./Sarasota FL	813-371-2360
Synapse Films/Atlanta	404-688-8284
Take 1 Productions/Coral Gables FL	305-442-1577
Tel-Air Interests, Inc./Miami	305-944-4621
Tele-Visual Aids/Miami	305-854-1424
Tomorrow Prods./Nashville TN	615-259-2204
Tri-Comm Prod'ns./Atlanta	404-892-0808
Tri-Comm Productions, Inc. Hilton Head Island SC	803-785-5920
Turner Video/Atlanta	404-876-5555
Twenty-First Century Prods./Nashville	615-244-5000
Video Atlanta, Inc./Atlanta	404-874-2252
Video South/Nashville	615-383-4916
Videotape Associates of Florida, Inc. Ft. Lauderdale FL	305-587-9477
Video Tape Associates/Atlanta	404-634-6181
Videoworks Prods., Inc./Miami	305-665-5556
Viscount Communications Inc./Atlanta	404-261-6240
Visual Productions/Miami	305-661-9631
Waga Productions/Atlanta	404-875-5551
WANX-TV 46/Atlanta	404-325-3103
Wometco Videotape Prods./Miami	305-377-8241
WTVT Prods./Tampa FL	813-876-1313

MIDWEST

Academy Film Prods./Chicago	312-642-5877
Actor's and Director's Studio Columbus OH	614-235-9831
AGS & R Studios, Inc./Chicago	312-836-4500
Aiko/Broadview IL	312-280-9177
Alpha Corp of America/Mundelein IL	312-566-0580
Gilbert Altschul Prods/Evanston IL	312-328-6700
Ken Ancell Films/Chicago	312-664-2447
Aratole Prods, Inc./Chicago	312-778-2100
Aniforms Midwest/Parkridge IL	312-823-5890
Anemators Above/Chicago	312-944-7350
Ansel Prods/Chicago	312-337-8045
Arocom Productions/Akron OH	216-867-7950
Ash Film Productions/Madison WI	608-238-9997
Assoc. Audio-Visual Corp/Evanston IL	312-866-6780
Audio Visual Prods./Chicago	312-276-1400
Automated Marketing Systems, Inc. Detroit	313-272-1000
Avsense Productions/Minneapolis	612-333-4581
Fred Badiyan Productions/Minneapolis	612-888-5507
Marv. Bailey Prod, Inc./Chicago	312-440-1030
Bajus-Jones/Minneapolis	612-835-4490
Baldwin Films/Chicago	312-642-6966
Ball Communications, Inc./Evansville IN	812-425-2271
John Ball & Assoc/Chicago	312-332-6041
Betzer Productions Inc./Chicago	312-664-3257
Michael Birch Inc./Chicago	312-329-9350
William Birch & Assoc./Chicago	312-527-2135
Larry Bloodworth/Chicago	312-477-8282
Blume-Liebeck/Chicago	312-736-8200
Brand Productions/Cincinnati	513-721-1462
Bright Light Productions, Inc. Cincinnati	513-721-2574
Burd & Cavan Communications Chicago	312-266-8661
Butler Associates, Inc./Dayton OH	513-298-7462
Calvin Communications, Inc. Kansas City MO	816-571-7800
Cavalcade Prods/Wheaton IL	312-668-6363
Celebrities Productions/St. Louis	314-862-7800
Centron Corp., Inc./Lawrence KS	913-843-0400
Chapman/Spittler, Inc./Omaha	402-348-1600
Chias Prods Inc./Chicago	312-281-6320
Christopher Prods/Chicago	312-642-2280
Cinecraft, Inc./Cleveland	216-781-2300
Cine-Groff Motion Pictures Chicago	312-327-9200
Cinema One Productions, Inc. Cleveland	216-228-1080
Cine-Mark/Chicago	312-337-3303
Cinemation & The Optical Center Minneapolis	612-861-4481
Cine Specialists/Wichita KS	316-267-6648
Communications Corp./Chicago	312-467-9575
Communico/Fenton MO	314-225-6000
Computer Creations Chicago	312-477-1122
Computer Creations/South Bend IN	219-233-1020
Contact Visual/Evanston IL	312-475-4656
Coronet Instructional Media/Chicago	312-977-4000
Cottonwood Productions/Wakonda SD	605-267-2859
Countryman-Klang, Inc./Minneapolis	612-332-2538
C-P Films/Omaha	402-453-3200
Ron Crawford/Evanston IL	312-328-3456
Creative Establishment/Chicago	312-642-7700
Creative Productions, Inc./Chicago	312-332-4076
The Creative Works, Inc./Chicago	312-644-1555
Dean Crow Productions/Indianapolis	317-926-3335
Crunch Bird Studios, Inc./Detroit	313-342-6066
Cusack Prods./Chicago	312-943-2118
Cutting Room Floor Prods./Park Ridge IL	312-823-6430
Cybern Film Systems Inc./Chicago	312-774-2250
Design in Motion/Chicago	312-943-6533
Dexter Prods, Inc./Evanston IL	312-328-1050
William Ditzel Productions/Dayton	513-298-5381
Diversified Cinema/Detroit	313-371-8557
Dix & Assocs. Inc/Kansas City MO	816-531-4455
John Doremus Inc./Chicago	312-664-8944
Dove Films/Chicago	312-787-7045
Victor Duncan, Inc./Madison Hgts MI	313-589-1900

TV, FILM AND VIDEO

Col Dunn Studios Inc./Chicago 312-644-7600
Edcom Productions, Inc./Cleveland 216-261-3443
Editel/Chicago 312-440-2360
Empyrean, Inc./Chicago 312-787-8382
Edward Feil Productions/Cleveland 216-771-0655
Toni Ficalora Film & Tape Prods., Inc.
Chicago 312-787-0085
Filmark Studios/Chicago 312-427-3395
Film-Art Inc./Cincinnati 513-621-4930
The Filmakers, Inc./Minneapolis 612-870-8691
Filmart Productions/Minneapolis 612-788-4054
Film Factory/Minneapolis 612-871-2811
Film Fair Inc./Chicago 312-822-9200
Film Comm/Chicago 312-329-0185
Filmedia, Inc./Minneapolis 612-888-9231
Film Production of Indianapolis 317-924-5163
Alan M. Fishburn Prods/Chicago 312-332-0657
Fox & Associates, Inc./Cleveland 216-621-8520
Freese & Friends Inc./Chicago 312-642-4475
Galbreath Media Group, Inc./Fort Wayne IN 219-478-1587
Gaughan-Michitsch Films/Cleveland 216-621-0599
General Television Network/Oak Park MI 313-548-2500
The Gilbert Group/Overland Park KS 913-642-9600
Educational Productions/Raytown MO 816-353-1010
Goessel & Assoc. Inc./Chicago 312-787-5300
Edward Goldberger Prods./St. Louis 314-647-7112
Goldshall Assoc. Inc./Northfield IL 312-446-8300
G3Prods/Arlington Hgts IL 312-398-2672
Jim Handy Organization/Detroit 313-875-2450
Hardcastle Film Associates/St. Louis 314-647-4200
Harley-McDaniel Film Prod/Whitefish Bay 414-444-4240
Hellman Design Assoc./Waterloo IO 319-234-7055
Fran Hunt Creative Services/St. Louis 314-842-1686
Industrial Film Group/Chicago 312-792-1290
Infocom Productions, Inc./Cleveland 216-431-9163
Innervision Prods. Inc./St. Louis 314-822-0258
Int'l Photographic Center/Sheridan IL 815-496-2393
Jamieson & Assocs., Inc./Minneapolis 612-333-4581
Jenkins-Covington/Chicago 312-951-0330
David Kallaher, Inc./Cincinnati OH 513-621-6007
Kapsalis, Fran/Chicago 312-787-7045
Kartemquin Films Ltd/Chicago 312-472-4344
Kartes Productions, Inc./Indianapolis 317-844-7403
Mel Kaspar Ltd/Chicago 312-528-7711
The Kerbawy Company/Troy MI 313-649-4400
Kinetics/Chicago 312-266-9300
Kleinman Productions, Inc./St. Louis 314-725-5583
LaClede Communication Services Inc.
St. Louis 314-961-1414
N. Lee Lacy/Assoc/Chicago 312-944-4156
Ed Lang, Inc./Dayton OH 513-433-3133
Lemorande Production Co./Milwaukee 414-271-3358
Lenco, Inc./Jackson MO 314-243-3147
Les Images/Chicago 312-871-4700
Don Levey Studio/Chicago 312-329-9040
Jack Lieb Prods Inc/Chicago 312-943-1440
Low & Assoc., Inc./Minneapolis 612-854-8036
Lukas Film Prods, Inc./Chicago 312-764-0600
Sidney A. Lutz & Associates, Inc.
Southfield MI 313-642-3101
Magic Lantern/Southfield MI 313-356-7030
Magic Theatre Co./Chicago 312-222-0229
Gerry Mandel/Westood Forest MO 314-822-4645
Don Manelli & Assoc. Inc./Chicago 312-368-8600
Marcom/Barrington IL 312-382-1202
Tom Marker Co./Detroit 313-822-9100
Markle-Goins, Inc./Minneapolis 612-338-7550
Dick Marx & Assoc/Chicago 312-440-7300
Media-4 Productions/ 805-963-4840
The Media Group, Ltd./Grand Rapids MI 616-774-8338
Don Meier Prods./Chicago 312-222-1755
Metromedia Prods./Chicago 312-467-5200
Metro Productions/Minneapolis 612-546-1111
Midwest Film Studios/Chicago 312-743-1239
Tom Morris, Inc./Park Ridge IL 312-825-7182
Moshier/Maloney Rep/Chicago 312-943-1668
Movie Makers, Inc./Cleveland 216-432-0411
Moynihan Associates/Milwaukee 414-645-8200
Multimedia Forum/Kansas City MO 816-274-8321
Burt Munk Prods. Inc./Chicago 312-337-0034
Nat'l TV News, Inc./Oak Park IL 313-541-1440
Nauman/Custer SD 605-673-4065
Nelson Productions, Inc./Milwaukee 414-962-4455
Net Television, Inc./Ann Arbor, MI 313-971-3600
Nightingale Conant Coys/Chicago 312-627-3100
Fred Niles Communications/Chicago 312-738-4181
Nordine Group/Chicago 312-262-8500
Northwest Teleproductions/Chicago 312-664-3914
Northwest Teleproductions, Inc.
Minneapolis 612-835-4455
Chuck Olin Assoc/Chicago 312-822-9552
Omnicom Proudctions/Lansing, MI 517-393-2476
PAR Prods/Chicago 312-828-0322
People Reaching Prods 312-642-3789
Portafilms, Inc./Drayton Plains, MI 313-674-0489
Premier Film & Recording/St. Louis 314-531-3555
Producers Group Ltd./Chicago 312-467-1830
Producers Int'l. Corp./Indianapolis 317-924-5163
Puck Productions/Chicago 312-266-0339
Rainbow Prods/Chicago 312-525-7701
Regan Productions Inc./Detroit 313-368-3000
The Remote Unit, Inc./Indianapolis 317-923-2349
Ritter-Waxberg & Assoc., Inc./Chicago 312-664-3934
RMI Film Prod'ns./Kansas City 816-523-4004
RMS Prods./Chicago 312-266-2762
Gerald T. Rogers Prods./Skokie IL 312-967-8080
Ross Roy, Inc./Detroit 313-568-6400
Salay/Miles Prods./Birmingham MI 313-647-6665
Richard Solt Prods./Southfield MI 313-557-6720
Sandy Corporation/Southfield MI 313-569-4000
Sarva Inc./Chicago 312-944-5151
Scientificom/Chicago 312-787-8656
Sedelmaier Film Prods./Chicago 312-822-0110
Jack M. Sell & Assoc./Chicago 312-337-2092
The Shana Corporation/Birmingham MI 313-643-0919
Sheppard Prods./Glenview IL 312-729-9080
Jay J. Sheridan & Co./Chicago 312-943-4666
Shield Prods./Chicago 312-642-6441
Richard Shirley/Chicago 312-943-3033
Shooting Gallery/Chicago 312-664-2447
Sinnott & Assoc./Chicago 312-440-1875
Sight & Sound /Chicago 312-337-6640
Sly-Fox Films, Inc./Minneapolis 612-336-3608
Jerry Smith Studio/Milwaukee 414-765-0080
Bill Snyder Films/Fargo ND 701-293-3600
Gil Sorensen Prods./Chicago 312-266-2929
Sorgel-Lee-Riordan, Inc./Milwaukee 414-224-9600
Sportlite Films/Chicago 312-236-8955
Spot Shop Chicago/Chicago 312-329-0044
Station 12 Producers Express/Southfield MI 313-569-7707
Storycraft Incorporated/Lakewood OH 216-221-4722
Studio Seven Inc./Chicago 312-337-6264
Swanson Prods., Inc./Milwaukee 414-271-8774
Take Ten Inc./Des Plaines IL 312-297-1010
Technisonic Studios, Inc./St. Louis 314-727-1055
Telecasting Services/Chicago 312-738-1022
Telecine Film Studios Inc./Park Ridge IL 312-823-1418
Telecom Prods Inc./Chicago 312-944-4211
Telemation Prods./Glenview IL 312-729-5215
Teletronics/Des Plaines IL 312-298-7700
Television Corp of America/St. Louis 314-428-2280
Tilimon Prods./Highland Park IL 312-831-5757
The Tom Thomas Organization, Inc./Detroit 313-681-8600
Topel & Assoc. Ltd/Chicago 312-929-1000
Transmedia, Inc./Dayton 513-298-1189
Turk Films/Chicago 312-944-2435
Twin Arts Studio/Morton Grove IL 312-965-3121
Ultramedia/Bloomfield Hills MI 313-645-5530
Universal Training Systems/Wilmette IL 312-251-8700
Henry Ushejima Films Inc./Rosemont IL 312-692-3828
Video Films Incorporated/Detroit 313-393-0800
Video III Inc/Arlington Hgts IL 312-439-4040
V.I.P. Studios Inc./Arlington Hgts IL 312-439-9250
Vipro Inc./Chicago 312-664-7111
Visual Concepts Inc./Troy MI 313-649-2833
Visual Impact Productions/Detroit 313-833-1313
Gordon Weisenbron/Chicago 312-248-5689
Weituschat & Assoc, Inc./Chicago 312-465-3630
Werthmann Group, Inc.
Grosse Pointe Woods MI 313-259-2460
WGN Continental Prods. Co./Chicago 312-528-2311
The White House Studio's/Kansas City MO 816-931-3608
Wilding Video & Film/Detroit 313-882-9166
Wilding/Southfield MI 313-569-2900
Wilson-Griak, Inc./Minneapolis 612-333-3571
Woting/Kowalski & Co./Chicago 312-871-1228
WTMJ-TV/Milwaukee WI 414-332-9611
WUAB Productions/Cleveland 216-845-6043
DD Zabel Inc./Chicago 312-943-2144

SOUTHWEST

ACA Recording Studios, Inc./Houston 713-783-1771
AIE Studios/Houston 713-781-2110
Alpine Film Prod./Denver 303-777-3406
Another Production Co./Denver 303-623-6616
Arlette Studio Film Prods./Albuquerque 505-831-9615
A-V Corporation/Houston 713-523-6701
Bob Bailey Studios, Inc./Houston 713-864-2671
Bandelier Films, Inc./Albuquerque 505-242-2679
David Berman Films/Houston 713-961-4020
Buffalo Sound Studio/Fort Worth 817-335-7733
Carlocke/Langden Inc./Dallas 214-826-9380
Century Studios/Dallas 214-522-3310
Cine/Design Inc./Denver 303-777-4222
Cinema Services/Denver 303-573-5411
Cinema Services Prod./Denver 303-320-5811
The Cinematographers/Dallas 214-247-2047
Cinemax Productions/Dallas 214-231-1331
Cine Media Productions/Salt Lake City 801-973-4500
Coconut Grove Productions/Dallas 214-748-2755
Communi-Creations/Denver 303-759-1155
The Company/Dallas 214-361-9189
Creative Communications Group/Dallas 214-358-4461
Computer Image Corp./Denver 303-934-5801
Creative Visions Corporation/Dallas 214-247-4865
Morey Engle Productions/Denver 303-758-4436
Film House/Austin TX 512-474-8671
Kim Dawson Agency/Dallas 214-638-2414
The Tom Doades Co., Inc./Dallas 214-361-9189
Victor Duncan, Inc./Dallas 214-369-1165
ECI Video/Dallas 214-745-1292
Englander/Take Two/Dallas 214-521-1570
The Great Shooting Gallery/Dallas 214-742-1668
Ken Heckmann Productions/Dallas 214-369-5529
Imagehouse/Dallas 214-691-3255
KDFW-TV/Production 4/Dallas 214-744-4000
KHTV-39 Production/Houston 713-781-3930
K & H Productions, Inc./Dallas 214-526-5268
J. Darrell Kirkley, Inc./Richardson TX 214-231-1051
KPHO-TV 5/Phoenix 602-248-7474
KTVT-Channel 11/Dallas 214-363-9321
KTVT Videotape Productions/Fort Worth 817-738-1951
KTVY Productions/Oklahoma City 405-478-0021
KXAS-TV Productions/Fort Worth 817-429-1550
Linsman Film & Tape Prods./Scottsdale AZ 602-949-9008
Roy Manley Film Prods./Tucson 602-623-0307
Stephen Marks Prods./Albuquerque 505-266-7100
MCI Productions/Austin TX 512-282-1015
MCI Productions/Dallas 214-630-1262
MCI Productions/Houston 713-627-9270
MFC Film Prod./Houston 713-781-1580
Midtown Video/Denver 303-778-1681
Mulberry Square Prods./Dallas 214-369-2430
Osmond Commercial Prod'ns/Salt Lake City 801-224-4444
Pearlman Productions/Houston 713-523-3601
Phoenix Video Center/Phoenix 602-263-8866
PRC of America/Dallas 214-634-7774
PSI Film Lab, Inc./Dallas 214-631-5670
Carl Ragsdale Assocs., Inc./Houston 713-729-6530
Reyna Animation Co./Dallas 214-750-0194
Rocky Mountain Cine Support/Denver 303-795-9713
Loyd C. Senn & Assocs./Lubbock TX 806-745-7000
Silver Mountain Prod./Manitou Spring CO 303-633-3108
Silvertree Productions/Dallas 214-741-1035
Pat Sims Productions/Dallas 214-691-6200
Soljay Productions, Inc./Dallas 214-231-1331
Southwest Producers Service, Inc./Dallas 214-243-5719
Bill Stokes Associates, Inc./Dallas 214-363-0161
Studio Seven, Inc./Dallas 214-748-7776
Sullivan Prods./Dallas 214-634-9686
Sumet-Bernet Sound Studios/Dallas 214-691-0001
Suncountry Prods./Tucson AZ 602-792-3194
Sundance Productions/Dallas 214-688-0081
Swartwout Productions, Inc./Scottsdale AZ 602-994-4774
Tannebringrose Associates/Dallas 214-363-3464
TecFilms/Dallas 214-339-2217
Telescene, Inc./Salt Lake City 801-973-3140
Texan Productions/Dallas 214-747-0333
Texas Coast Productions/ 713-528-8209
Texas & Pacific Film Co., Inc./Austin TX 512-478-8585
Tom & Jerry Productions/Dallas 214-692-0216
Video Aide Corp. of Colorado/Loveland TX 303-667-3301
Video Central Productions/Dallas 214-824-0942
Jay West Productions/Houston 713-784-5280
WFAA-TV Productions/Dallas 214-748-9631
Rudine Wittman Prods./Dallas 214-634-0430
Zachry & Assoc., Inc./Abilene TX 915-677-1342

WEST COAST

Robert Abel & Assoc., Inc./Hollywood CA 213-462-8100
Academy Prod. Corp./Hollywood CA 213-985-5988
A & G Concepts/San Diego 714-291-7690
Aleman Films/LA 213-256-0868
American Mobile Video, Inc./Hollywood CA 213-465-7146
American Zoetrope/SF 415-788-7500
Amvid Communication Services
Manhattan Beach CA 213-545-3165
Animation Filmakers Corporation
Hollywood CA 213-851-5526
Animedia Prod. Inc./N. Hollywood CA 213-769-7469
Animagraphics/LA 213-464-4315
Ansel Prod./Hollywood CA 213-934-1101
Araiz Condoy Productions/Hollywood CA 213-464-5111
Associates &Toback/Hollywood CA 213-464-2157
Richard Audd/Encino CA 213-990-1416
AV-ED Films/Hollywood CA 213-466-1344
Avery/Tirce Prods./LA 213-466-5404
Banbury Films/SF 415-346-5727
Steve Banks, Inc./LA 213-667-0671
Barzman & Co./Hollywood CA 213-462-7261
Saul Bass & Assoc./Hollywood CA 213-466-9701
Bay Area Mobiletape/San Carlos CA 415-593-7124
Marvin Becker-Filmmaker/SF 415-567-2160
Cal Bernstein Prods./LA 213-461-3737
BFA Educational Media/Santa Monica CA 213-829-2901
Biddick Co./Northridge CA 213-349-9526
Bluebird, Inc./Hollywood CA 213-651-5180
Boardwalk Film & Tape/Venice CA 213-399-3261
Carl Borack Prods./Venice CA 213-399-3261
Ron Bourke Co./Seattle 206-282-4600
Stephen Bosustow Prods./Santa Monica CA 213-450-3936
Broverman Prods./Hollywood CA 213-278-5444
Bravura Films, Inc./SF 415-928-4273
Bresee, Frank/LA 213-933-6666
Wally Bulloch/Anicam/Hollywood CA 213-465-4114
The Burbank Studios/Burbank CA 213-843-6000
Bill Burrud Prods./Hollywood CA 213-937-0300
California Communications Int'l. LA 213-466-8511
Cali-Filmery/Tarzana CA 213-881-7128
Cameron Film Productions/Seattle 206-623-4103
George Carlson & Assoc./Seattle 206-623-8045
Paul Carlson Cartoons, Inc./Hollywood CA 213-842-7174
Catusi & Assoc./Marina Del Rey CA 213-821-0700
Cavalcade Pictures Inc./Hollywood CA 213-654-4144
CBS-TV/Studio City CA 213-763-8411
Centipede Films West/Hollywood CA 213-462-1330
Centre Films Inc./Hollywood CA 213-466-5123
Centurion Films, Inc./San Diego CA 714-224-0950
Chambers & Assoc./Westwood CA 213-470-1353
Chipman & Olsen Film Co./Hollywood CA 213-461-3294
R.B. Chenoweth Films/LaHabra CA 213-691-1652
Chris-Craft Videotape Center/LA 213-851-2626
Christopher Productions/Hollywood CA 213-462-6021
Chuck Blore & Don Richman, Inc.
Hollywood CA 213-462-0944
Ciccolini Film, Inc./SF 415-957-1705
Cine Rent West/Stage A/SF 415-864-4644
Cinema Research Corp./Hollywood CA 213-461-3235
Cineservice, Inc./Hollywood CA 213-463-3178
Douglas Clark Assoc./Sausalito CA 415-332-0754
Dick Clement Prods., Inc./Hollywood CA 213-462-6185
Coast Prods./Hollywood CA 213-876-2021
Coast Video/Newport Beach CA 714-557-2100
Coffin & Company/Seattle 206-282-1941

TV, FILM AND VIDEO

Fred Cohen Productions/SF	415-543-0822
Color Video Recording Service/San Diego	714-278-0734
Communications Group West/Hollywood CA	213-462-7353
Compact Video Systems/Burbank CA	213-843-3232
Consolidated Film Industries/Hollywood CA	213-462-3161
Cooper, Dennis & Hirsch/Hollywood CA	213-655-9610
CPC Associates, Inc./Hollywood CA	213-467-5900
Fred Craig Productions/San Gabriel CA	213-287-6479
Cornerstone Productions/Van Nuys CA	213-994-0007
Corporate Prods., Inc./Toluca Lake CA	213-760-2622
Creative Film Arts/Hollywood CA	213-466-5111
Creative Services Div.-G.E.S./Las Vegas NV	702-457-2376
Creative Video Associates, Inc. Hollywood CA	213-930-1127
CRM/McGraw Hill Films/Del Mar CA	714-481-8184
Cally Curtis Co./Hollywood CA	213-467-1101
Datafilms/LA	213-385-3911
Davidson Films, Inc./San Anselmo CA	415-457-1203
Dawson Productions/SF	415-391-7620
Del Rey Communications/San Gabriel CA	213-799-9782
Hal Dennis Prods./Hollywood CA	213-467-7146
Denove Prods./LA	213-650-0704
DePatie-Freleng Enterprises/Van Nuys CA	213-988-3890
Design Concepts/Scenic Studios Las Vegas NV	702-736-8333
DHP Video Mobile/Don Hagopian Productions North Hollywood CA	213-980-3320
D Prods., Inc./LA	213-930-2800
Dibie-Dash Prod./Hollywood CA	213-663-1915
Dick & Bert/Hollywood CA	213-462-4966
Dimension Films/Hollywood CA	213-657-2910
Walt Disney Prods./Burbank CA	213-845-3141
Harry Dorsey & Assoc./Westwood CA	213-270-4101
Dove Films/Hollywood CA	213-461-3737
Duck Soup Productions, Inc. Santa Monica CA	213-451-0771
Charles East Co./Seattle	206-623-2355
Eggers Films/Hollywood CA	213-851-7100
Richard Einfeld Prods./Hollywood CA	213-461-3731
The Elliot Concern/LA	213-874-9400
EYE/Hollywood CA	213-851-6377
EUE-Screen Gems, Inc./Burbank CA	213-843-3221
Jerry Fairbanks Prod./LA	213-462-1101
FM Motion Picture Svcs./Burbank CA	213-849-7618
Feury & Assoc./LA	213-273-0284
Filmation/Resada CA	213-345-7414
Film Communicators/Hollywood CA	213-766-3747
Film Consortium, Inc./Hollywood CA	213-550-0190
Film/Core/Hollywood CA	213-464-7303
Film Effects of Hollywood/Hollywood, CA	213-469-5808
Filmfair/Studio City, CA	213-877-3191
Film Harmonies/Billings, MT	406-248-3027
Filmline Prod. Assoc./Hollywood, CA	213-466-8667
Leo Diner Films, Inc./SF	415-775-3664
The Film Tree & Reagan/Hollywood, CA	213-659-9350
Film Ventures Int'l, Inc./LA	213-659-0545
The Film Works!/SF	415-552-8505
Imero Fiorentino Assoc./Hollywood, CA	213-476-4020
Flagg Films Inc./N. Hollywood, CA	213-985-5050
Flicker Makers Prods./LA	213-655-6099
Roger Flint Prods./Hollywood, CA	213-650-6546
Format Productions, Inc./Tarzana, CA	213-987-3900
Fraser, Tom/Sherman Oaks, CA	213-784-0765
Freberg, Ltd./Hollywood, CA	213-657-6550
Gary Freund Prods./LA	213-569-1444
Furman Films/SF	415-282-1300
George Gage Prods. Inc./Hollywood, CA	213-874-7400
Vern Gillum & Friends/Hollywood, CA	213-659-6100
GN Prods/LA	213-463-5693
Golden West Broadcasters/Hollywood, CA	213-469-3181
Richard Goldstone Prods./Hollywood, CA	213-931-1305
Graphic Films Corp./Hollywood, CA	213-851-4100
Great American Cinema Co./LA	213-475-0937
The Groot Organization/SF	415-543-9920
Randy Grochoske Films/SF	415-982-3857
Gerry Gross Prods./Hollywood, CA	213-467-1493
Group One Productions/SF	415-777-9777
G.T.A. West Inc./Hollywood, CA	213-937-6100
The Haboush Co./Hollywood, CA	213-466-4111
Richard Haboush Company/Hollywood, CA	213-851-8955
Don Hagopian Prods./N. Hollywood, CA	213-980-3320
Hanna-Barbera Prods. Inc./Hollywood, CA	213-851-5000
Keith Harrier Prods./Hollywood, CA	213-930-2727
Harris, Burton/Hollywood, CA	213-874-3883
Denny Harris, Inc./Hollywood, CA	213-826-6565
Harris-Tuchman Prods./Burbank, CA	213-841-4100
Harvest Films, Inc./Hollywood, CA	213-464-7307
Hawaiian Holiday Films/Hollywood, CA	213-462-1011
Bill Hendricks Films/Burbank, CA	213-843-6000
John J. Hennessy/S. Pasadena, CA	213-682-2353
Alfred Higgins Prods./Hollywood, CA	213-878-0330
Lenny Hirschfield Prods./LA	213-657-6124
Hollywood Video Corp./Hollywood, CA	213-467-3278
Image Transform, Inc./N. Hollywood, CA	213-985-7566
Image West Ltd./Hollywood, CA	213-466-4181
International Producers/Hollywood, CA	213-851-3595
Riley Jackson Prods./Hollywood, CA	213-464-4708
Jean-Guy Jacques Et Co./Hollywood, CA	213-936-7177
Jeffries Films/Hollywood, CA	213-876-1132
Johnson-Cowan Inc./Hollywood, CA	213-466-5301
Jones, Douglas/LA	213-783-1456
Terry Kahn Org./Hollywood, CA	213-278-9181
Kaleidoscope Films Ltd./Hollywood, CA	213-465-1151
Larry Katz & Co./Marina Del Rey, CA	213-821-5866
Stacy Keach Prods./N. Hollywood, CA	213-762-0966
Kenworthy Snorkel Films/LA	213-476-4100
Konikow & Company/San Diego	714-292-4462
KTVU-TV/Oakland, CA	415-834-2000
Kurtz & Friends Films/Hollywood, CA	213-461-8188
N. Lee Lacy/Assoc. Ltd./LA	213-852-1414
Lajon Films Inc./Burbank, CA	213-841-1440
Lyon Lamb Video Animation Systems/LA	213-277-2633
Landor Associates/SF	415-955-1200
Landry Video Systems/Hollywood, CA	213-462-3539
Learning Garden/Hollywood, CA	213-874-6632
Leawood/Hollywood, CA	213-464-8914
Gene Lester Prods./N. Hollywood, CA	213-769-6160
Rich Levine Prods./Hollywood, CA	213-874-4222
Harry Liles, Photo./LA	213-466-1612
Lou Lilly-Films/West Inc./LA	213-659-0024
Lori Productions, Inc./LA	213-466-7567
Magus Films Inc./SF	415-788-8527
Howard T. Magwood Prods./Hollywood, CA	213-874-9611
Marcom Prods. Ltd./LA	213-820-6867
Marujara, Art/LA	213-660-6276
Marvin Prods./LA	213-851-6813
Ed Marzola & Assoc./Hollywood, CA	213-652-7481
McGraw-Hill Films/SF	714-453-5000
McIndoe, Geoerge/Santa Monica, CA	213-396-4775
Cameron McKay Prod./LA	213-463-6073
Medallion TV Enterprises/Hollywood, CA	213-652-8100
Bill Melendez Prods./LA	213-463-4101
Lee Mendelson Prods. Inc./Burlingame, CA	415-342-8284
Merrick Studios/Hollywood, CA	213-462-6781
Meta/4 Prods. Inc./Hollywood, CA	213-273-6075
Metrotape West/Hollywood, CA	213-462-7111
Micromedia/Hollywood, CA	213-468-8777
Midocean Motion Pictures/Hollywood, CA	213-462-7272
Mobilcolor/San Diego, CA	714-571-0591
Mobile Video Systems/Hollywood, CA	213-464-7151
Motion Picture Marine/Marina Del Rey, CA	213-822-1100
Motion Picture Service Co./SF	415-673-9162
Multi Image Productions, Inc./San Diego	714-560-8383
Murakami Wolf Swenson/Hollywood, CA	213-462-6474
MPTVT Prods./LA	213-461-2951
NBC Telesales/Burbank, CA	213-845-7000
Northwestern, Inc./Portland, OR	503-226-0170
Noel Nosseck Films/Malibu, CA	213-456-9893
Number One Video Prod, Ltd./Seattle	206-322-5824
One Pass Video, Inc./SF	415-777-5777
Orange Coast Video/Irvine, CA	714-556-9292
Otto Glenn Studios/LA	213-933-5679
Pacific Video/Hollywood, CA	213-462-6266
Pacific Title & Art Studio/Hollywood, CA	213-464-0121
Pantomine Pictures/N. Hollywood, CA	213-980-5555
Paramount Communications N.Hollywood, CA	213-506-1402
Parthenon Pictures/Hollywood, CA	213-385-3911
Pasetta Prods./Hollywood,CA	213-655-8500
M.B. Paul Studios, Inc./Beverly Hills, CA	213-271-8396
Perland Prods./Burbank, CA	213-841-1530
Pentangle/Hollywood,CA	213-652-8330
Phoenix Films Corp./LA	213-654-1660
Photo-Art Studios/Portland, OR	503-224-5665
Playhouse Pictures/Hollywood, CA	213-851-2112
Piscetello, Charles/LA	213-464-7734
Premore, Inc./Culver City CA	213-559-4850
Productions West/LA	213-464-0169
Producers Assocs./LA	213-851-4123
Professional Arts/Stanford CA	415-365-6630
Project Films, Inc./LA	213-466-9651
John Purdy, Inc./Hollywood CA	213-874-7289
Pyramid Films Corp./Santa Monica CA	213-828-7577
Quartet Films Inc./LA	213-464-9225
Ramic Productions/Newport Beach CA	714-833-2444
Bill Rase Productions, Inc./Sacramento CA	916-929-9181
RKA Pictures/Seattle	206-682-4628
RFT Productions Ltd./Hollywood CA	213-651-3042
RKO General/Hollywood CA	213-462-2133
Robe/Ackerman, Inc./Hollywood CA	213-463-2133
John Robert Productions/SF	415-392-8408
Jim Rose Assoc./Hollywood CA	213-653-9240
Roundtable Films, Inc./Beverly Hills CA	213-657-1402
Jack Rourke Prods./Burbank CA	213-843-4839
Danny Rouzer Studio/Hollywood CA	213-936-2494
Ruxton, Ltd./Burbank CA	213-845-3724
Sage & Assoc./Hollywood CA	213-656-3024
Salenger Educational Media Santa Monica CA	213-450-1300
Scenografix/Sausalito CA	415-332-0103
Screen Images/Hollywood CA	213-462-4383
Frank Sentry Group/LA	213-655-6099
Edward Shaw Prods./Beverly Hills CA	213-274-5123
Jerry Sims Prods./Studio City CA	213-766-4363
Snazelle Films, Inc./Hollywood CA	213-466-4307
Snazelle Films, Inc./SF	415-431-5490
Sonex Int'l Corp./Burbank CA	213-843-7484
Rich Spalla Video Prods./Hollywood CA	213-469-7307
Spectrum Video/Burbank CA	213-843-7195
Don Stern Prods./Hollywood CA	213-851-3673
Andre Stojka & Assoc./Hollywood CA	213-934-1439
Stop Frame, Inc./SF	415-543-5344
Robert Story Moving Pictures/Hollywood CA	213-467-6700
Strickland, Robert/Los Gatos CA	408-374-1407
Herbert L. Strock Prods. Inc./Hollywood CA	213-461-1298
Studio 16, Inc./SF	415-982-2097
Sunlight Pictures/Hollywood CA	213-650-8145
Sunrise Canyon Video/Glendale CA	213-241-5173
Sunset Films/SF	415-495-4555
Sunwest Prods., Inc./Hollywood CA	213-464-5111
Super Colossal Pictures/LA	213-876-6770
Superior Video Services, Inc. N. Hollywood CA	213-786-7060
Swanson Prods. Inc./Hollywood CA	213-851-8930
Tapestry Video Prods./Burbank CA	213-469-5891
Tartan Prods./LA	213-461-2877
Teleprompter Production Services Santa Clara CA	408-247-4210
Telepros/Belmont CA	415-595-1169
Jim Terry Prod. Services Inc./Century City CA	213-277-7535
Thomas Brothers Film Studio/SF	415-957-9700
Roger Tilton Films, Inc./San Diego	714-233-6513
Roger Tilton Films, Inc./Hollywood CA	213-467-3191
Trans-American Video/Hollywood CA	213-466-2141
Trans-American Video, Inc./Las Vegas	702-873-3660
Trio Productions/LA	213-874-9400
Universal Commercial/Universal City CA	213-985-7321
UPA Pictures Inc. /LA	213-842-7171
Uplift Prods./Santa Ana CA	714-751-5393
Valley Video/Burbank CA	213-841-2387
Van Der Veer Photo Effects/Burbank CA	213-841-2512
VCI Studios/LA	213-380-2722
Versatile Video, Inc./Sunnyvale CA	408-734-5550
The Video Center/Hollywood CA	213-467-6272
Video Concepts/Burbank CA	213-841-0295
Video Craftsmen, Inc./Hollywood CA	213-464-4351
The Videography Studios/Hollywood CA	213-204-2000
Video Production Artists/Marina Del Rey CA	213-821-0755
Video Production Services/Berkeley CA	415-526-6741
The Video Tape Co./N. Hollywood CA	213-985-1666
Video Tape Enterprises/Hollywood CA	213-466-3273
Videotape Works/Hollywood CA	213-464-5891
Video Transitions, Inc./LA	213-653-2244
The Vidtronics Co., Inc./Hollywood CA	213-466-9741
Vid West/Studio City CA	213-766-3701
Vik-Winkle Prods./Burbank CA	213-843-1920
Vista Productions, Inc./SF	415-626-2927
Visual-Istics/San Diego	714-235-0843
Kent Wakeford & Assoc./Hollywood CA	213-273-7595
Jay Ward Prods./LA	213-654-3050
Warner Bros. TV/Burbank CA	213-843-7280
Alan Waite Prods./N. Hollywood CA	213-985-3905
Washington State Dept. Commerce. Olympia WA	206-753-5610
WE Prods./Century City CA	213-277-0597
Western Video Systems/San Diego CA	714-292-0337
Wexler Film Prods., Inc./Hollywood CA	213-462-6671
Wexler/Holt Prods./Hollywood CA	213-655-6800
Bill White Prods./LA	213-934-1412
Carl Wikman Video/Tape/Portland OR	503-234-3562
Wildwood Films North/SF	415-543-2885
Carter Wright Enterprises/Hollywood CA	213-469-0944
Richard Williams Animation/LA	213-461-4344
L.J. Wood Film Prod./Las Vegas	702-739-7705
Marvin Young Assoc./N. Hollywood CA	213-763-5347

W

**THE ART DIRECTOR'S
ESSENTIAL GUIDE
TO PHOTOGRAPHY**

hen booking a shooting date with a photographer, remember that you will have ample time later to discuss details like lighting, models, camera angles and composition. The first and most important communication between an art director and a photographer should concern itself with the most crucial aspect of the booking—the luncheon.

A seasoned art director will instinctively sense what foods will satisfy the palates of even the most demanding clients, and will take great care to choose the photographer accordingly. ANY PHOTOGRAPHER WORTH HIS SALT CAN FEED YOU, BUT ONLY A HANDFUL OF PROS CAN PROVIDE THAT MEMORABLE GASTRONOMICAL NUANCE.

The beginning art director can refer to the indispensible Fuscia Book which contains a listing of photographers by menu. Notice that although there's been a big upsurge lately of Hunan and Japanese fare (with Macrobiotic starting to catch on in the inner circles) the safety of the American Spread is still available for the less daring. AN ACCOUNT CAN BE JEOPARDIZED BY SERVING RAW OCTOPUS, BEAN CURD OR TOFU SALAD TO THE WRONG PEOPLE.

The second most essential aspect to consider is the type of music to be played during the shooting session. Top art directors will search out photographers whose knowledge of current music is so profound that anything recorded even the week before the shooting date will already be classified by them as baroque.

Once the music is chosen, the art director must be assured that it will be played as loudly as modern acoustical technology will allow. This means that if any conversation at all can be heard in the studio, it is obvious that the photographer has failed to provide a suitable atmosphere. Beginning art directors should beware of photographers who try to pass themselves off as "cool" simply by taking Montavani and turning the volume up to a deafening pitch. NEVER, I REPEAT, NEVER USE A PHOTOGRAPHER WHO RELIES SOLELY ON FM RADIO STATIONS.

Last, but certainly not least, is the way the art director handles himself at the shooting. Not only is the respect of the photographer at stake, but that of the ad managers, account supervisors, assistant product managers, account trainees and anyone else who finds it absolutely necessary to be there.

Try not to tire out the photographer with information, so that his creative juices aren't hampered with such boring details as what he's going to shoot or how or why or what the ad is for. Just remember to say "Yeah" and "Great, Man" when he shows you Polaroids.

Talk the photographer's language and repeat "neutral density filters," "F-stops" and "bracketing" as much as possible, so the assembled crowd can note your incredible grasp of the situation.

During the actual shooting, try to stand right in back of the photographer, nearly touching, and constantly talk in his ear or, better yet, talk to the models or rearrange the still life until you get it almost the way you want it. AN ART DIRECTOR IS THERE TO DIRECT. SO DAMN IT…DIRECT!

It's impressive to use the telephone as much as possible. Save up as many return calls as you can for the day of the shoot and don't forget to tell anyone at all that you can be reached at the studio.

Develop a slightly worried, pensive look. This will make it appear that you're working very hard, and make everyone else aware that the photographer is completely responsible for not being able to execute your brilliant concept.

At least everyone will be able to get together again at the reshoot, have another great lunch, and hear the latest sounds—"YEAH." "GREAT, MAN."

**ARNIE ARLOW
Creative Director
Martin Landey, Arlow Advertising, Inc.
New York City**

MATHEW BRADY FILMS INC.
31 West 27th Street
New York, New York 10001
(212) 683-6060

Producer /Sales: Maria Giordano

EDSTAN STUDIO
240 Madison Avenue
New York, New York 10016
(212) 686-3666

Animation stand photography for the
thinking Art Director/Designer.

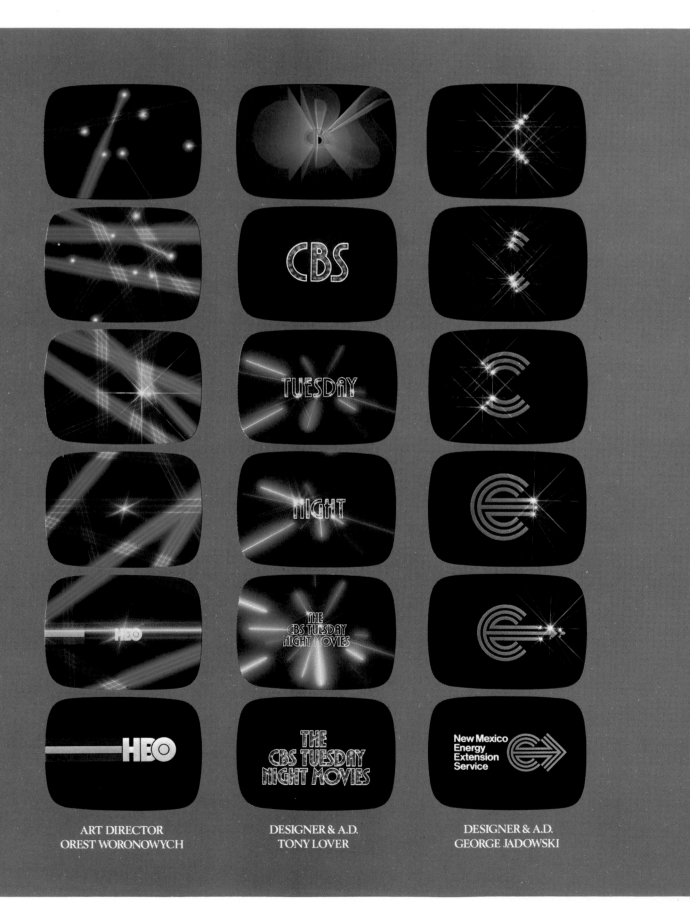

ART DIRECTOR
OREST WORONOWYCH

DESIGNER & A.D.
TONY LOVER

DESIGNER & A.D.
GEORGE JADOWSKI

GLUCK DURHAM FILMS INC.
108 Fifth Avenue
New York, New York 10011
(212) BU8-6394

Contact: Magi Durham

Specializing in
tabletop, food, animals.

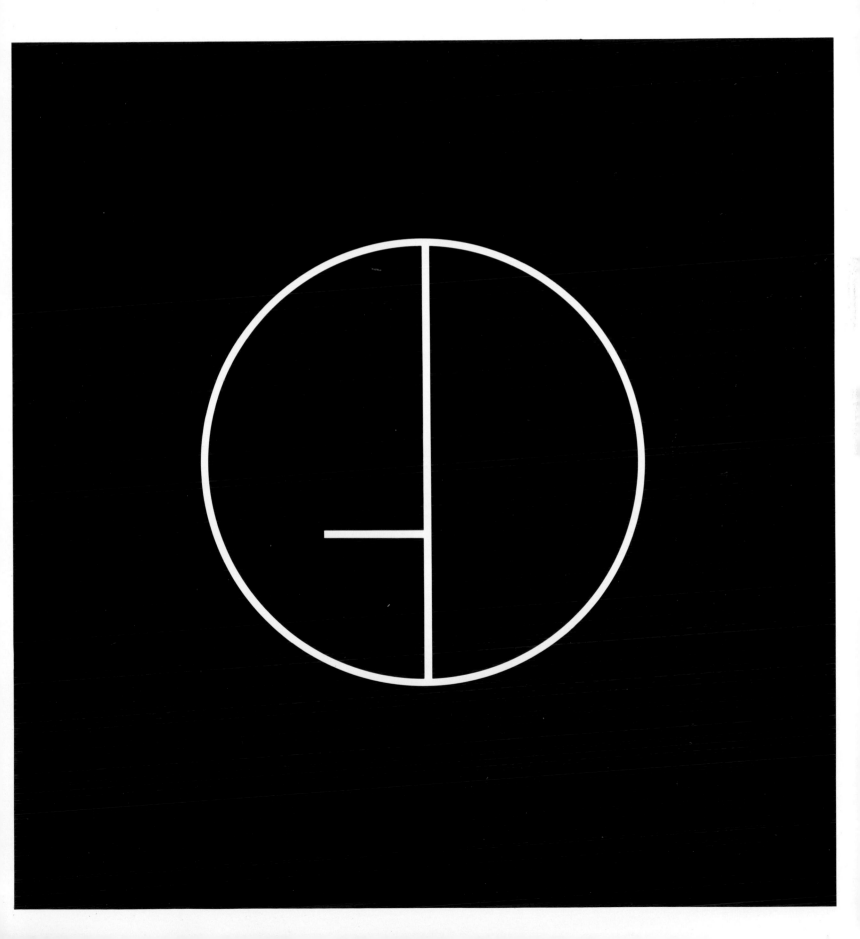

S I LOVE IT

So many people in my business are always putting down the business I'm in. They're even afraid to call it by name. They call it "The Business"; as if it were show business or something. Well it isn't. It's advertising. And I've got to tell you, I love it.

People say advertising burns you out at 30. Well I'm 35 and I haven't burnt out yet. In fact, when I get a new assignment, I usually feel like a rookie in my first big game. I love it.

Advertising has always been good to me.

I love doing what I want to do.

I love the freedom.

I love the competition (with a passion).

I love the money.

I love to overhear people talking about my ads or the products and services I work on.

I love the diversity of people in advertising.

I love the absurd sense of humor most of the people in advertising seem to have.

I love the discipline.

I love the excitement of deadlines.

I love the fact that no matter how much experience you have in advertising, it's constantly changing and presenting a new challenge every day.

I love solving "problems."

I love how advertising brings together creativity, analogy, psychology, marketing and work.

I love how advertising keeps me current.

I love learning about so many different businesses and products.

I love working on my craft.

I love to sit with a writer and think up stuff.

I love to come up with what I know is a great concept.

I love to design a page or a commercial.

I love getting ready for and experiencing "The Big Presentation."

I love to produce music.

I love to shoot with a good photographer or director.

I love to direct a good illustrator.

I love to hear that sales are going through the roof on my accounts.

Most of all, I love to experience the finished product, by chance, on TV or radio, or in print. I love to say to myself, "Hey, I did that. It's not bad."

IVAN LIBERMAN
Art & TV Production Supervisor
Ogilvy & Mather/2
New York City

PHIL MARCO PRODUCTIONS
104 Fifth Avenue
New York, New York 10011
(212) 929-8082

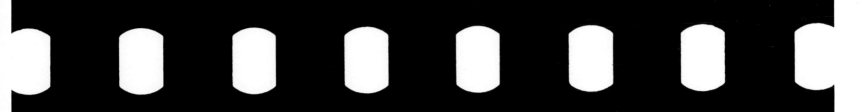

S LAUNCH THE CONDOR!

Some years ago, the story of the condor was widely circulated in automotive advertising circles. It seems that the production crew, agency people, clients and all others who can turn a normal shoot into a "Ben Hur production" had travelled to South America on behalf of a campaign that featured a car traversing the Andes Mountains.

Not unexpectedly, the creative people at the agency had come up with an idea for one of the spots in the series to feature the car driving down an Andean mountainside road simultaneously on camera with a giant condor gliding majestically across the steep ravine that the road of the car's route rimmed—an exciting visual idea that obviously required a lot of pre-production work to set up for a one-take shot.

Much prep-time later the shot was set—light, clouds, mountainside and other conditions being perfect, the car and giant bird were ready on top of the steep precipice. The director and his camera crew had it all in the lens as the director gave the "roll 'em" to his camera and via a highly magnified bull horn bellowed, "Launch the condor!"

The car started the drive downhill on cue, and the condor-keepers pushed the magnificent bird over the rim of the precipice expecting him to stretch his great wingspan and soar across the ravine. Instead, he accomplished the avian equivalent of a human "sailor dive" and plummeted straight down to a feathery death thousands of feet below.

It was only then realized that this particular bird had been purchased from a zoo in which he had been hatched and raised all of his life, until show biz called, with neither the need nor the opportunity to learn to fly!

When asked to write this piece which would, hopefully (by whom?), contain some words of advice to the more neophyte photographers' agents (the classy title is "representative"—I prefer "agent" for some perverse reason), I tried to put the primer of photography salesmanship on paper: know the advertising business; let the pic-

tures speak for themselves; take the job, not yourself, seriously; don't spill coffee on the portfolios; and so forth. One point kept coming up—we agents are, in the long run, only as successful as the talent we represent. Great agents represent great talent, and one fault, in our never-ending quest for immediate success for a photographer (with the accompanying immediate commissions!) is to push him or her too fast.

How many times have we seen a portfolio of very good pictures with not one of them being an actual assignment? What an opportunity, the novice agent thinks, to take this virgin talent right into the big time (and $$$).

But there's a vast difference between an undirected shoot without a client and/or layout and a photographic assignment that requires preparation to satisfy a client's specific requirements. A young, even if very talented, photographer cannot make great pictures if "forced" (and pride will rarely allow him to exert the common sense/intuition of turning down big stuff) into an important shoot that's over his or her head.

So what if you have a brother-in-law art directing a bouillabaisse account that produces 20 ads a year? Let the photographer install a kitchen and learn to overcome his allergy to seafood before you dump the first 10 (of the 20) layouts on his desk.

So what if an A/D who loves you gets a major Detroit automotive account? Let the photographer shoot some foreign car editorial pictures before facing "Detroit metal."

So what if your buddy designs two Sunday Times color fashion pages each week of the year? Let the photographer shoot some "back of the book" fashion before you take your buddy's layouts and possibly blow your (and the photographer's) chances for a nice on-going account.

Have I made my point clear? In other words, find out if the photographer knows how to fly before grabbing your bull horn and shouting, "Launch the condor!"

NOB HOVDE
(who has been an agent for various photographers and film directors for the past two decades)

PS: Time has a way of dimming the memory, and I beg the forgiveness of those who actually experienced the condor story if some of the facts are not accurate. The point I attempted to make still works, even if the facts have shifted over the years. Thanks.

295 Fifth Avenuc
Penthouse
New York, New York 10016
(212) 532-9670

Phillip Collins, Sales Representative

Jeffrey Metzner Productions
295 Fifth Avenue
New York City 10016 (212) 532-9670

Houston Office:
(713) 961-1961

Parkersburg Office:
(304) 485-4481

Washington D.C. Office: Shari Hall
(703) 437-4978

New York Office: Margery Andrews
(212) 679-8554

Dallas Office: Jack Jordan
(214) 521-3250

Denver Office: Henry Associates, Inc.
(303) 756-4811

IF YOUR STANDARDS EXCEED THOSE OF EXCELLENCE IN FILM PRODUCTION AND PHOTOGRAPHY

HARRY SEAWELL

Research and scripting (non-fiction)
High impact films from reality
Unscripted political commercials (on acceptance)
Multimedia research, development and production
Oscar winning location photography

TRY CONVINCING HARRY SEAWELL THAT "IT CAN'T BE DONE"....

**LET ME PUT YOUR
TRANSPARENCIES,
ART,
DESIGNS...IN MOTION...**

...by making movies from slides, drawings, graphics.

Your stills become exciting motion pictures, TV spots, sales and industrial movies when I shoot them on my trusty Oxberry animation camera with pans, zooms and dissolves.

How about sophisticated opticals? Easy. Wipes, moving mattes, strobe action, split screens are all simply added with "ANI-MATTES" by Al Stahl. ANI-MATTES are sets of animated mattes—10 to 20 Kodalith frames that are sandwiched over your slides and projected one at a time. A totally new concept in audio visuals. With them, you produce wipes, push-offs, panning, zooming mattes, just like the pros.

My portfolio of samples is best demonstrated when you screen my free 16mm color MINI-REEL of actual film clips of "moving" effects. However, without a movie projector, let me try to illustrate some of the effects, for example, a zoom into a 3/8-inch width of any transparency or art:

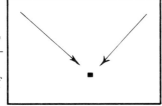

It's like moving into 1/50 of your 8x10 transparency (that's one-to-one for you macro-minded photographers).

Now, try this! Pan your 103 mm portrait lens over five city blocks! I'll duplicate that pan on a 2x2 slide like this:

Art directors, photographers, artists! Are you worried about how your color slides and art reproduce on movie film? I'll surprise you with fabulous results, retaining the original skin tones of your transparencies. This is possible because I shoot your actual slide on the animation stand, not a retouched blow-up or projected image.

There's a limit to how much movement you can add to a movie from slides (or art) with just pans and zooms. I've solved this problem of more motion with ANI-MATTES, the greatest technological advance in 25 years of slide show production.

Here's an example of a four-way split using only three frames from a 50-slide set. You can pan, fade or pop in quadrants, wipe in one section, spin in another:

 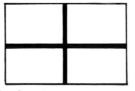 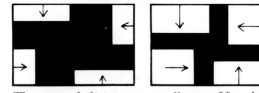

The possibilities are endless...Here's a clock wipe:

a flip:

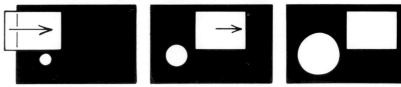

and mattes that pan and zoom at the same time:

Push offs, reveals, barn doors, checker boards, circle wipes, explosions, star bursts—you name it, I'll do it. ANI-MATTES, in addition to camera zooms and pans, produce professional opticals for your audio-visual presentations that are truly unique in concept and design:

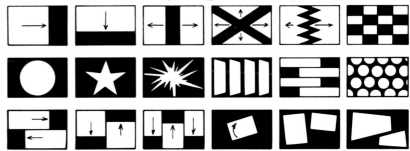

You also eliminate many slides, extra projectors, and simplify programming by combining two or more scenes of the same slide. For example, this six-frame diamond wipe zooms from pinpoint to full, revealing a second scene inside the first:

And when you transfer your stills to video tape, ANI-MATTES produce wipes at a fraction of the cost of the electronic effects generator.

Want to see a conversion of a whole multi-screen show to a one-screen movie? Then request a sample reel of any one of the films I've made for IBM, Goodyear, ATT, Western Union, Citibank, Time-Life, Celanese, Dennyson. Or see TV commercials for Norelco, Bloomingdale's, Ajax, Scotties, Columbia Records, Viva, Hasbro, Contac...and 2,000 more!

Phone for my versatile free MINI-REEL, "How to Make Movies From Slides," with 30 assorted movie clips from TV spots, sales, promotion and industrial reels.

**AL STAHL ANIMATED
1600 Broadway
New York, New York 10019
212-265-2942**

ILLUSTRATION AND GRAPHIC DESIGN

CREATIVE SPECIALIZATION...
A TWO-EDGED SWORD
(OR A CHEER AND A BOO
FOR SPECIALIZATION)

Today, specialization is taking over in the creative area (just as it seems to be doing everywhere else in advertising).

What is an art director?

Today, they want to be known as communicators.

What's communication?

TV. Radio. Print. Posters. Collateral. Matchbook covers. And so on.

The question is...can all of today's art directors/communicators hack it in all those areas?

The second question is...do they have to?

As for the first question, no, I don't think they hack it in all areas of communications.

As for question two, it's a matter of whether or not they want to broaden themselves.

As a case in point, the art director who does automobile advertising is in danger of being typecast as being able to do only automobile advertising (this typecasting is great if the A/D wants to switch from Toyota to Ford for more money—it's not so great if he tries to break out of his mold and work in a new area).

The A/D doing television knows the route to go in creating and executing a TV commercial—but give him a booklet to design and a lot of these fellows get lost. They don't know anything about paper and haven't the foggiest notion of how type works (luckily, a lot of these A/D's have some great type specialist in the production department to call on for help). A TV A/D specialist can get along without a flair for graphic design in his television work, but that lack will kill him when he tries to do a booklet.

Then there's the print A/D who knows who the best photographers and retouchers are, but can't design a logo. And the consumer A/D who can't do industrial and/or corporate advertising. And vice versa.

Maybe we should change the all-encompassing art director title to, say, TV communicator, trade print communicator, consumer print communicator, collateral communicator, matchbook communicator, and so on.

Specialization can be very efficient—especially in the bigger advertising agencies. But while it's important to be efficient, I wonder if it isn't often done that way with a considerable sacrifice in the quality of the work. Also, it seems to me that it would be more fun for the art director to be working on a broader range of projects, rather than being locked into one area. I also am convinced that a chunk of diversification actually helps the A/D turn out better work (and anybody in advertising can tell you there's an awful lot of dull stuff around and so little great stuff—so anything that will help improve creative work deserves some careful thought).

The A/D "specialist" as opposed to the "diversified" A/D is part of the endless struggle in our business between the business end and the creative end. No one ever wins this struggle completely—but any creative person worth his salt should be aware of it and find his right place in it.

My own personal feeling is that it's better for the art director to broaden out of his specialty—perhaps not for the whole gamut of creative work, but at least three or four areas. I'm convinced it will improve his overall creative output. And it's also good job insurance.

SALVATORE VENTI
Art Director
Creamer, Inc.
New York City

STANISLAW FERNANDES
35 East 12th Street
New York, New York 10003
(212) 533-2648

As well as being an illustrator, I am an accomplished graphic designer, typographer/letterer and art director. Although I enjoy decorative illustration, I am principally interested in solving all forms of visual problems, creating new and interesting images and forming the total look of a design—the fusion of type and image. Over the years, I have received numerous awards from various internationally well known societies and magazines that specialize in this field. My clients include some of the country's top advertising agencies and publishing companies. I handle advertisements, movie and general posters, paperback covers, magazine cover and editorial illustration, record albums, brochures, pharmaceutical and science fiction illustration, logotypes and typography.

TIM GIRVIN
Represented by: Sam Walsh
Post Office Box 5298 University Station
Seattle, Washington 98105
(206) 522-0154

Tim Girvin illustrates language. With an extremely versatile design capability—derived from extensive American and European studies with master type designers and calligraphers—he can capture any nuance in statement, from the dazzling to the classical.

He has worked with ad agencies, interior designers and architects, and top U.S. graphic designers to open anew the world of the letterform as art. He has contributed his talents to fashion design, packaging, signage, interior wall treatments, book and book jacket design, album covers, headlines and sig lines, illustrative spreads, logotypes identity systems, and posters. In addition to winning numerous awards, his work and writing has been featured in U&lc, Graphics Today, Rainbow, and Art Direction Magazines.

Tim Girvin lives and works in Seattle, and he regularly travels to job sites to provide his design, consultation, and artistic services firsthand.

HOWARD GOLDSTEIN
7031 Aldea Avenue
Van Nuys, California 91406
(213) 987-2837

A problem solver who listens.

Third generation of a publishing /advertising family. Designer /director of numerous award winning publications, illustrations, etcetera. Corporate art director for major communications media, medical, computer and manufacturing firms. Design, illustration, concept and copy to fit the unique needs of the individual client.

Catalogs, trade magazines and tabloids, collateral and direct mail campaigns, logos and corporate image programs, advertising and packages that win awards, get response…sell product, service and message.

Attention getting designs and illustrations in ink, paint, dyes, markers, wood, welded steel and found objects. (Medium dependent upon client, message, artist.)

© Howard Goldstein 1979

LES KATZ
367 Sackett Street
Brooklyn, New York 11231
(212) 625-4741

Illustration in a painterly manner.
I also approach my work from a dramatic
design standpoint. Some of my clients
(more than satisfied, naturally) are
Redbook, Doremus & Co., Emergency Medicine,
National Lampoon, GQ, and The Literary Guild.
If the work illustrated below stimulates
your imagination, call me.

DOREMUS-SALVATION ARMY—JOHN STROHMEYER, A.D.

McGRAW-HILL—BOB MITCHELL, A.D.

LILI LAKICH/NEON ILLUSTRATION

1632 Lemoyne Street
Los Angeles, California 90026
(213) 413-2404 /934-4853

Light years ahead of its time...until now.
For print, film, display.

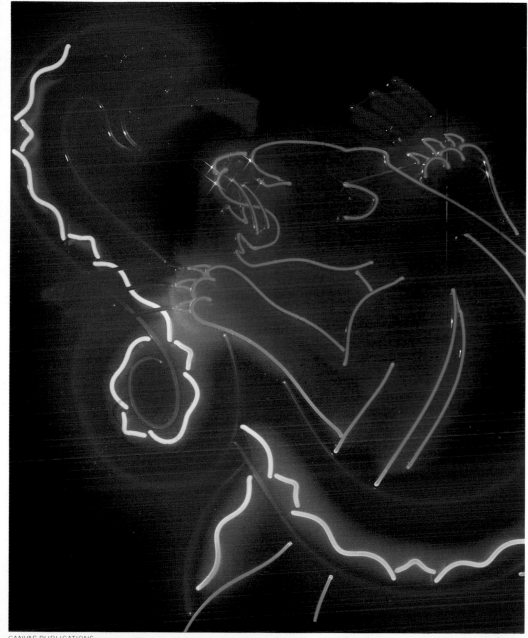

CANVAS PUBLICATIONS

OLIVIA RECORDS

20TH CENTURY FOX

THE BLISS BAND — COLUMBIA RECORDS

METRO-GOLDWYN-MAYER

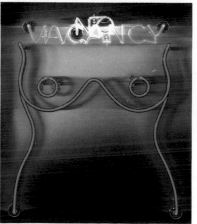

BANTAM BOOKS

COLUMBIA RECORDS

BERNHARDT FUDYMA DESIGN GROUP
133 East 36th Street
New York, New York 10016
(212) 889-9337

1. Series of cover sheets for inter-departmental news releases
   for W.R. Grace & Co.
2. Financial brochure for State Street of Boston
3. Color card for Klopman, a division of Burlington Industries
4. Booklet for Manufacturers Hanover Trust
5. Poster for Penguin Books
6. Calendar for Book-of-the-Month Club
7. Employee/shareholder magazine for W.R. Grace & Co.
8. Brochure for Fiduciary Trust Co.
9. Employee magazine for Seagram Distillers Co.
10. Logo for trade publication: Electrical Digest
11. Logo for Burlington House Awards, a division of Burlington Industries

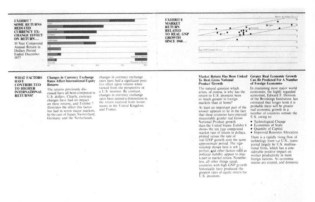

(2)

(1)

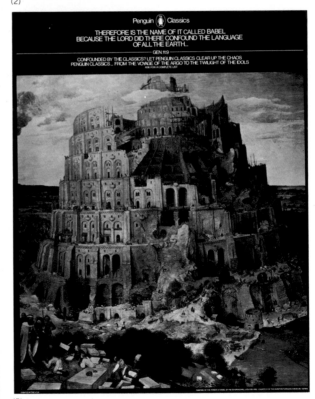

(5)

(3)

(4)

(6)

(7) Springtime in the Rockies — Grace's Colorado coal country

(8)

(9)

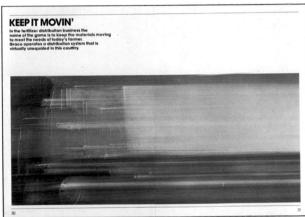

(10)

(11)

ELY BESALEL
235 East 49th Street
New York, New York 10017
(212) 759-7820

"When you can see positive results…my personal goals in the visual communication process have been met."

Our design/consultant firm produces total corporate design systems, integrated communications programs, package design and illustration, annual reports, logotypes, and advertising and promotion graphics.

Great clients have helped us earn 28 major awards. Here are a few of the clients we've served in 19 years: CBS, ABC, Philip Morris, Equitable Life Assurance, WRVR, Alitalia Airlines, Thermex, American Airlines, Dry Dock Savings Bank, St. Regis Paper, Georgia-Pacific, Love Cosmetics, Avon, Union Carbide.

ROD DYER, INC.
Design & Marketing Consultants
5550 Wilshire Boulevard, Suite 301
Los Angeles, California 90036
(213) 937-4100

Rod Dyer, Inc. is a full service graphic design studio specializing in conceptual solutions to advertising and marketing
problems. Ideas are conceived directly with the client and
taken through all stages of application from copy concepts
to finished art. Their projects include corporate identity
programs, brochures and catalogues, packaging design,
advertising campaigns and film /video production. The studio
has distinguished itself with numerous international design
awards and is one of the leading suppliers for the record,
film and television industries.

ANNOUNCEMENT FOR THE WALT DISNEY FEATURE "THE BLACK HOLE"

ANNOUNCEMENT FOR THE FEATURE "CABOBLANCO"

TRADEMARK FOR
LA FAMIGLIA RESTAURANT

TRADEMARK FOR
CAROLCO MOTION
PICTURE DISTRIBUTION

TRADEMARK FOR
EAGLE RECORDS

ALBUM COVER FOR MARSHALL HAIN

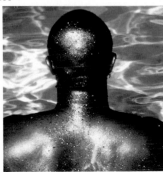

ALBUM COVER FOR ISAAC HAYES

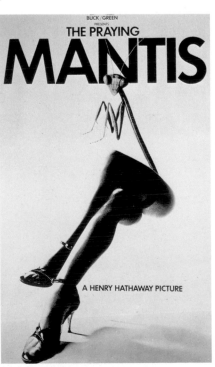

PARAMOUNT NON-THEATRICAL CATALOG

ALBUM COVER FOR THE STATES

ALBUM COVER FOR IAN HUNTER

ANNOUNCEMENT FOR THE PRAYING MANTIS FEATURE

WINE SPREAD FOR NEW WEST MAGAZINE

JOHN FOLLIS & ASSOCIATES
2124 Venice Boulevard
Los Angeles, California 90006
(213) 735-1283

Architectural signing and graphics, corporate identity, printed graphics, environments, exhibits, interiors, furniture and cabinets.

JF&A is internationally known for signage programs—for airports, corporations, office complexes, zoos, theme parks, and hotels—and provides complete services from planning and traffic flow analysis to design, installation supervision and manuals. We wrote the book on it: Architectural Signing and Graphics, by John Follis and Dave Hammer (Whitney Library of Design, 1979), large format, many illustrations.

THE GRAPHIC EXPRESSION, INC.

150 East 58th Street
New York, New York 10022
(212) 759-7788

FUNCTION...OBJECTIVE...FULFILLMENT

Our function is to conceptualize and design annual and interim reports, capability and recruitment brochures and other corporate literature.

Our objective is to help communicators communicate. With clarity, impact, individuality and creative resourcefulness. By identifying and positioning corporate strengths in fresh and imaginative ways. On time and within budget.

While we have the plaques and scrolls to prove it, our most fulfilling reward is a long-term relationship with a multitude of leading manufacturing, financial and service companies. Proving that excellence is its own reward.

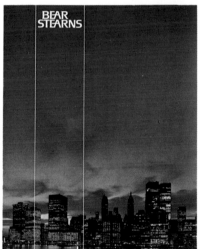

Warner-Lambert Annual Report 1978

Saxon Is The Star System

GRIBBITT! LTD.
5419 Sunset Boulevard
Los Angeles, California 90027
(213) 462-7362

Gribbitt! provides the broadest possible range of communication services for our clients. With an internationally known award-winning staff, we offer advertising campaign concepts, design, art direction and layout, copy, illustration, photography, hand-lettering, marketing, merchandising, public relations, point of purchase, packaging, direct mail brochures and catalogs, audio-visual presentations, radio, television and video production. Our client list provides us with impeccable endorsements. Further information on request.

JOHN HEINEY & ASSOCIATES, INC.
200 East 33rd Street
New York, New York 10016
(212) 686-1121

Designers and producers of corporate literature

AUTOMATIC DATA PROCESSING, INC.

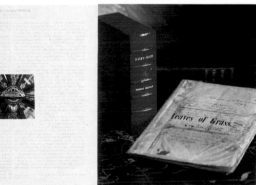

JLG INDUSTRIES, INC.

U.S. TRUST CORPORATION

STONE & WEBSTER, INC.

CHARTER NEW YORK·CORPORATION

PNEUMO CORPORATION

NATIONAL CARRIERS, INC.

MUELLER & WISTER STUDIO
1211 Chestnut Street, Suite 607
Philadelphia, Pennsylvania 19107
(215) 568-7260

For the past twelve years Mueller & Wister Studio has been creating effective visual communications for a wide range of corporate clients. Our talented staff offers a unique blend of corporate advertising and agency experience.

Our services have been utilized by Air Products and Chemicals, Inc., Rohm and Haas, Betz Laboratories, Inc., RCA, Insurance Company of North America, Wyeth Laboratories and a variety of other corporations.

We are big enough to handle your most challenging assignments, yet small enough to provide the kind of top management and personal attention your project deserves.

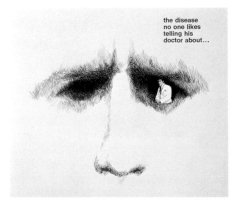

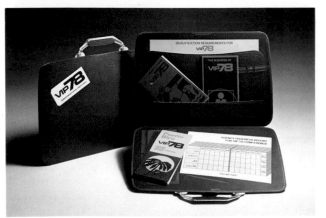

Overlock Howe & Company is a design and marketing communications consulting firm, specializing in packaging, corporate identification and collateral materials. We bring to each project a depth of experience, analytical thinking and the creative insight to meet or exceed marketing objectives.

Member: Package Designers Council

1. Packaging system for laboratory animals feeds—Ralston Purina Company
2. Packaging for mileage improvement product—The Gaid Company
3. Identification system for Public Television/St. Louis
4. Consumer packaging—Dean Foods, Inc.
5. Corporate identification control manual—Wilson Foods Corporation
6. Packaging program for line of vitamins—Rexall Drug Company
7. Mini-appliance packaging—McGraw-Edison
8. Packaging for new dog food product—Ralston Purina Company

© Overlock Howe & Company

1

2

3

4

5

8

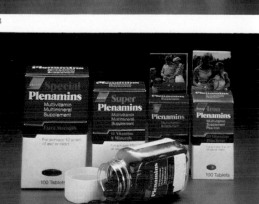

6

7

RIDGEWAY, ZAKLIN AND ASSOCIATES, INC.

Visual/Verbal Communicators
East Coast Office:
Suite 303/305 Valley Plaza
99 Kinderkamack Road
Westwood, New Jersey 07675
(201) 664-4543

West Coast Office:
Suite 1006 Park Westwood Towers
969 Hilgard Avenue
Los Angeles, California 90024
(213) 824-9602

Ridgeway, Zaklin and Associates creates and develops product, service and corporate literature for corporations sincerely concerned with the thoughtful balance of the visual image and the written word.

1. Consumer program which includes: introductory brochure/poster/p.o.p./product mailer/banner/sales guide
2. Multiphase program for trade introduction which includes: brochures/audio-visual presentation/flip chart presentation/folders/mailers
3. Graphic for brochure entitled, "a perspective"
4. Annual report cover and spread
5. 3-D motif developed for a series of sales/marketing guides entitled, "target"
6. Posters for p.o.p. display

1.

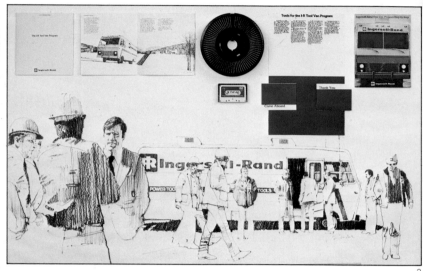

2.

3.

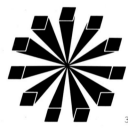

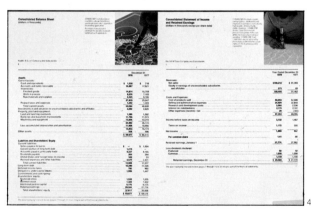

4.

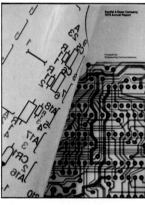

5.

6.

Y THE VISUAL/VERBAL RELATIONSHIP

You've heard the expression, "There are two sides to every story." By this time we all know when someone will throw the sentence into a conversation. It's become one of the givens of our language. But, nonetheless, as with most belabored cliches, the truth of the statement is virtually irrefutable. That truth is very self-evident in the creative process of preparing product, service and corporate literature—the segment of the communications business often referred to as collateral material.

It could be argued that this segment, the segment my company has selected to devote its energies and resources to, is many-faceted and has many more than two sides. But there are only two primary ingredients: the visual image and the written word.

These two elements are what create the whole. They are not independent of one another, albeit we are forever being reminded of a world which is becoming more and more visual. These elements, results of the creative process translated into distinctive expressions, must be cohesive, unified and work together from the beginning of an assignment to its conclusion if a client is to impart information, solve marketing problems and meet objectives.

It's a proven method. Agencies primarily concerned with ads and TV commercials team a writer and art director to create concepts and follow through with a complete manuscript and finished artwork. They've realized the visual/verbal combination is the nucleus of effective communication with the client's target audience.

Our company has assumed a similar posture in our segment of the communications business. We've found the visual/verbal combination to be most effective when it is prepared with comparable expertise and enthusiasm. My partner and I, from the beginning, sit down and work on a concept together from both points of view and guide our thoughts simultaneously. Time after time, the results are a visual/verbal presentation which singularly relates the message called for by the problem and/or objective as given by our client.

We've found that being supplied a script or a visual and having to work one side against the other often creates a situation in which the visual and verbal, although competently prepared, appear to be mutually exclusive of one another when the finished product rolls off the press. On the other hand, when we've offered a client our in-house ability to take a project, from its commencement, utilizing our individual talents and putting them to work towards the same goal, the client recognizes the difference, and the logic to our approach becomes very apparent.

Effective communications are, at their source, a two-sided story. We've proven it day after day. Effective communications, results oriented communications, are more valuable and enhance a client's opportunity when there is the thoughtful balance of the visual image and written word.

JOEL M. ZAKLIN
Ridgeway, Zaklin and Associates, Inc.
Visual/Verbal Communicators

Corporate publications
Company and product identification
Packaging

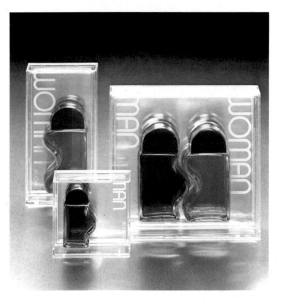

STUDIO ARTISTS, INC.
638 South Van Ness Avenue
Los Angeles, California 90005
(213) 382-6281

Studio Artists has offered just one thing
for 28 years: Service. Our staff of twenty-
plus has dedicated itself to the highest
performance for many of the area's
top agencies, and some of the nation's
leading corporations.

Studio Artists. For concepts, design,
illustration, calligraphy, retouching,
mechanical productions, audio/visual
presentations, etc.

UNIGRAPHICS
350 Pacific Avenue
San Francisco, California 94111
(415) 398-8232

After years of designing and producing annual reports for many of the nation's largest corporations, we at Unigraphics are convinced that the "battle of the annual report" has become a needlessly traumatic experience for all concerned. To help ease and simplify this annual exercise in corporate self-examination, we have created a manual for our clients: "The Annual Report System". It is a method for organizing and planning an annual report within eight basic areas of concern. This simplified and practical system relieves the day to day problems which hinder the smooth production of an annual report, enabling a corporation to concentrate on objectives without being harassed by the multiple details related to budgets, scheduling and quality control. Unigraphics has an international reputation for quality design, communications and production management.

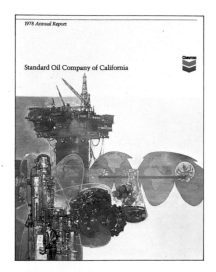

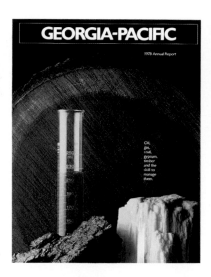

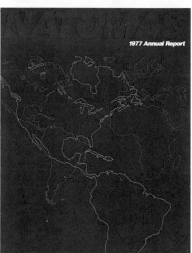

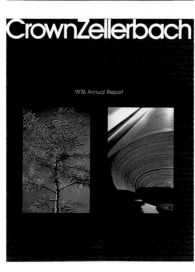

WARDELL-BERGER DESIGN, INC.

1450 Broadway
New York, New York 10018
(212) 398-9355

33 West Main Street
Elmsford, New York 10523
(914) 592-6170

Graphic design for all aspects of industry
including advertising, sales promotion, packaging,
brochures, displays, corporate identity,
slide presentations and others. Provided are all
services from concept to finished piece.

1. Presentation kit and booklets for Metropolitan Life Insurance Co.
2. Three-dimensional lucite construction for Chesebrough-Pond's flyer
3. Cutex shade chart for Chesebrough-Pond's
4. Angel Face flyer for Chesebrough-Pond's
5. Prototype package of a rust-proof paint for Dutch Boy
6. Brochure cover for ASARCO
7. Page from a Cutex shade chart for Chesebrough-Pond's
8. Compact design for Angel Face
9. Camera carton for GAF
10. Brochure page on bumper system for INCO
11. Logo for U.S. Pencil Co.
12. Logo for Terrace Realty
13. Logo for General Fluidics Corp.
14. Logo for Exxon Research and Engineering benefits program
15. Symbol for Ogden Corp. benefits program

1.

15.

2.

3.

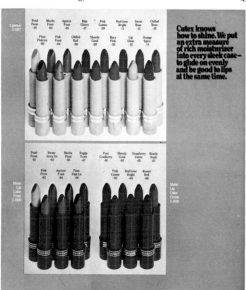

4.

14.

5.

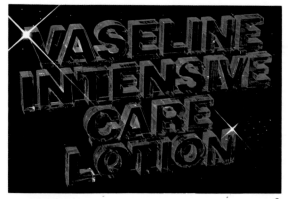

6.

7.

13.

8.

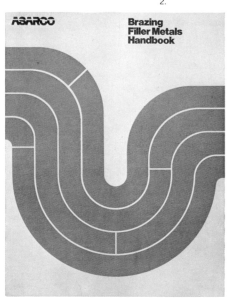

9.

10.

11.

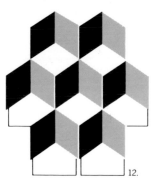

12.

Graphic design, annual reports,
corporate brochures, sales promotion,
corporate identity, packaging,
publication design, catalogs
and illustration.

PHOTOGRAPHY/N.Y. METROPOLITAN AREA

"Divorce"

Nichols: Mrs. Van Rennep, Mr. Van Rennep has asked me to discuss the divorce settlement with you.
May: Yes, Mr. Hager.
Nichols: He wants it to be a happy divorce. He suggests that you have the house in town, the house in Cortina D'Impezzo
May: Don't want it.
Nichols: The house in Terra Del Fuego
May: Don't want it.
Nichols: The Rolls Royces, both children, the dog, um, he'd like to keep the two cats and Le Car.
May: Yes. I don't want the children. I do want Le Car. I only want one Rolls and I'll take the house in town.
Nichols: Mrs. Van Rennep, the children of course can be discussed. But I'm afraid Le Car is out of the question. I know that Mr. Van Rennep was very firm about that. He said it's the only quality and fun left in his life.
May: Mr. Hager. The Rolls is boring, the house in town is unspeakably dull. I'm 28 years old —I've given him the best year of my life.
Nichols: Mrs. Van Rennep, would you consider letting Mr. Van Rennep keep Le Car if he throws in Hawaii?
Anncr: That was Mike Nichols and Elaine May for Le Car by Renault.

Gold Award Winner
The One Show
Consumer Radio—Single Commercial
Produced for Renault by
   Marsteller Inc.
Copy written by Mike Nichols and
   Elaine May

"Das Car"

He: Miss. (German accent)
She: Yes.
He: Come here immediately!
She: Can I help you?
He: Is this Das Car by Renault?
She: Ah, yes. This is Le Car by Renault. We…
He: Das Car.
She: Well, we call it Le Car.
He: Silence.
She: Sorry (laughing)
He: Frauline, please, what is the precise mileage on Das Car?
She: It's 41 miles per gallon on the highway, twenty-five miles per gallon in the city…according to EPA tests, and these mileage are of course, estimates.
He: Estimates? These are estimates? I cannot take estimates. I must know the exact, <u>precise</u> mileage on Das Car!
She: Le Car. Le Car. We really would prefer that you call it Le Car.
He: I call it Das Car.
She: Right, well, you see Le Car is written on the side here, call it what you like. Le Car's actual mileage …(trails off)
Anncr: That was Mike Nichols and Elaine May for Le Car by Renault.

Gold Award Winner
The One Show
Consumer Radio—Commercial Campaign

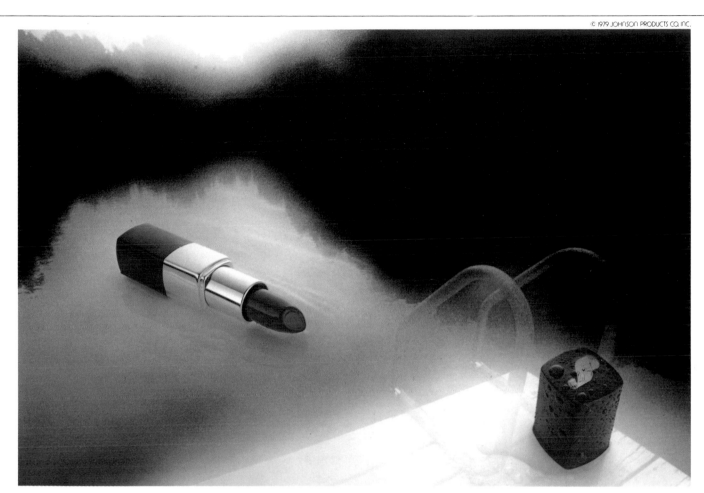

A NEW ERA IN LIPCOLOUR. MOISTURE FORMULA LIPCOLOUR. CHECK IT OUT.
NEW FROM *SP* ULTRA SHEEN COSMETICS.

Earth Care. We challenge any plant food to measure up.

NOBU ARAKAWA
40 East 21st Street
New York, New York 10010
(212) 475-0206

A photographer with wide international experience, Nobu worked for two years in Japan and two years in Rio de Janeiro, Brazil before settling in New York.

Nobu has taken photos in almost every continent of the world; a sampling of his locations include The Sahara desert, Iceland, Morocco, Rio de Janeiro, Paris, Tokyo, Amsterdam, and the American South-West.

He specializes in still life and travel photography.

THE IMAGE BANK

AVEDIS
381 Park Avenue South
New York, New York 10016
(212) 685-5888

Advertising, editorial, beauty,
still life & illustration.

ROBERT AZZI
Represented by: Woodfin Camp
Woodfin Camp & Associates
415 Madison Avenue
New York, New York 10017
(212) 355-1855

Telex: 428788 CAMPFOT
Cable: CAMPFOTO

PHILIP BENNETT
1181 Broadway
New York, New York 10001
(212) 683-3906

Representatives: Nob Hovde and Laurence
(212) 753-0462

GENTLEMAN'S QUARTERLY

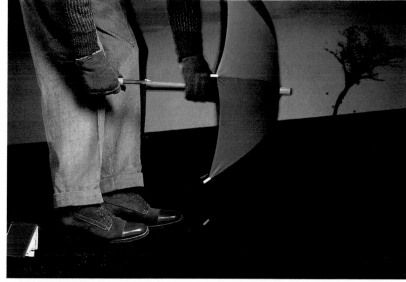

GENTLEMAN'S QUARTERLY

LEO BURNETT

YOUNG & RUBICAM

DOYLE DANE BERNBACH

BEVILACQUA
202 East 42nd Street
New York, New York 10017
(212) 490-0355

Representative: Tony Stathis
(212) 490-0355

Perrier/self promotion © Bevilacqua 1979 ASMP Member
Concept: Tony Stathis
Art Direction: Tony Stathis
Design: Tony Stathis-Joe Bevilacqua

Clients include: Avon, Phelps Dodge, Pepsico, Durotest, Helena
Rubinstein, Fleishmann distillery, United States Embassy.

Portfolio available

General Electric, May Company, Fairchild Industries, Reynolds Metals, Xerox, Continental Telephone, Nation's Business, L'eggs, Bell Telephone, Marriott Corporation, Quality Inns, Holiday Inns, Hilton Hotels, Garfinckel's, Brooks Brothers, Miller & Rhoads, Aeromaritime, Life Magazine, U.S News & World Report, Department of Health, Education and Welfare, Department of Labor, Pepsi Cola, Smithsonian Magazine, National Geographic Magazine, NUS Corporation, Rubbermaid, National Public Radio, Colt 45, Glass Packaging Institute, Pyramid Publishing, Avon Books, London Fog, Dynastar Skis, Paternayan Brothers, Aftatrol, United Virginia Bank, First & Merchants National Bank, Riggs National Bank, John F. Kennedy Center for the Performing Arts, Psychiatric Institute, Union Camp, Myer-Emco, Britches, Sound Gallery, Atlantis Sound, Hyatt Corporation, America Magazine, Ketchum, MacLeod & Grove, A/C Pipe Corporation, Peoples Drug Stores, American Express, Norwegian Travel Association, University of California at Santa Barbara, Brick Institute of America, and Amtrak.

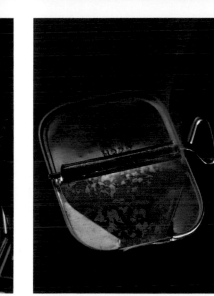

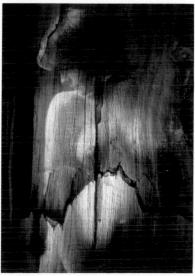

THOUGHTS ON SEEING

The questions that come up when visual matters are being discussed with almost any group except designers or artists almost invariably have to do with the possible value of being able to see....Never has anyone asked me if seeing makes life richer, or more entertaining. It has to be <u>worth</u> something.

More of our seeing goes on in the brain than in our eyes...

We see what we are looking for, what we have been trained to see by habit or tradition. The notion that we come upon a scene and see everything has no truth in it ...We see what interests us...

To see...is to think. To think is to put together random bits of private experience in an orderly fashion. Seeing is not a unique God-given talent, but a discipline. It can be learned.

It is a general rule that we like what is familiar to us and that we tend to back off from anything unfamiliar. Company managements are acutely aware of this, and one of the results is that products on the market at any given moment tend to look alike, whether they are cars, household furniture or stereo sets.

In a functionally blind society, the role of art is widely misunderstood. Art, for the visually illiterate, has some vague connection with "beauty," "the finer things," "aesthetics," and none at all with its real role of coming to grips with various aspects of perceived reality...

...My view of the work of many contemporary artists is that at first glance much of it appears to be crazy, but that further examination and thought strongly suggest that it is the society which has abandoned sanity. The artist, in continuing to pursue his traditional role of sensitive observer and reporter, is merely pointing this out.

GEORGE NELSON
Excerpts from <u>How to See</u>,
A Guide to Reading Our Manmade Environment.
Copyright ©1977 by George Nelson
by permission of Little, Brown and Company,
Boston

BARBARA BORDNICK
Photographer/Director
39 East 19th Street
New York, New York 10003
(212) 533-1180

Print and film.
Fashion/beauty advertising, editorial and illustration.
Celebrity and corporate portraiture.
President/Chairwoman/ASMP.

JOSEPH B. BRIGNOLO
Oxford Springs Road
Chester, New York 10918
(914) 496-4453

International assignments smooth
as silk with the expertise of 32
trips around the world.

ASMP Member

Active Clients:
Combustion Engineering
Conoco
du Pont
Firestone
G.E Corporate Communications
G.E. International Communications

G.E. Jet Engine
G.E. Mobile Radio
GTE
Gulf
IBM World Trade
IBM Think Magazine
R.J. Reynolds
Texaco

JOSEPH B. BRIGNOLO
Oxford Springs Road
Chester, New York 10918
(914) 496-4453

Assignments completed in 113 countries.

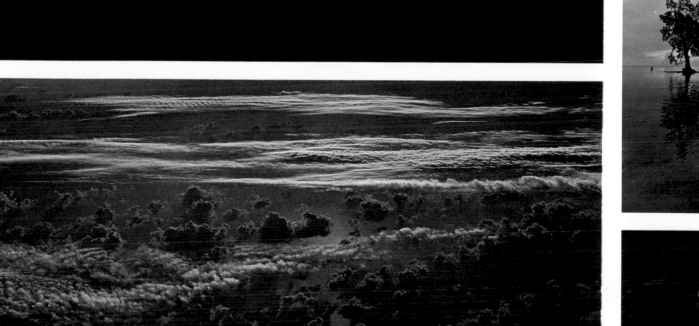

ED BROWN
100 West 92nd Street
New York, New York 10025
(212) 580-2483

Ed Brown...on 92nd Street.
He shoots black and white and color.
Go up and see him!

NANCY BROWN-DAVE BROWN

6 West 20th Street
New York, New York 10011
(212) 675-8067

Stock: The Image Bank.

Clients: Avon, Glamour, Kodak, Bride's, Cone Mills
Marketing, Woman's Day, Good Housekeeping,
Proctor & Gamble, Jack Morton Productions,
Signature Magazine, Co-ed, Avon Books, Lipton
Tea, Good Humor, Wallace-Church, Joe Kardwell
Associates, GAF, Redbook, E.T. Howard, Compton
Advertising, Working Mother, Ogilvy & Mather,
Playboy, Muller Jordan Herrick, Inc.

THE IMAGE BANK

AVON

COMPTON-PERT

CONDE NAST-BRIDE'S

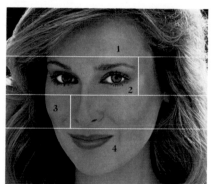

OGILVY & MATHER

RUMRILL-HOYT

WALLACE-CHURCH-GAF

JOHN BRYSON
12 East 62nd Street
New York, New York 10021
Phone: 212-755-1321

22258 Pacific Coast Highway
Malibu, California 90265
Phone: (213) 456-6170

Representative: Frank Beilin
(212) 751-3074

Library: The Image Bank
(212) 371-3636

THE IMAGE BANK

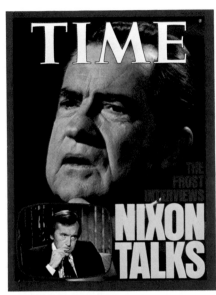

LONDON SUNDAY TIMES MAGAZINE

TIME

JOHN BRYSON
12 East 62nd Street
New York, New York 10021
Phone: 212-755-1321

22258 Pacific Coast Highway
Malibu, California 90265
Phone: (213) 456-6170

Representative: Frank Beilin
(212) 751-3074

Library: The Image Bank
(212) 371-3636

THE IMAGE BANK

ALI MACGRAW—LOOK

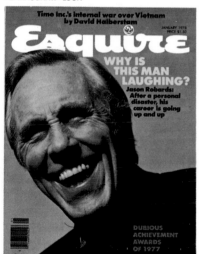

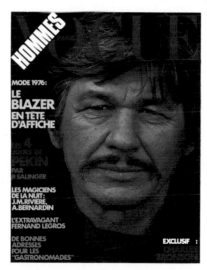

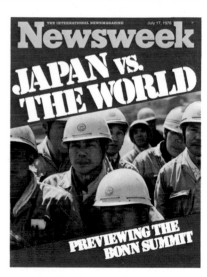

WOLF von dem BUSSCHE
7144 Norfolk Road
Berkeley, California 94705
(415) 845-2448

Annual reports for over seventy Fortune 500 companies.
Editorial assignments for Time-Life Books, Fortune, and
Life. Represented in permanent collections of museums in
New York, in other U.S. cities, and abroad.

Selected stock through The Image Bank.

See West Coast, page 230

DON CARROLL PHOTOGRAPHY, INC.

Focus 2000, Ltd.
33 East 60th Street
New York, New York 10022
(212) 371-3648

"The Special Effects Man"

Want to do a multi-image shot against something other than black? Need a far-away or dangerous looking background but don't have the time or budget? Need help with an unusual concept for your product? We solve problems! Shoot your multi-images against any color you choose, including white. Use front projection in the studio to create any background effect and provide variety and realism a strip-in never can. Make any layout come to life, no matter how "far out". We do montages and multidimensional images. These photos are not retouched or stripped together. They are all 35 mm camera originals.

Stock available through the Image Bank.

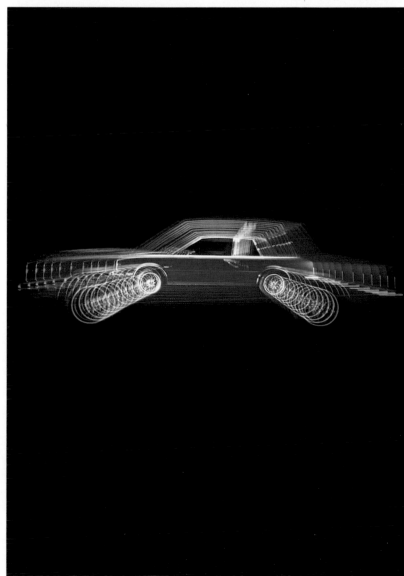

WALTER CHANDOHA
R.D. 1, P.O. Box 287
Annandale, New Jersey 08801
(201) 782-3666
Representative: Sam Chandoha

A specialist in animal and horticulture /nature photography, Walter Chandoha's pictures have appeared on over 200 magazine covers and he has written and /or illustrated 24 books. (The Literary Cat, published by Lippincott is his latest.) His advertising clients have included such blue-chips as Eastman Kodak, Johnson & Johnson, General Foods, Nabisco, General Mills, Quaker Oats, 3M, Merck, Ralston Purina, Eli Lilly, EG and G, and others.

Hallmark, Norcross, Brown & Bigelow, U.S. Playing Card, Wallace Berrie have all used his photographs on their calendars, greeting and playing cards and other paper goods.

Chandoha's photographs are widely used in text books, encyclopedias and film strips by Encyclopedia Britannica, Xerox, Grolier, Field, Bowmar, Scott Foresman and numerous others.

In addition to supplying his accounts with Chandoha-made stock photographs, he makes original photographs to layout in his fully equipped studio 60 miles west of New York City in Annandale, N.J., or on location anywhere in the world.

WALTER CHANDOHA
R.D. 1, P.O. Box 287
Annandale, New Jersey 08801
(201) 782-3666

Representative: Sam Chandoha

Vegetables and herbs, fruits and berries, sunrises and scenics, the four seasons, trees, flowers and gardens occupy about half of Chandoha's stock file of over 100,000 animal and horticulture/nature photographs. All animals are represented in the fauna file with special emphasis on cats, dogs and horses.

In both these broad Chandoha specialties—flora and fauna photography—using stock photographs makes sense. There's no wondering if the required pictures will have the right feeling or mood or the

exact expression or pose. With a stock photograph it's all there! There's no doubt—no headaches—no retakes.

Admittedly, some stock photographs have been previously used—but many more have not. So a Chandoha stock photograph can be just as exclusive and as fresh as a Chandoha custom photograph made on assignment.

Chandoha stock photographs are available immediately. Chandoha custom photographs made to layout take just a little longer.

JAN C. COBB
381 Park Avenue South
New York, New York 10016
(212) 889-2257

Stock photography: The Image Bank

THE IMAGE BANK

GEORGE M. COCHRAN
381 Park Avenue South
New York, New York 10016
(212) 689-9054

Free.
A new book of explicit photographs in full color involving people you know in advertising.

LARRY COUZENS
124 East 27th Street
New York, New York 10016
(212) 684-6585

Still life, beauty & illustration

Polaroid, Olympus, General Foods,
Quaker Oats, Dannon, L'Oreal,
Revlon, Avon, Movie Star, Seagrams,
Ballantine, TWA, Ford, STP, Bulova,
Atlantic Records.

Editorial: Food & Wine, Americana,
Family Circle, Cosmopolitan,
New Times, Esquire, Redbook.

CROSS/FRANCESCA
502 East 88th Street
New York, New York 10028
(212) 988-8516

William Cross
Carole Francesca

Bill: "Heraclitus says that Homer should be taken out and thrashed, and also Archilochlus."

Carole: "These movies were made before I was born: Night And Day,
The Woman In White, The Two Mrs. Carrolls, Rhapsody In Blue, Any Number
Can Play, Morocco, The Blue Angel, Blond Venus, A Woman Commands, Blythe
Spirit, Design For Living, The Awful Truth, Sylvia Scarlet, Queen Christina,
My Favorite Wife, Mother Didn't Tell Me, Nancy Drew—Detective."

Spiritual advisor: Barye Phillips
© 1979 Cross/Francesca

DARWIN K. DAVIDSON
32 Bank Street
New York, New York 10014
(212) 242-0095

Location photography of home furnishings
and residential and contract installations
for advertising, editorial, publicity
and catalogue use.

NEW YORK: 321 E. 62 ST. / LOS ANGELES: 8936 BEVERLY BLVD. / CHICAGO: MERCHANDISE MART / MIAMI: 47 N.E. 36 ST.
BOSTON · CHICAGO · DALLAS · HOUSTON · LOS ANGELES · MIAMI · NEW YORK · SAN FRANCISCO · SEATTLE
5200 BIG SADDLE LEATHER CONFERENCE TABLE SERIES / DESIGN: G. FALESCHINI

pace

We've just given our competition
something else to try to imitate. The Levolor Valance.

We didn't invent the window blind. We
improved it. We did away with wide slats, thick
tapes, confusions of cords and no-color color.
Now, we've got another improvement for our
improved Levolor Blind. A matching valance
cleverly conceals the working head to give
you the luxury of a clean sweep of color, from
the bottom of the blind, right up and over
the top. No one else gives you that, yet. But,
sooner or later, somebody just might. Meanwhile,
our list of "firsts" is one "first" longer.
Levolor Lorentzen, Inc., 720 Monroe St., Hoboken, N.J. 07030

Levolor. Our love is blinds.

What's New? This shiningly remodeled kitchen by Barbara
Ross (shown above) and Barbara Schwartz of
Dexter Design, Inc., both members of Formica
Corporation's Design Advisory Board.
  Says Mrs. Ross, "To achieve a sleek, elegant,
yet warm and inviting look, we chose Roseline
cabinets surfaced with Formica's Brushed
Chrome laminate, matched with countertops
surfaced with their warm Pumice color laminate."
  FORMICA® brand products are perfect for
residential remodeling, cabinetry and casework.
With all the benefits that have made Formica
Corporation the leader in laminate design,
quality and innovation.
  To see what else is new, write us for your free
subscription to FORMICA TODAY. Excite your
imagination with the unique and beautiful things
being created using FORMICA®
brand products. Write to: Formica
What's Next! Corporation, Advertising Services
Department T, Wayne, N.J. 07470

FORMICA® is a registered trademark of Formica Corporation.
Formica Corporation, subsidiary of American Cyanamid Company,
Wayne, N.J. 07470

BOB DAY
29 East 19th Street
New York, New York 10003
(212) 475-7387

Clients: AT&T, American Can, American Express, Beatrice Foods,
Bell Magazine, CNA Insurance, Exxon, Frank B. Hall, Forbes,
General Foods, Harvey Hubbell, Home Insurance, Homequity/Homerica,
Hustler, IBM, Ingersoll-Rand, Johnson & Johnson, L.S. Good,
Maryland Cup, MOAC, Mobil Oil, Newspaper Ad Bureau, New York
Magazine, The Reader's Digest Association, Schaefer Brewing,
Texaco, Touche Ross, Warner Communications, West Point Pepperell,
W.R. Grace.

© Bob Day 1979/1980

LEN DE LESSIO
110 East 23rd Street
New York, New York 10010
(212) 254-4620

Advertising and editorial
Still life photography

All photographs © 1979 Len DeLessio

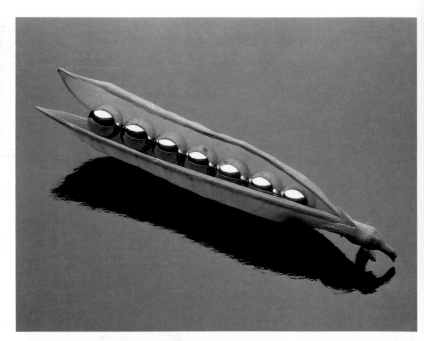

BART J. DEVITO PHOTOGRAPHY

Bohmark Ltd.,
404 Park Avenue South
New York, New York 10016

Representative: Kitty DeVito
(212) 889-9670

Still life/Food

My wife, Kitty, thinks the illustration typifies my
personality...tenacious as a crab when given a
problem (not cranky, sweetie) and as sweet as a berry.

Enjoy problem solving. Love food, both photographing
it and devouring it.

The Image Bank

73

DAVID DOUBILET
Representative: Anne L. Doubilet
1040 Park Avenue
New York, New York 10028
(212) 348-5011

The best in underwater photography.

Editorial, advertising, and annual report assignments—
on the sea, under the sea, and over the sea. Complete
stock library from world-wide work under all the seven
seas—shrimps to supertankers, sharks to submarines.

PHOEBE DUNN
20 Silvermine Road
New Canaan, Connecticut 06840

Representative: Tris Dunn
(203) 966-9791

"Phoebe and Tris Dunn are internationally known for their sensitive pictures of babies, young people, children and families…their work for magazine and TV advertisers appears regularly throughout the world." U.S. Camera World Annual.

Fairfield County studio plus wide range of suburban and country locations. Team has mastered the delicate psychology of working with babies and children.

Clients include: Avon Products, Campbell Soup, Eastman Kodak, General Foods, Gerber, Hasselblad Cameras, Eli Lilly, Procter & Gamble, Sierra Club, Sterling Drug, Union Carbide, Redbook, 3M Company, Woman's Day.

Available photographs through Al Forsyth at DPI (212) PL2-3930

75

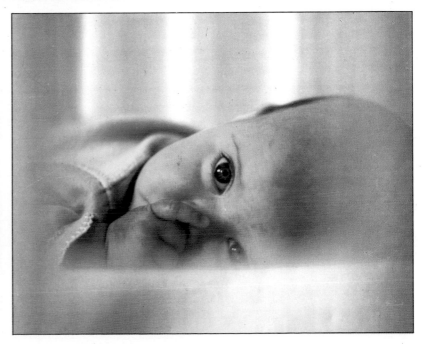

TIMOTHY EAGAN
39 East 12th Street
New York, New York 10003
(212) 777-9210

Representative: Woodfin Camp and Associates
(212) 355-1855

Graphic images for advertising, annual reports,
corporate/industrial, editorial and travel.

Clients include: Johnson & Johnson; AT&T; Warner Communications,
Inc.; Nikon; Texaco, Inc.; Merrill Lynch; Texas International Airlines;
McGraw-Hill; Random House; Fortune; Horizon; Carnegie Museum of
Natural History; Standard Brands, Inc.; Hilton International.

COLORADO HERITAGE CENTER—PELLEGRINI & KAESTLE

NEW YORK CITY, 1978

BOY'S LIFE

JOHNSON & JOHNSON—GEORGE TSCHERNY

MICHAEL EVERETT PHOTOGRAPHY, LTD.
16 East 17th Street
New York, New York 10003
(212) 929-4461

Representative: Meagan Longcore
(212) 929-4461

"I'd like to thank the Academy,
my Director, Producer and all
those who have gotten me
where I am today…"

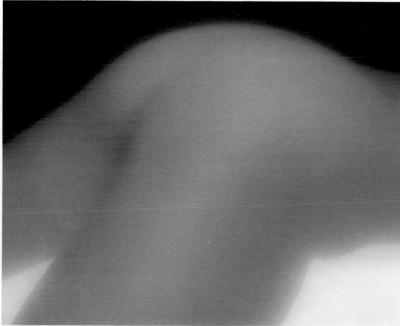

DOUGLAS FRASER
45 East 34th Street
New York, New York 10016
(212) 689-8853

Represented by: Sol Shamilzadeh
1155 Broadway
New York, New York 10001
(212) 532-1977

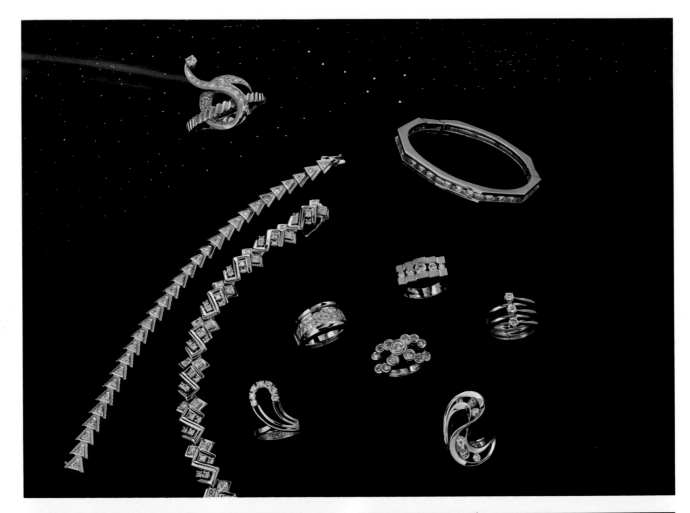

LIONEL FREEDMAN
Camera 73 Inc.
325 East 73rd Street
New York, New York 10021
(212) 737-8540

Still life, interiors, people and industrial films: on location, or in spacious studio facilities equipped to photograph everything from the monumental to the minute.

Among the clients, through the years: Columbia Records, Gillette, Champion International, Karastan, Ethan Allen, Pande Cameron, Time-Life, Certainteed, Pennsylvania House, Kittinger, JC Penney, Sears, Springmaid, American Olean, Congoleum, Whirlpool, DuPont, Armstrong Cork, Kentile, Amtico, Seiko, Johnson & Johnson, Ladies Home Journal, McCall's, Rohm & Haas, Geico, S&H, J.P. Stevens, Amstar, Jaguar, Westinghouse, Burlington,

US Plywood, InterRoyal, Lysol, Simmons Co., General Foods, GAF, Glidden, Seatrain, Alcoa, General Motors, Seventeen, Collins & Aikman, House Beautiful, House & Garden, Container Corp., Carrier Corp., Merck, Worthington Pump Inc., National Distillers, Mosaic Tile, Bigelow, Corning, Stauffer Chemical, Ciba-Geigy, Avon, Revlon, McGregor Sportswear, Fiberglas, Goodyear, Scotchgard, Samsonite, Magnavox, Knabe, Dixie Cup, Lever Bros., Parker Bros., Westclox, Medaglia D'Oro, Cannon, Fleischmann Distilling, Fieldcrest, RCA, Folger's Coffee, Lightolier, American Standard, Reynolds Metals, Pepperell, General Electric, etc.

MITCHELL FUNK
500 East 77th Street
New York, New York 10021
(212) 988-2886

Problem solving photography with a variety of creative styles
and techniques; type, titles, logos, graphic symbols, products,
people and multiple images.

Concepts and innovative photography for advertising, corporate,
editorial and record album assignments.

Partial list of clients include: IBM, AT&T, TWA, Newmont Mining,
Nikon, Litton Industries, Inmont, Robert Stigwood Organization,
Fortune, Newsweek, Business Week, Women's Day, Psychology Today.

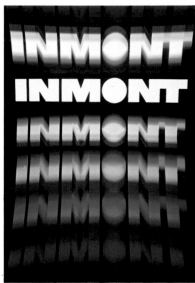

MITCHELL FUNK
500 East 77th Street
New York, New York 10021
(212) 988-2886

Industrial, location, and annual report photography.

I have photographed nuclear plants, above and below-ground
coal mines, oil rigs, steel and paper mills, sugar harvesting,
automotive assembly lines, power companies, computers, oil
exploration, etc.

Companies I have worked for include: IBM, The Williams Companies,
Inmont, Newmont Mining, North American Philips, AT&T, Time Inc.,
ABC, Ciba-Geigy, North American Mortgage Company.

MICHAEL FURMAN PHOTOGRAPHER, LTD.
113 Arch Street
Philadelphia, Pennsylvania 19106
(215) 925-4233

Client: "Hey Mike, have you ever shot dishware?"
Furman: "Nope."

AL GIESE
Represented by: Mary Hottelet
156 Fifth Avenue
New York, New York 10010
(212) 675-2727

AL GIESE
Represented by: Mary Hottelet
156 Fifth Avenue
New York, New York 10010
(212) 675-2727

AL GIESE
Represented by: Mary Hottelet
156 Fifth Avenue
New York, New York 10010
(212) 675-2727

CORPORATE IDENTITY: A COMPLEX COMPLEX AS COMPLEXES GO!

Most of you probably remember a film, made some years ago, called "The Three Faces of Eve." It related the true story of a young schizophrenic woman who had, in effect, developed three totally separate personalities for dealing with the rest of the world. When things got a little rough, she wouldn't just turn the other cheek, she'd put on a whole new face.

Her schizophrenia made it almost impossible for her to adopt any coherent approach to life, and didn't help her domestic affairs either. No husband likes to have an extra-marital affair with his own wife without even knowing it. In fact, since Eve was a menage a trois all by herself, her husband was something of an unintentional bigamist—which just goes to show that schizophrenia makes strange bedfellows.

Eve suffered from what we might call today an "identity complex" (and a pretty complex complex as complexes go). Where do you turn for help when you've a split personality? Eve asked herself this very same question. After much consideration, she explained to herself that schizophrenia was nothing to be ashamed of, and that she should seek professional help.

At first she wouldn't hear of it, of course, and even covered her ears so as not to hear her own advice. But she was persistent, and at last convinced herself. After all, it was two against one, which is a strong working majority.

So Eve agreed to take her problem lying down—on the doctor's couch—twice weekly at $60 an hour. (The doctor had wanted to charge $180 for her three personalities; but he eventually settled on a group rate.)

The psychiatrist's verdict was swift and to the point. "Eve," he said (I'll spare you an imitation of his Viennese dialect), "Eve, just be yourself."

"But we are myself," she replied.

Anyway, the point of this story about Eve is, I'm sure, obvious to all of you: Never give a schizophrenic a straight line.

But beyond that, I think there is also a connection between this case history and the theme of my talk: "Corporate Design," for the design and identity problems of a multi-faceted corporation are akin to those of a multi-faceted schizoid.

And don't think that a corporation has no problems simply because it's big and powerful. Size only exacerbates the problem. An organization with a thousand employees—or, like CBS, with 35,000—has thousands of different faces. Compare that to Eve's difficulties with only three. Indeed, the larger an organization, the more diversified its activities and interests, the harder it is to maintain cohesion, coherence, or unity. A score of different faces don't make for a handsome profile.

The actual marketing value of one's public profile and appearance, or—to use that terrible trendy word—"image" is intangible; yet nonetheless real. The personality a company projects often has ramifications beyond its actual performance. All things being equal, an appearance of quality often tips the scale in your favor. It is frequently the intangibles of style that—in the end—determines one's effectiveness in the marketplace.

Appearance, then, should not be sneered at, but neither should it be treated as a panacea. A face lift is a very ingenious operation; but there's a limit to what it can achieve. My aunt on Pitkin Avenue could have a dozen face lifts and she still wouldn't be mistaken on the street for Farrah Fawcett.

If one's public profile is contorted by the lack of a unified or coherent identity, one might well follow Eve's example and go to that old Viennese psychiatrist. And his advice will be largely the same as before. A memo will go out couched in Freudian terms:

"After consultation with the Board of Directors (the memo will read) I have observed a latent tendency toward diffusion of concentration, leading to preliminary pseudo-schizophrenia, melancholia, and a rather bad cough. The only responsible diagnosis to be drawn is that you—as a corporate entity—are suffering from visual confusion and loss of direction."

The doctor's prescription will be for the corporation to indulge in some rigourous soul-searching in an attempt to find itself.

But of course there's a danger in trying to find oneself: You're liable to succeed. And if you succeed, there's a good chance you won't like what you find; because if your inner being was in good shape, you probably wouldn't have developed an identity complex in the first place.

So a new kind of doctor is usually called in: a designer. This kind of doctor not only puts his patients on the couch, but he tells them what color couch to use.

Can a design "doctor" cure all the patient's identity problems? Probably not. Much of his treatment will, of necessity, be superficial—and the development of a personality is a very complex process.

The role or success of a designer in bringing cohesion to a corporation depends, to a great extent, on the designer himself and on the outlook of the corporation's top management. It can vary from simple cosmetics to substantive contributions.

The cosmetic aspect should not be underrated or disparaged, though. Even if design were purely cosmetic—which good design isn't—so what? I'm pleased to report that lipstick has not caused the decline and fall of kissing. At worst, cosmetics are harmless; and at their best, there is much to be said for transforming an old complex into a new complexion.

And the physical working environment of a company is important in many different respects. For one thing, a company obviously makes a statement about its style, standards, and aesthetic awareness in the design of its living quarters.

GARY GLADSTONE
The Gladstone Studio, Ltd.
237 East 20th Street
New York, New York 10003
(212) 982-3333

Annual reports, capability books, business & industry–strong executive portraiture, financial community, aviation, college. Author of juvenile books and craft books (major publishers). Very strong design emphasis in all phases of work– people, places and things. Has graphic design background and enjoys working as a team with designer. Among clients are: AMAX, American Can, Business Week, Celanese, Cerro, Chesebrough-Ponds, C.I.T., Citibank, Colt Industries, Continental Oil, Fortune, General Cable, General Electric, (Does anybody read this stuff?) International Paper, Johnson & Johnson, Kraft, Inc., Merrill Lynch, Moore McCormack, Nabisco, St. Joe, Sperry Rand, Time Inc., U.S. Industries, United Technologies, Xerox.

Stock Photography through The Image Bank

TIB THE IMAGE BANK

BURT GLINN
New York Representative: Magnum Photos, Inc.
15 West 46th Street
New York, New York 10036
Contact: Barbara Fine:
(212) 541-7570 Telex: 420339
(212) 832-8914

European Representative: Magnum Photos
2 rue Christine
75006 Paris, France
325·90·09 Telex: 200254

Assignments and stock photography.

THE GLOBUS BROTHERS
One Union Square West
New York, New York, 10003
(212) 243-1008

"PHOTOGRAPHY IN MOTION"
High Speed Sports (Stroboscopic)
Slit-Scan Product Transformations
Scientific Imagery
360° Panoramic Views
Fashion & Personality Sequences
Computerized Logos
All made possible with our
Globuscope® Cameras...

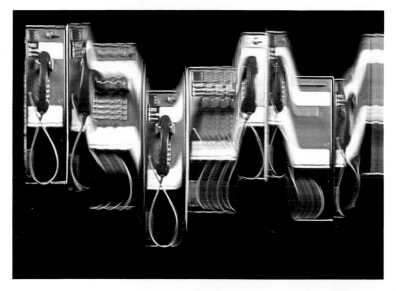

RICHARD ROY GOLDMAN
36 West 20th Street
New York, New York 10011
(212) 675-3021

The Goal: The enhancement of your concept,
by utilizing the proper elements of lighting,
casting, directing and styling.
Versatility: To meet your needs for still life
and industrial shootings.

JOEL GORDON PHOTOGRAPHY
5 East 16th Street
New York, New York 10003
(212) 989-9207

Creating the right photograph for his
clients' special needs is Joel's art.
Versatility is his talent.

Advertising, annual reports, audio-visual,
editorial, still life.
Location or studio.

©Joel Gordon 1979

HAVE WE FORGOTTEN WHO PAYS FOR ALL THIS BEAUTY?

A lot is made about the relationship—the perfect marriage—between art director and photographer. And obviously, it's got to be a good one. But what's equally important, at least to me, is the marriage between the client and the agency creative team. Having spent many years on the business side of the business before switching to the creative end of things, I'm particularly aware of how essential it is to have a client who truly appreciates and demands quality. It's an attitude that filters down through every level of an agency, through every aspect of a job, and ultimately affects all who contribute to the finished product. We're lucky to have clients who continually press us for our best. And we in turn, press the photographers we rely on. So the end result is one we can all be proud of.

PETER ROGERS
President & Creative Director
Peter Rogers Associates
New York City

STEPHEN GREEN-ARMYTAGE
171 West 57th Street
New York, New York 10019
(212) 247-6314

Represented by: Ursula G. Kreis
(212) 562-8931

105 East 28th Street
New York, New York 10016
(212) MU3-2558
Cable: Haliphot

European Representative: Grazia Neri
Via Senato 18
20121 Milano, Italia
Telex 33575/Telefono 799275

The results of your assignment should reflect the concern and
invention of a photographer you can count on. You've found one.

This partial client list and sampling from my Nikon House Exhibit
are intended to give you an idea of the energy, enthusiasm and scope
I've brought to bear on visual problems for nearly two decades.

AMERICAN CAN

SAVE MONO LAKE

INMONT

GEORGE WASHINGTON BRIDGE

D.C. HEATH

CORPORATE & ANNUAL REPORT /Alcoa; Amerace; American Can; Celanese; Champion International; Combustion Engineering; Consolidated Natural Gas; Citibank (N.Y.); GAF; General Cable; General Electric; Gimbels; Hartford Group Insurance; Indian Head; Inmont; Kimberly-Clark; The May Co.; Merrill Lynch; Metromedia; Mitchell-Hutchins; N.Y. Telephone; Otis; Pepsico; Salomon Brothers; Schlumberger Ltd; Seatrain; Sperry-Rand; Standard Oil; Travelers Insurance; United Fund; Wallace Murray; Xerox (numerous).

DESIGN & P.R. /Beau Gardner Assoc.; Boyer Org.; Chermayeff & Geismar; Cook & Shanosky; Corporate Annual Reports; Danne-Blackburn; Edward Howard Co.; John Haines; Richard Hess Inc.; Jack Hough & Assoc.; LSC&P Design Group Inc.; Edward Lefkowith Inc.; Noneman & Noneman; Page, Arbitrio & Resen; Russell & Hinrichs.

EDITORIAL & REPORTAGE /American Airlines; Camera (Switz.); D.C. Heath Co.; Esso Rivista (Italy); Fortune; Grazia (Italy); Holiday; Horizon; Infinity; Ladies Home Journal; Lamp (Standard Oil); La Scala Opera (Milano); London Daily Telegraph; Mitchell Beazley Ltd. (London); Robert Mondavi Winery; Museum of Natural History (Calendar); N.Y. Times Books; Progresso Fotografico (Italy); Réalités (France); Stern (Germany); Time-Life Books (numerous); Toronto Calendar Magazine.

TRADE & NATIONAL ADS /ABC; Advertising Council; American Airlines; Borg Warner; Bristol-Myers; Bulova-Accutron; CBS; Ciba-Geigy; Greenwood Mills; IBM; National Airlines; NBC; Newsweek; RCA; Sony; Sylvania; TWA; Union Dime Bank (N.Y.).

WALLACE–MURRAY

SHLUMBERGER

JELLY BEAN FACTORY

CAMPAGNA ROMANA

XEROX

GREGORY HEISLER
611 Broadway, Room 900
New York, New York 10012
(212)

The not-so-still life: on location or in my studio.

Corporate, editorial, record industry, and advertising clients including: Life Magazine; Fortune; Money; Time; Avenue Magazine; United Artists Records; Polydor, Mercury; Barber Blue Sea, Barnwell Industries; Bear, Stearns & Co.; Bradford National Corp.; Citicorp; Du Pont; Hardwicke Inc.; E.F. Hutton; International Harvester; Norfolk & Western Railway; Norwegian America Line; PBS; Vivitar; United States Surgical Corp.; United Technologies.

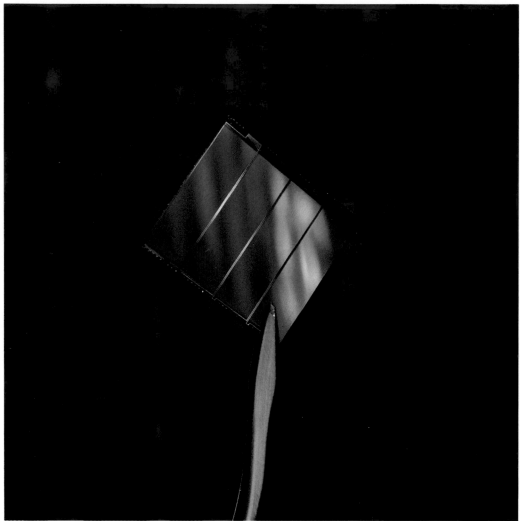

FORTUNE MAGAZINE

BARNWELL INDUSTRIES

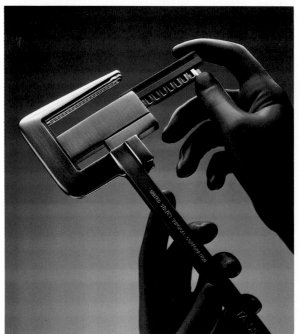

UNITED STATES SURGICAL CORPORATION

BARBER BLUE SEA

GREGORY HEISLER
611 Broadway, Room 900
New York, New York 10012
(212) 580-2712

Real people: alive with warmth and design, on location or in
my studio.

Corporate, editorial, record industry, and advertising clients
including: Life Magazine; Fortune; Money; Time; Avenue Magazine;
United Artists Records; Polydor; Mercury; Barber Blue Sea;
Barnwell Industries; Bear, Stearns & Co.; Bradford National Corp.;
Citicorp; Du Pont; Hardwicke Inc.; E.F. Hutton; International
Harvester; Norfolk & Western Railway; Norwegian America Line;
PBS; Vivitar; United States Surgical Corp.; United Technologies.

UNITED STATES SURGICAL CORPORATION

AVENUE MAGAZINE

FORTUNE MAGAZINE

HARDWICKE INC

UNITED ARTISTS RECORDS

BILL HELMS, INC.
1175 York Avenue
New York, New York 10021
(212) 759-2079

Representative: Jennifer Sims
Yellowbox, Inc. (New York)
(212) 532-4010

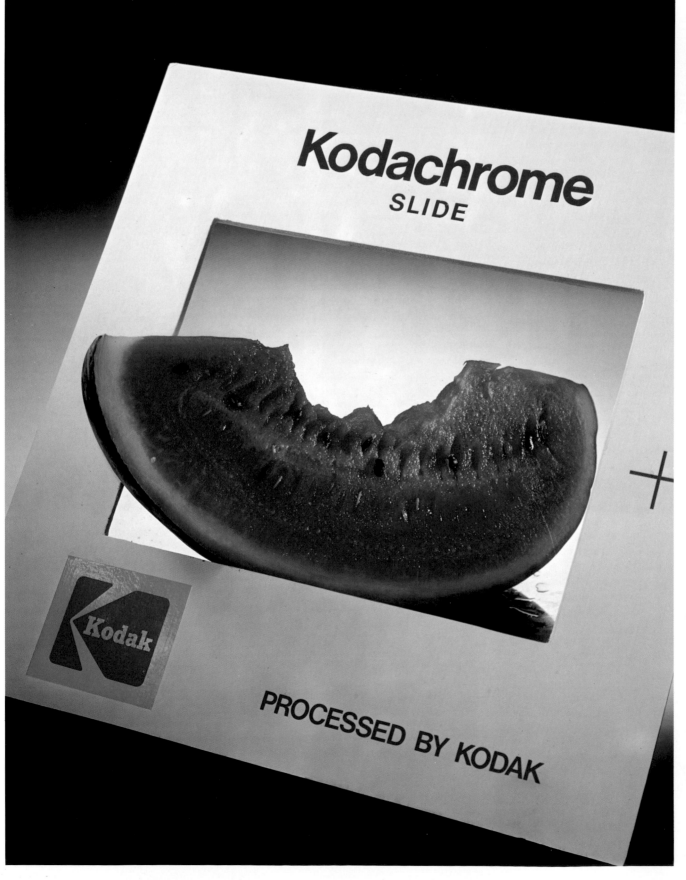

APARTMENT LIFE

APARTMENT LIFE

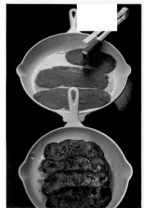

APARTMENT LIFE

APARTMENT LIFE

CORSON HIRSCHFELD
316 West Fourth Street
Cincinnati, Ohio 45202
(513) 241-0550

TED HOROWITZ
8 West 75th Street
New York, New York 10023
(212) 595-0040

Covers the world of international megabusiness. Photographs steel mills, oil rigs, refineries, research labs, chemicals, computers, shipbuilding, mining, manufacturing, agriculture, banking, finance, energy, and the environment. Shoots corporate presidents, farmers, physicists, log rollers and lab techs, bankers and bakers, welders and workers world-wide. Assignments encompass advertising, annual report, editorial, and corporate applications. Extensive client roster includes AMF, U.S. Steel, Bank of America, Union Carbide, Burroughs Corporation, AT&T, Continental Grain, Westvaco, Celanese, Time, Business Week and IBM.

Selected stock photography available through the Image Bank.

TED HOROWITZ
8 West 75th Street
New York, New York 10023
(212) 595-0040

Running the gamut of editorial, advertising, travel, and illustrative work for such clients as AMF, AT&T, W.R. Grace, New York Times Publishing, Western Union, Union Carbide, and Time, Inc., Ted Horowitz covers a wide range of subjects and events. Whether shooting workers in Wyoming, banking in Bombay, violinists in Vienna, or scenics in San Francisco, he photographs each situation with versatility and skill, displaying a graphic sense of design and a strong appreciation of color and light. Photographing people throughout the world with enthusiasm, Ted Horowitz adds spirit and energy to his assignments, bringing warmth, insight, and excitement to his work.

WILLIAM HUBBELL
Hubbell Associates
57 Wood Road
Bedford Hills, New York 10507
(914) 666-5792

Representative: Marian Hubbell
(914) 666-5792

Selected Stock: Woodfin Camp & Associates
(212) 355-1855

Areas of work include: Corporate, audio-visual, advertising
and illustration; 35mm through 8 × 10.

LOUIS H. JAWITZ
13 East 17th Street-Penthouse
New York, New York 10003
(212) 929-0008

Stock photography: The Image Bank

Avon, Clairol, Revlon, Nikon, Sigma, Sony, IBM, Grumman, Lafayette, Pratt & Whitney, United Aircraft Products, National Airlines, Eastern Air Lines, Finnair, Americana Hotels, American Express, G.Q., Swank, Popular Mechanics Magazine, Show, Viva, Scholastic Magazine, Dell Publishing, Pinnacle Books, Holt Rinehart & Winston, Avon Books, Ziff-Davis Publishing, CBS, ABC, WNEW, RCA Records, Johnny Walker Red, Miller Brewing, Nabisco, Kool, L'eggs, Bic Pen, Cibachrome, Famolare, Howell, Toshiba, Sanyo, Corning Electrical Products, Tyler Pipe Co. (Texas), Occidental Petroleum, Combustion Engineering Inc., Kendall Oil Co., Continental Can Co., Saxon-3, Unitron, and Bio-Tec.

THE IMAGE BANK

SIMPSON KALISHER
Roxbury, Connecticut 06783
(203) 354-8893

A quarter of a century of outstanding photography
has earned Simpson Kalisher a roster of clients
that include a host of Fortune 500 corporations,
our country's leading graphic designers and our
top ad agencies. His work has often been cited
by the AIGA, The Mead Library, as well as art
director clubs in New York, Chicago, Philadelphia,
New Jersey and Boston.

In addition, he is also the author of
Railroad Men: Photographs and collected stories;
Clarke & Way, 1961 and
Propaganda and other Photographs,
Addison House, 1977.

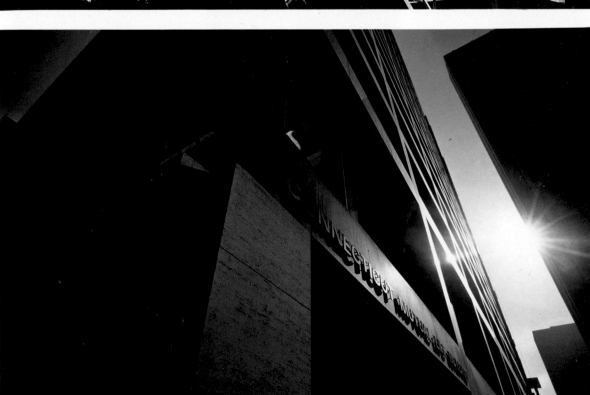

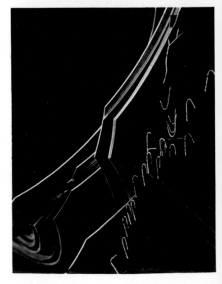

PAUL KATZ
381 Park Avenue South
New York, New York 10016
(212) 684-4395

Paul has photographed people, places, and things for: Texaco; IT&T; Dancer Fitzgerald Sample; Citibank; Citicorp; Grey Advertising; Gilbert, Felix & Sharf; The U.S. Army; Kenyon & Eckhardt; Nikon House; Rums of Puerto Rico; Air France; McAdams; New York University; MBA Magazine; Lipman Advertising; Medical Tribune; Guidepost Associates; Gene Wolfe & Company; World Tennis Magazine; Ted Barash & Company; Medigraphics; Pace Advertising; Industrial Development of Puerto Rico; Taylor Wine Co.; Banco Do Brasil; Garrison & Elliot; NLP&F Advertising; Cooper Union.

Stock Photography: The Image Bank:
(212) 371-3636

THE IMAGE BANK

CURT KAUFMAN
320 East 58th St.
New York, N.Y. 10022
(212) 759-2763

For portfolio, call: GITA
(212) 759-2763

Clients include: Dancer Fitzgerald and Sample, Marsteller, Diener Hauser & Bates, BBD&O, Grey Advertising, Rosebud Studios, Toyota, IBM, IT&T, Chromalloy America Corp., Dow Jones & Co., Sterling Optical, Sears, American Airlines, Berkey Photo, Franklin Mint, Warner Paperback Library, Costa Lines, Chandris America Lines, Time, Life, Viva, Playboy.

Also: American Broadcasting Company, Columbia Pictures, EUE/Screen Gems, Paramount Pictures, Universal Pictures and Warner Brothers.

THE IMAGE BANK

TED KAWALERSKI
52 San Gabriel Drive
Rochester, New York 14610
(716) 244-4656

Stock Photography: The Image Bank

Location photography for advertising and corporate
communications, specializing in annual reports.

Partial list of clients: Bausch & Lomb, Corning Glass, Eastman
Kodak, Gannett, Louis Harris & Associates, Holiday Inn,
Lincoln First Banks Inc., Security New York State Corporation,
Vornado, Washington Post Company, Xerox.

ASMP Member

All photographs below © Ted Kawalerski 1979

MATTHEW KLEIN STUDIO
15 West 18th Street
New York, New York 10011
(212) 255-6400

Still life and photographic illustration

110

PALMA KOLANSKY
155 West 13th Street
New York, New York 10011
(212) 243-4077

DAN KOZAN PRODUCTIONS, INC.
89 Fifth Avenue
New York, New York 10003
(212) 691-2288/9

LET THERE BE NEON

Rudi Stern/Abe Rezny
451 West Broadway
New York, New York 10012
(212) 226-7747

LET THERE BE NEON is a workshop/
studio for neon graphics, sculpture,
interiors, environments, architectural
projects, and displays of all kinds. Since
1972, we have been developing neon as
a creative resource.

Neon photography for posters, brochures, all
print media: Abe Rezny.

CUNARD LINES—BETH VOGEL, JOHN TUR, RUDI STERN, CHRISTOPHER RICHARTZ

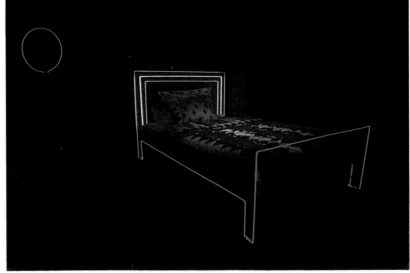

WAMSUTTA—WAYNE LITTLE, ABE REZNY, RUDI STERN

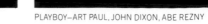

PLAYBOY—ART PAUL, JOHN DIXON, ABE REZNY

KLAUS LUCKA
35 West 31st Street
New York, New York 10001
(212) 594-5910

Represented by: Joe Cahill, New York   Jack Petz, Detroit   Mark Ramon, West Germany
(212) 751-0529   (313) 643-6000   40-826444

Jack Kapes, Chicago   Yuko Arai, Tokyo
(312) 664-8282   03-451-4178

Clients: Noxema, Oldsmobile, Benson & Hedges, Revlon, Clairol, Monet, Levis, Wrangler, Max Factor, Helena Rubinstein, Almay, Anheuser-Busch, Sony (U.S. & Japan), Michelob, National Panasonic (Japan), Lord Extra Cig. (Germany), Peer Export Cig. (Germany), Belvedere Cig. (Canada), Export "A" Cig. (Canada), Motorola, Chrysler, Volkswagen, Swiss Air, Coca Cola, United Brands, Procter & Gamble, Now Cig., More Cig., Vantage Cig., Usher Scotch, Rochas Parfumes, Dana Parfumes, Hagger Slacks, Asbach Brandy, Seagram, Maybelline, Avon, Coty, Klopman Fabrics, Hart Schafner & Marx, Frye Boots, Esquire, G.Q., Ladies Home Journal, Town & Country, Harpers Bazaar, Prell Shampoo, Posner, Ultra Sheen, Caress Soap, Gilette, Cutex, Q-Tips, Maxi Pads, La Coste, Sealy, American Standard, Secret Deodorant, Haynes Hos., Ballentine Scotch, Buick, Cadillac, Fieldcrest, General Foods, Johnson & Johnson, American Express...

F THE ENERGY CRISIS... IN ART DIRECTION

ocus group interviews, marketing, strategy plans, media research, copy concept, pre-testing, Starch scores, Burke scores, in-store check and so on.

Advertising's come a long way. But the technology isn't worth a damn if the cumulative parts aren't executed with **ENERGY**.

ENERGY is the power of the advertising to be seen over the deluge.

ENERGY transmits the concept in its best light.

ENERGY is the context pushing the content. It's the visual that makes your mouth water in one ad and your eyes water in another.

ENERGY is additive. It's the image that strengthens the concept, the layout that amplifies the personality of the product, the typography that complements the headline.

ENERGY is the work it takes to develop a visual concept, the image idea, the visual headline.

ENERGY is the desire to take the art direction beyond compliance, it's the computer graphics in Un-Cola, the exquisite look of Piaget ads, the bold design of Life trade ads.

ENERGY is more than is asked for. More sensuous, more refined, more dynamic, more sophisticated, more dramatic, more outstanding.

The **ENERGY** of the advertising is the responsibility of the art director.

ENERGY is the work it takes to sell a well designed ad. It takes **ENERGY** to educate copywriters, account executives and clients to the benefits.

ENERGY is on top of "Concept." "Concept" was the key of the sixties. "Concept" became the mystique of the hot creative shops. It added dimension, content, and progress.

"Creative" advertising had a competitive edge.

By the early seventies "Concept" was being taught in art school ad classes.

Now that "Concept" is part of the standard formula used by most agencies in developing advertising, how does one's advertising keep ahead of the pack?

It takes more **ENERGY**.

CHARLES DAVIDSON
V.P. Creative Services
North American Watch Corporation
New York City

DICK LURIA PHOTOGRAPHY, INC.
5 East 16th Street
New York, New York 10003
(212) 929-7575

117

"A photographer must listen to his clients—focus in on their needs, solve their problems and most importantly give them what they want (even if they don't ask for it directly). In addition, he should bring an extra-special excitement and enthusiasm to his work. I do."

Corporate and industrial advertising and annual reports for over forty of the 'Fortune 500': Allied Chemical, American Airlines, Babcock & Wilcox, Bear Stearns, Braniff International, Burroughs Corporation, Caesar's World, Chemical Bank, Eastern Airlines, Engelhard Minerals & Chemicals, Entenmann's Inc., Fortune, General Electric, General Signal, Getty Refining, Hazeltine, E.F. Hutton, IBM, IT&T, Ingersoll-Rand, International Paper, Lever Brothers, Merrill Lynch, North American Philips, Pratt & Whitney, Savin, Sperry & Hutchinson, Stromberg-Carlson, Teltronics, Texasgulf, Toshiba, TWA, U.S. Steel, U.S. Surgical, Warner-Lambert, W.R. Grace.

The fascinating thing about photography, beyond the wonderful design and the beautiful lighting, is that it captures moments in time. Moments in time that most of us spend little of our lives in. We live with one foot in the future and one foot in the past, and very seldom truly experience right now. Right Now. Right now.

Photography has a way of holding a moment for us to look at. A moment that would have slipped by barely noticed.

Everything is always moving, always changing, and for me, photography is a reminder that the way it is, is the way it is.

RONALD TRAVISANO
President
DellaFemina, Travisano & Partners Inc.
New York City

PHIL MARCO PRODUCTIONS
104 Fifth Avenue
New York, New York 10011
(212) 929-8082

JOHN MARMARAS
235 Seventh Avenue
New York, New York 10011
(212) 741-0212

Representative: Woody Camp
(212) 355-1855

Advertising, corporate & editorial assignments.

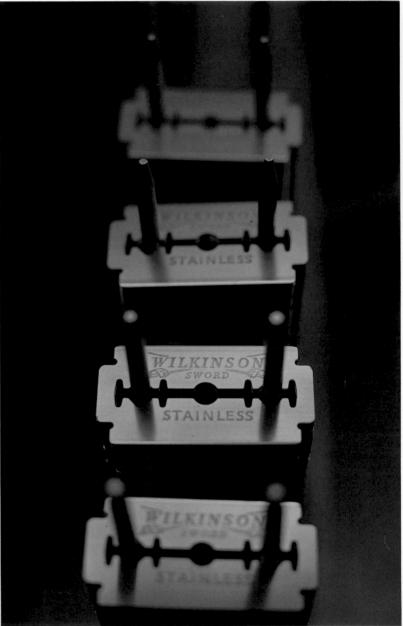

Advertising, album covers, fashion,
travel, editorial and annual reports.

D.W. MELLOR
Darby and Marple Roads
Haverford, Pennsylvania 19041
Studio: (215) 649-6087

Annual Reports
People
Still life
Advertising
Editorial

RELIANCE INSURANCE COMPANIES

CAR AND DRIVER MAGAZINE

FERRARI EAST COAST IMPORTER

ERIC MEOLA STUDIO, INC.
134 Fifth Avenue
New York, New York 10011
(212) 255-8653

Representatives:

New York: Les Klein (212) 832-7220
Chicago: Bill Rabin (312) 944-6655
Tokyo: P.P.S. Tsushinsha (03) 264-3821

Major campaigns, ads, corporate and editorial work for domestic and foreign clients including Porsche, IBM, Polaroid. Color, graphics and concept applied to still life, travel, beauty, illustration and corporate communications. Three self-promotion booklets available on request, with more than fifty pages of color. Direct sales of 30″ x 40″ dye transfers to corporations, designers and collectors.

Campagnes de grande ampleur, annonces publicitaires, travaux sur brochures d'entreprises et sur magazines pour clients français et étrangers, dont Porsche, IBM et Polaroid. Réalisation couleur, graphisme et création pour les articles de style nature morte, les voyages, les produits de beauté, les illustrations symboliques et les publications des sociétés. Trois brochures auto-publicitaires contenant plus de cinquante pages en couleur sont disponibles sur demande. Ventes directes de transferts de couleurs (dimensions 76 cm x 101 cm) aux entreprises, dessinateurs et collectionneurs.

Bedeutende Kampagnen,Werbeanzeigen, Aufträge von deutschen und ausländischen Zeitschriften und Unternehmen wie Porsche, IBM und Polaroid. Farbvorschläge, graphische Darstellungen und Konzepte für fotographische Stilleben, für die Reise-und die Kosmetikindustrie, symbolische Darstellungen und Veröffentlichungen von Firmen. Drei erläuternde Broschüren über uns selbst mit mehr als fünfzig Farbseiten stehen auf Anfrage zur Verfügung. Direktverkauf von Farbübertragungen (76 cm x 101 cm) an Unternehmen, Designer und Sammler.

ポルシェ，IBM，ポラロイドを含む海外，及び国内顧客用の大規模なキャンペーン，宣伝広告，及び会社やマスコミ用の資料。静物写真，旅行業，化粧品業，イラスト，及び企業刊行に応用した色彩，グラフィックス，及び概念。50面以上のカラー・ページを含む自己振興のパンフレット 3 冊を要求により提供。企業，デザイナー，収集家に 76×101 センチのダイ・トランスファー作品の直売。

LOUIS MERVAR
29 West 38th Street, 16th Floor
New York, New York 10018
(212) 354-8024

Portfolio on request.

126

MARTIN MISTRETTA
91 Fifth Avenue
New York, New York 10003

Represented by: John Clements
(212) 348-6806

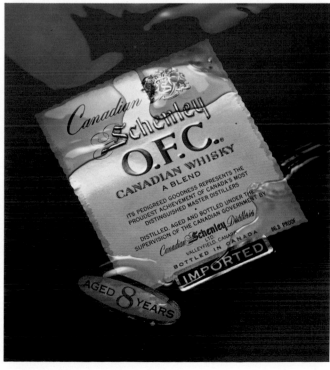

MICHAEL NELSON
7 East 17th Street
New York, New York 10003
(212) 924-2892

Clients: AT&T; Sudler & Hennessey; Doyle
Dane Bernbach; J. Walter Thompson;
Young & Rubicam; William Douglas McAdams;
New York Times; Seligman & Latz; Cosmopolitan;
Yardley of London; Scali, McCabe, Sloves.

"The real challenge for me on a shooting
is to bring out from my subjects a real
sense of feeling."

128

TERRY NIEFIELD
210 Fifth Avenue
New York, New York 10010
(212) 686-8722

PALMER/KANE, INC.
269 Lyons Plains Road
Weston, Connecticut 06883
(203) 227-1477

Palmer is the photographer. The work speaks for itself.
Strong graphic design. Saturated color. He is rapidly
becoming one of the most sought after corporate/industrial
photographers in the country.

Kane is the former client. Corporate communications from
the client's point of view. She is concept, planning,
print production, logistics and logic.

Stock photography available through The Image Bank.

ROBERT T. PANUSKA
Representative: Al Forsyth
521 Madison Avenue
New York, New York 10022
(212) 752-3930

Graduate of L. A. Art Center. Awards include: Andy, Clio, One Show,
Addys, C. A., Print, etc. Extensive experience in travel and resort work,
including aerial, underwater, and other specialized types of outdoor
photography. Clients include: National, Eastern, American, and
Northwest Orient Airlines, Bertram Yachts, Kodak, Jamaican Hotel
Association, Norwegian Caribbean Lines, Monarch Cruise Lines, Playboy
Magazine, Dunhill Cigarettes, Tiffany's, Burger King, Coca-Cola,
Ryder Trucks.

Stock available.

STEPHEN POFFENBERGER
P.O. Box 15
Sarasota, Florida 33578
(813) 957-0606

Ideas into impact images

Stock photography: The Image Bank

As we grow older in life, our senses become
gradually numbed and our vision of life is
warped by too much preoccupation with cold,
trivial realities. I wish to restore in you
a freshness of vision. Cast your eyes
into my mirror.

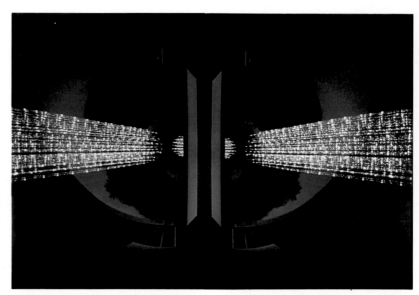

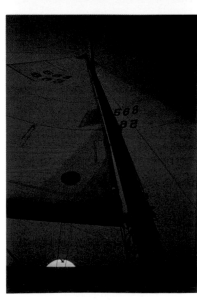

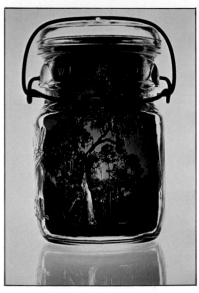

SCOTT PURVIS
49 West 27th Street
New York, New York 10001
(212) 889-9898

Representative: Paula Krongard
(201) 783-6155

Stock Photography: The Image Bank

THE IMAGE BANK

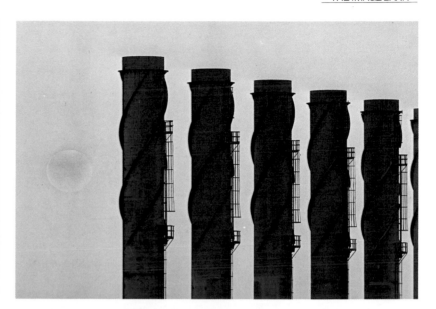

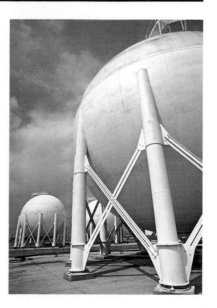

NEIL RICE STUDIO, INC.
91 Fifth Avenue
New York, New York 10003
(212) 924-6096

Representative: Ed Susse
(212) 477-0674

HENRY RIES
204 East 35th Street
New York, New York 10016
(212) 689-3794

HELIOPTIX© is a unique photographic concept.
Controlled motion of light and lens creates
designs of imaginative shapes and colors
around words, logos, products and symbols.

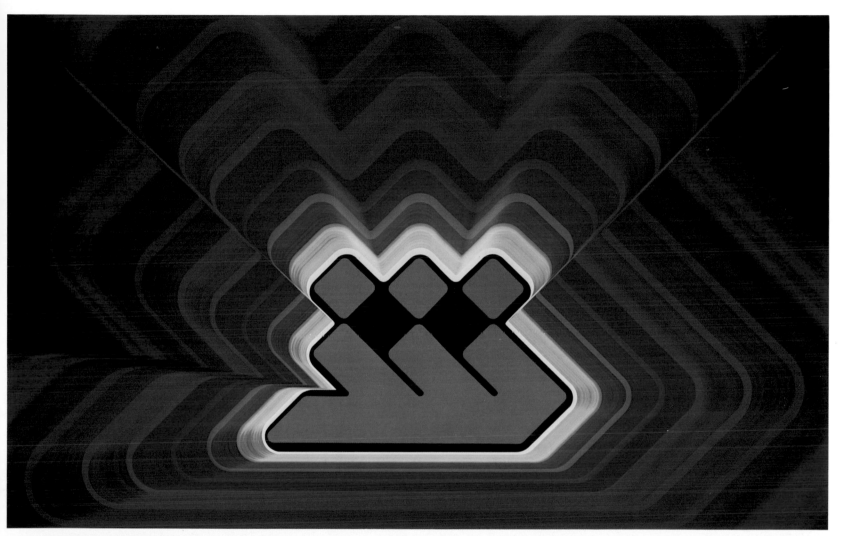

A commercial solution   to a military problem.

Introducing the TFE1042   low bypass turbofan engine.

JON RILEY
12 East 37th Street
New York, New York 10016
(212) 532-8326

Representative: Catherine Riley
(212) 532-8326

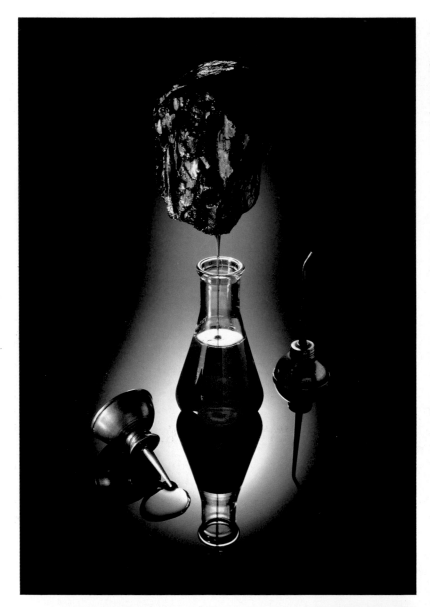

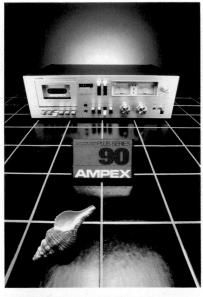

BEN ROSE
91 Fifth Avenue
New York, New York 10003
(212) 691-5270

Representative: Sol Shamilzadeh
1155 Broadway
New York, New York 10001
(212) 532-1977

Multiple imaging. Space, time motion
studies. Stroboscopy. Image programming
techniques. Time selection in micro
seconds. Freezing short events—sports.
Logos in motion. Sophisticated
electronics in photography. Outer
space events. Illusions.

THE IMAGE BANK

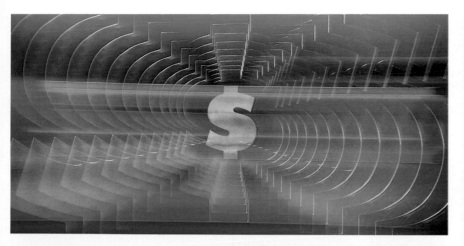

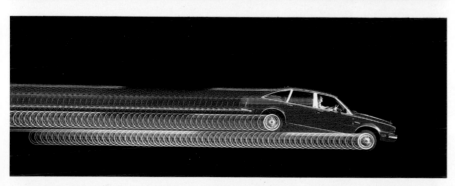

BARRY SCHEIN PHOTOGRAPHY
Represented by: Kathy Sorkin Associates
127 Lexington Avenue
New York, New York 10016
(212) 685-1606
(212) 849-7808

Still life and illustration photography

Some of our clients include: General Foods,
General Mills, American Express, Anchor
Hocking, New York Racing Association,
Burlington Mills, Pfizer, Avon,
Bigelow Carpet Mills, Procter & Gamble,
Standard Brands, Quality Mills.

VICTOR SCOCOZZA
117 East 30th Street
New York, New York 10016
(212) 686-9440

Representative: Richard Mendelsohn
(212) 682-2462

Advertising and editorial photography.

IT&T—ROY FREEMANTLE

The <u>only</u> vodka
imported from Russia.

Stolichnaya.
(pronounced: Stol-itch-NYE-ya)

OGILVY & MATHER

BETTY CROCKER

GOOD HOUSEKEEPING

It seems to me a lot of art directors these days haven't a clear idea of what it is to be a professional.

They haven't paid their dues, and they don't seem to want to learn how. You start paying your dues by learning how to make postage-stamp-size trade ads interesting. And you work your way up from there. Maybe television is responsible for the demise of professionalism. Flying to the coast and hanging around in Levis and boots on a star-studded set is certainly a lot more alluring than sitting in an office doing small space black and white print. Ads that have to sell merchandise.

But the business is advertising, not flash.

And the Polo Lounge in Beverly Hills doesn't have much to do with the professionalism of advertising art direction.

What does?

Being an advertising as well as a graphics person. And as far as I'm concerned, that's as simple as being interested in selling somebody something; with the looks of it being the means and not the end.

Giving attention to the little assignments as well as the big fabulous ones; enthusiastically addressing even the stuff that probably won't make it into the shows.

Getting the right people to do the job. Not necessarily the hottest photographer or illustrator; but the one most genuinely equipped. Having the courage to hire somebody really talented, instead of a patsy whom you can shove around. Realizing that God gave you talent, but you have to supply the energy that converts it to professionalism.

I'm sure every art director in the business has his set of professional standards. For now, those are mine.

MARTIN STEVENS
Vice President Creative Services
Revlon
New York City

SEPP SEITZ
381 Park Avenue South
New York, New York 10016
(212) 683-5588/355-1855

An eye for graphics, ability to deal with people,
and cool professionalism on locations around the
world let me make my advertising and industrial
clients shine. List on request.

STAN SHAFFER
2211 Broadway
New York, New York 10024
(212) 595-2608

Represented by: Sue Mosel
(212) 288-9204

GENTLEMAN'S QUARTERLY

GENTLEMAN'S QUARTERLY

STAN SHAFFER
2211 Broadway
New York, New York 10024
(212) 595-2608

Represented by: Sue Mosel
(212) 288-9204

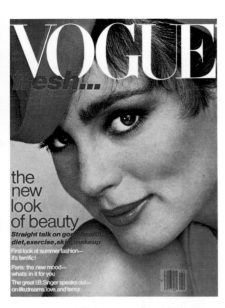

GUY J. SHERMAN
108 East 16th Street
New York, New York 10003
(212) 675-4983

Representative: Ora Able
(212) 751-3282

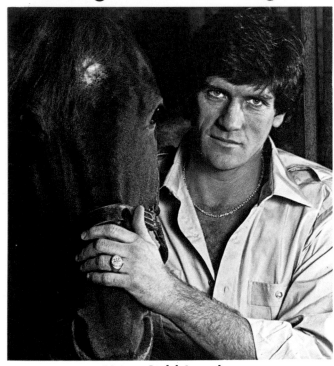

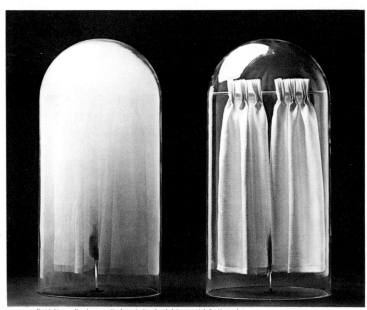

GUY J. SHERMAN
108 East 16th Street
New York, New York 10003
(212) 675-4983

Representative: Ora Able
(212) 751-3282

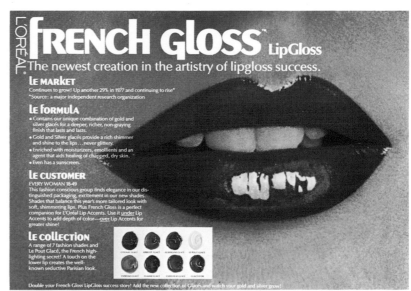

CARL SHIRAISHI
137 East 25th Street
New York, New York 10010
(212) 679-5628

Representative: Kim
(212) 679-5628

LEWIS SKOLNIK
33 East 60th Street
New York, New York 10022
(212) 758-5662

Graphic, corporate identity
and packaging presentations.
Product photography.

Member ASMP

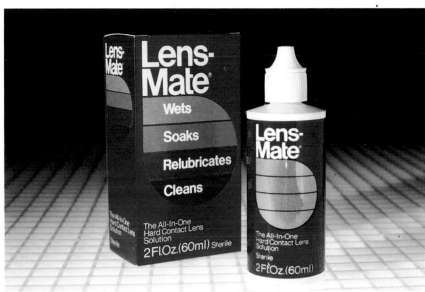

PRODUCT ILLUSTRATION

NEW LABEL PROMOTION

CONCEPTUAL PHOTOGRAPHY

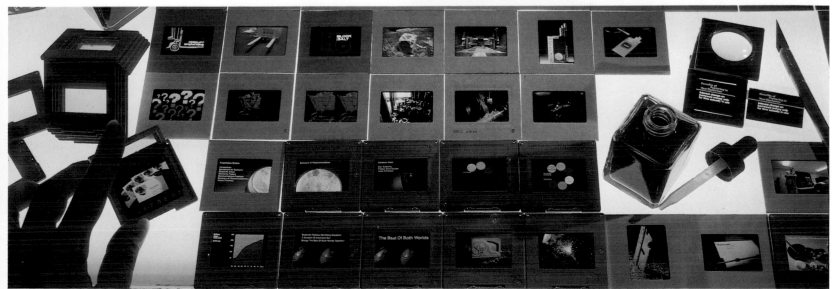

SLIDE PRODUCTION, PRESENTATIONS FOR CORPORATE/INTERNAL MEETINGS

NORMAN SNYDER
Norman Snyder Studios, Inc.
7 East 19th Street
New York, New York 10003
(212) 254-2770

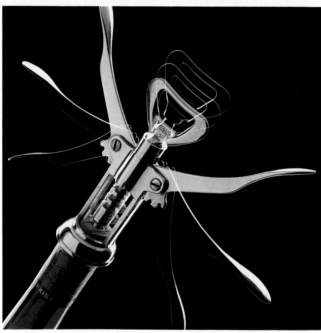

HOWARD SOCHUREK
680 Fifth Avenue
New York, New York 10019
(212) 582-1860 office
(914) 337-5014 home

Electronic imaging, color conversion and image enhancement.
Medical illustration, ultrasound, thermography, X-ray color.
Photojournalism for advertising, capabilities books,
and corporate reports.

Clients: IBM, SCM, AVCO, Revlon, Eastman Kodak, Squibb,
Time-Life, Pfizer, Gillette, Merrill Lynch, Pan Am, Carrier,
G.M., Western Electric, Newsweek, Boeringer-Ingelheim,
Forbes, Wheelabrator-Frye, Rockwell, Cameron Iron,
Belco Petroleum, McDonnell Douglas, Kimberly-Clark,
and many many more.

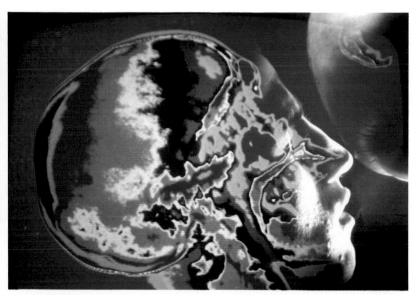

ANGIOGRAPHY

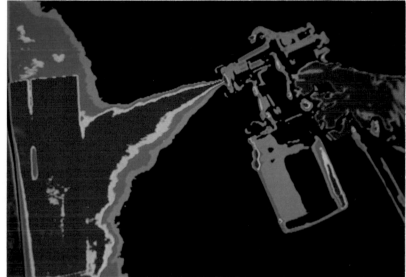

ELECTRONIC COLOR

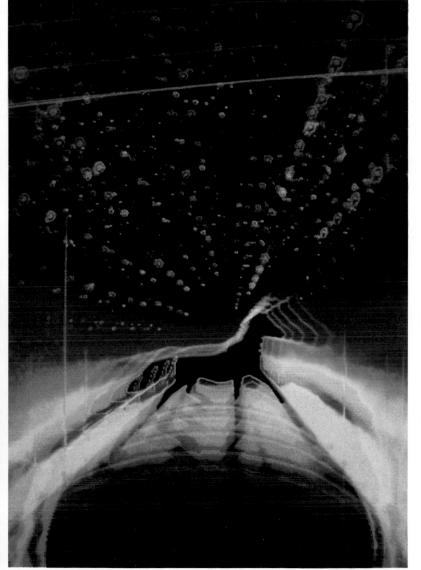

COMPUTER GRAPHICS

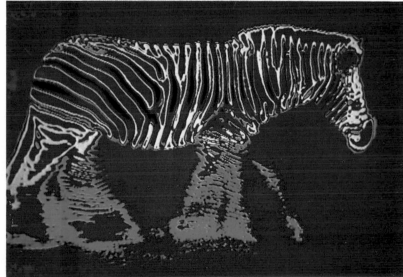

IMAGE ENHANCED ZEBRA

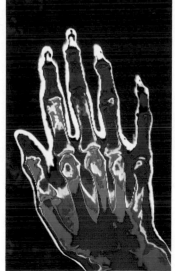

TOMOGRAPHY

THERMOGRAPHY

DAVID M. SPINDEL
18 East 17th Street
New York, New York 10003
(212) 989-4984

The smallest, most ordinary, most
insignificant things are neither
small, ordinary nor insignificant.

JOHN LEWIS STAGE
Iron Mountain Road
New Milford, New York 10959
(914) 986-1620

Stock agent: The Image Bank
New York, New York.
(212) 371-3636

© John Lewis Stage, 1979

JOE STANDART
377 Park Avenue South
New York, New York 10016
(212) 532-8268

Representative: Barbara Peters
(212) 475-2665

Joe does corporate, location, foreign travel, still life, interiors, food, illustration.

Clients include: American Express; AT&T; Baron, Costello & Fine; Bessen & Tully; Bundy Corporation; Cosmopolitan; DKG; Food & Wine; Glamour; House & Garden; International Marketing; Pan Am; Travel & Leisure; West Point Pepperell; and many others.

FOOD & WINE

COSMOPOLITAN

DENISE HARBIN, INTERNATIONAL MARKETING

DIVERSION

IRENE STERN
117 East 24th Street
New York, New York 10010
(212) 475-7464

Photography is the center of her life.

Whether it's advertising, editorial, or industrial, she dedicates herself to the assignment, in the studio or on location, ranging from a shot of 20 Christmas trees to the button on your shirt.

Special strengths in still life: foods, liquor, and just plain objects.

Some of her clients include:
Heinz Foods; Maxwell House; Best Food; Hereford Cow; Beefeater; Schaefer Beer; Piels; House of Seagram; Johnson & Johnson; Malox; Warner Communications; Exxon; American Express; Gilette; Procter & Gamble; Owens Corning Fiberglass; Leggs; Fitz & Floyd; Merrill Lynch; New York Magazine; Esquire; Food & Wine; Redbook; Ted Bates; Robert A. Becker; Benton & Bowles; Burson-Marsteller; Cunningham & Walsh; Dancer Fitzgerald Sample; Manoff; Geers Gross; Mathieu, Gerfen & Bresner; Ogilvy & Mather; Sacks & Rosen; SSC&B; Warwick, Welsh & Miller; Wells, Rich, Greene.

MICHEL TCHEREVKOFF
873 Broadway
New York, New York 10003
(212) 228-0540

Representative: Nob Hovde and Laurence
(212) 753-0462

THE SKY IS THE LIMIT...

Stock available through The Image Bank
(212) 371-3636

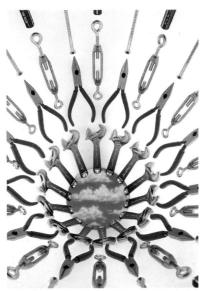

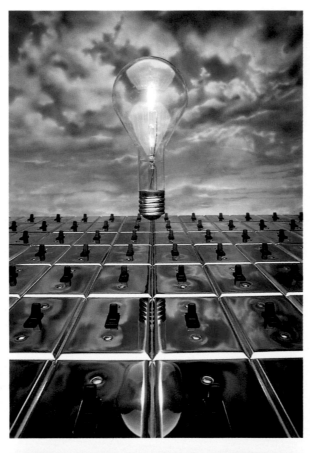

STEVE UZZELL
2505 North Custis Road
Arlington, Virginia 22201
(703) 522-2320

Representative: Woodfin Camp
(212) 355-1855

Print and audio visual production.

MICHAEL WAINE
873 Broadway
New York, New York 10003
(212) 533-4200

Representative: Bob Palevitz
(212) 684-6026

A still life photographer in every sense of the word—Michael specializes in all from advertising to editorial to pharmaceutical problem solving. His experience with assignments from clients and the still life camera is a very moving one indeed.

Some of the clients who have called upon Michael over the last few years are: Arnold Bakers, Breyers, De Beers, du Pont, IBM, Playboy, Philip Morris, Johnson & Johnson, Kraft, Ralston Purina, Swiss Bank, GQ, Colgate-Palmolive, Peugeot, Rossignol, Chesebrough-Ponds, Corning Glass Works, Hoffman-La Roche, Wyeth, Kool, American Express, Bantam Books, Kodak-Amphoto, Bergdorf Goodman, Bloomingdale's, Rosenthal, Orrefor's, American Distilling, Ballantine Scotch Whiskey, Mark Cross, Christian Dior, Estee Lauder, Aramis, Revlon, Germaine Monteil, Faberge, Chanel, L'Oreal, and the U.S. Air Force.

GEORGE R. WASCO
20 West 38th Street
New York, New York 10018
(212) 921-0917

32 South Strawberry Street
Philadelphia, Pennsylvania 19106
(215) 922-4662

Existing photography: The Image Bank

THE IMAGE BANK

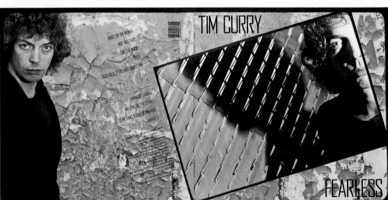

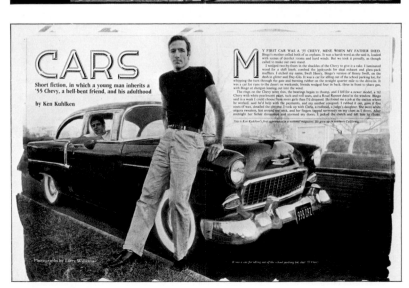

JOSEPH ZEDAR
29 West 26th Street
New York, New York 10010
(212) 685-5288
Advertising, still life, food and liquor photography.
ASMP member

A

s a commercial photographer, I deal with people's problems, visual problems, which they feel should be resolved photographically. They call us, we try to resolve those problems as best we can, given the time and the guidelines. Some of the problems aren't worth resolving, but that's somebody else's business, someone who wants to perpetuate his life, his involvement for himself. That's his thing, and we meet to resolve his problem.

* * *

Clients pay a lot of money for something they need. They have to give you the rules, and you have to take these rules and visually express them the way you feel is correct. Ultimately, I subscribe to the golden rule—the man with the gold makes the rules. Sometimes the rules are a little strange, and sometimes the people are strange. But the picture shouldn't be strange. You have to deal with it. That's the business. If you don't want to deal with it, then don't do the business, because it isn't going to change right away.

* * *

I am thoroughly dedicated to the business. Aside from my family and relaxing, I can't think of another interest that I have. I enjoy what I do. It's frustrating, it's a lot of things; but it's gratifying. It offers instant gratification. I can shoot a job today and see it this afternoon, or tomorrow morning, the latest. If I hate it, I can do it again. When the clients love it, they applaud. That's instant gratification, and I get paid very well.

* * *

I think deep down I don't know me at all. I think most people have very little ability to be introspective. I'm certainly one of those. But, what I do know is that I am me. One set of circumstances, one group of clients, one week's worth of shooting isn't going to change me. Clients can want whatever they want, as long as I control it. When it comes out of this church, whatever pew they're in is academic. I am tailoring a picture for them. When I walk out the door, I can say whatever, but I can still say that I'm me. All I have done is resolve a problem for a client on that day. Next time I have another someone who may be different, who may be closer to what I feel is me. And that's a nice occasion. One thing for sure, no matter who they are, no matter where they come from, we do the best we can.

* * *

When a photo-journalist documents a guy getting shot, he pushes the button, but he really doesn't do anything to create the picture. In still life, you have to control everything. So if a still life photographer were to show someone being blown away, it would have to be done <u>right</u>. He might have to go through four or five people to get the right expression…

I'm just joking, of course, but I do think still-life people have an advantage over the other photographers. We have total control, and that's what I enjoy. I like moving my highlights, I like finessing my props, I like knowing that I put them there. I like knowing they're wrong when I look at the chrome.

* * *

I know what I want, and it's to end up at a reasonable old age and with some modicum of sanity, and I'm not going to give it up for this business, because the business isn't worth it.

GEORGE COCHRAN

"Mistaken Identity"

(SFX)

Woman: Burt, don't actually look at him, but look at the man in the rear booth.

Man: In the rear—

Woman: No, don't look at him.

Man: But how can I— Isn't that, eh— Oh, it's, uh—

Woman: Isn't it?

Man: Oh, it's—

Woman: Am I right?

Man: Yeah, you're right.

Woman: Who is it?

Man: I don't know.

Woman: Oh, he's in the new issue of TIME Magazine.

Man: Oh, right! The science section. He's the inventor of the—

Woman: No! The theatre section; he's the new star of the youknowwhat—

Man: Yeah. What?

Woman: Burt, if he's famous, if he's in the news, where else would we have seen him but in TIME Magazine.

Man: The one I just picked up at the newsstand?

Woman: Oh, he's that new author or that old artist or something.

Man: That's silly. Come on—

Woman: Where are we going?

Man: Pardon me, sir.

2nd Man: Yeah?

Man: We know we've seen you somewhere—

Woman: Like TIME Magazine—

Man: But we just can't place it.

Woman: And we'd love your autograph.

2nd Man: Sure. Here.

Man: Thank you, Mr. Casmer—?

2nd Man: Casmerzack. Yeah. Casmerzack plumbing. I snaked out your pipes last month.

Man: Oh, right, you snaked out—

Woman: Why would that be in TIME Magazine?

Man: Okay. Thank you for the autograph.

Woman: Why would, would that be in TIME Magazine?

Man: Just keep walking backwards. He snaked out our pipes, for—

Woman: Bye, bye.

Anncr: TIME. The most colorful coverage of the week. Pick up a copy.

Silver Award Winner
The One Show
Consumer Radio—Single Commercial
Produced for Time Inc. by
   Young & Rubicam Inc.
Copy written by Dick Orkin and
   Bert Berdis

"Puffy Sleeves"

1st voice: Pardon me, sir, would you step over to the patrol car, please?

2nd voice: Oh! Hello, officer.

1st voice: Do you have business in this neighborhood, sir?

2nd voice: Yes. I live four blocks from here. It's the brick colonial with the crack in the driveway.

1st voice: What are you doing at this time of night, sir?

2nd voice: Well, I got all ready for bed, see, and darned if I didn't forget to pick up a copy of TIME Magazine at the newsstand today.

1st voice: What type of coat would you call that, sir?

2nd voice: This is a h-house coat. See I spilled cocoa on mine and I just grabbed my wife's. I guess the puffy sleeves look a little silly. (LAUGHS)

1st voice: Do you want to get in the car, sir.

2nd voice: In the car…in the car…see, I just don't go to bed without a TIME movie review or something from the modern living section…

1st voice: Yes, sir.

2nd voice: I tried reading something else but there just isn't anything like TIME. Do you know, officer, how many editorial awards TIME Magazine has won?

1st voice: No, sir.

2nd voice: And TIME is so respected. I'm a firm believer, along with Winston Churchill, that you are what you read.

1st voice: Uh, huh.

2nd voice: Oh, please don't send me up the river just for wearing puffy sleeves.

1st voice: You're home, sir.

2nd voice: I'm home. Oh! Thank—God Bless, OK, Bye…

Anncr: TIME. The most colorful coverage of the week. Pick up a copy.

Gold Award Winner
The One Show
Consumer Radio—Commercial Campaign

MIKE BLAKE
77 North Washington Street
Boston, Massachusetts 02114
(617) 523-3730

"Surprise!"—That's not what you need when you're
shooting with a photographer out-of-town. What you
do need is clean, competent product illustration—
a photographer that's proficient in 35mm to 8x10,
in studio or on location, and is easy to work with.
If you have an assignment coming up in the New
England area, give me a call and I'll surprise you
with a mini-portfolio.

Member ASMP

DICK DURRANCE II
Dolphin Ledge
Rockport, Maine 04856
(207) 236-3990

Advertising Representative: Photo-Artists
157 West 57th Street
New York, New York 10019
(212) 246-3737

Corporate Representative: Woodfin Camp and Associates
415 Madison Avenue
New York, New York 10017
(212) 355-1855

A former staff photographer for National Geographic now
shooting advertisements and annual reports world-wide for:
Leo Burnett; Scali, McCabe, Sloves; Ketchum, MacLeod & Grove;
Kurtz & Tarlow; Statig, Sanderson, & White; SCM; Pepsico;
Squibb; Ogden; Midland-Ross; and the Ethyl Corporation.

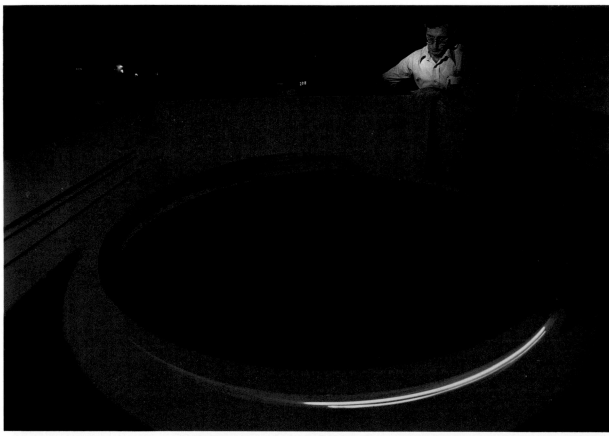

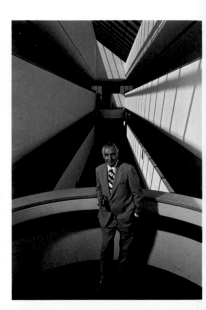

JAMIE EISMAN PHOTOGRAPHY, INC.
518 South 4th Street
Philadelphia, Pennsylvania 19147
(215) 922-7652

Representative: Joyce Schiff
(215) 625-9010

JOEL CARL FREID
812 Loxford Terrace
Silver Spring, Maryland 20901
(301) 681-7211

Specialties: Advertising illustration, corporate reports, editorial and film stills.

"Joel Carl Freid is one of those rare photographers who has truly blended the personal, involved eye of the photo-journalist with an impeccable sense of graphics. Poignancy doesn't embarass him or his subjects. Without any slick bravura, his portraits are haunting."
ART DIRECTION MAGAZINE

Assignments have taken me to South America, Africa, the Middle East, Eastern and Western Europe, Canada and through-out the United States. I have photographed ambassadors, corporate presidents and Nobel prize winners. I have been lowered into coal mines, hung 2,000 feet up from helicopter skids, photographed open heart surgery, research and manufacturing facilities, 3,000 year old religious groups and grandiose city scapes.

My greatest passion is my work.
My life is my studio.

JOHN HOLT
129 South Street
Boston, Massachusetts 02111
(617) 426-7262
Full-service commercial studio.

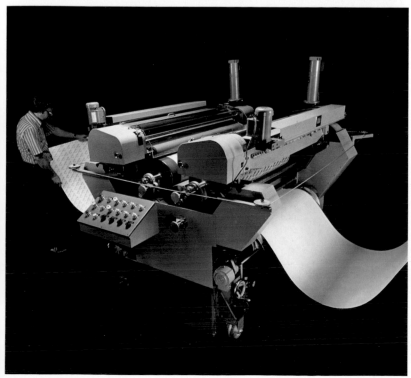

BRUNO JOACHIM
73 Newbury Street
Boston, Massachusetts 02116
(617) 266-7552

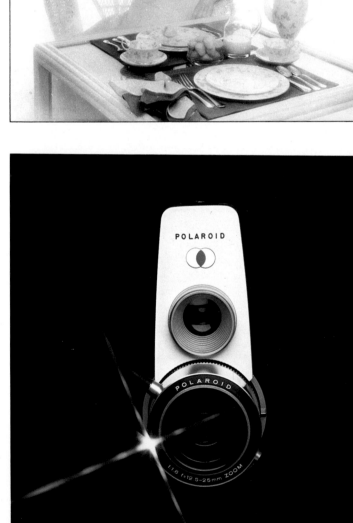

CAROL LEE

78 Chestnut Street
Boston, Massachusetts 02108
(617) 523-5930

Carol is a highly regarded industrial photographer whose work has appeared in numerous national and international business and trade publications and annual reports. She has done work on assignments in Europe, the Caribbean, and throughout the United States.

Clients include: Allegheny Ludlum Industries, BASF, Corning Glass Works, Fortune, Hublein, Medical World News, Mobil/Tyco Solar Energy Project, Olin, Philip Morris International, Quaker Oats, Raytheon, Time, Xerox.

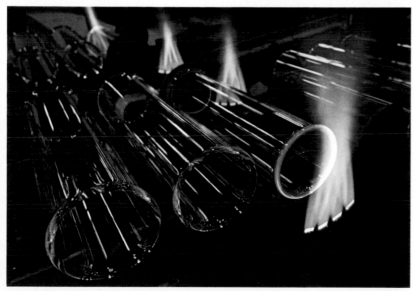

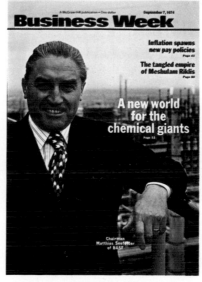

TOM MUSTO

225 South Main Street
Wilkes-Barre, Pennsylvania 18702
(717) 822-5798

New York Representative: James Forrest Smith
(212) 674-5569

To those concerned:
Tom Musto is:

Artistic	Hell-Raising	Rational	
Believable	Interesting	Sometimes Sensational	
Cognizant	Jovial	Tireless	
Demanding	Keen	Unbelievable	
Efficient	Loving	Venerable	
Friendly	Meticulous	Workaholic	
Gutsy	No-Nonsense	X-act	
	Open-Minded	Youthful	
	Practical	Zealous	
	Quick		

These words describe
Tom Musto as an artist with
a camera, and as a friend.

Fredd Orlando
V.P. Senior Art Director
Gann-Dawson, Inc.

DON NICHOLS
1241 University Avenue
Rochester, New York 14607
(716) 275-9666

Representative: Eva Nichols, Don Nichols

Advertising illustration, people,
still life, industrial, annual reports,
landscape/nature, food.

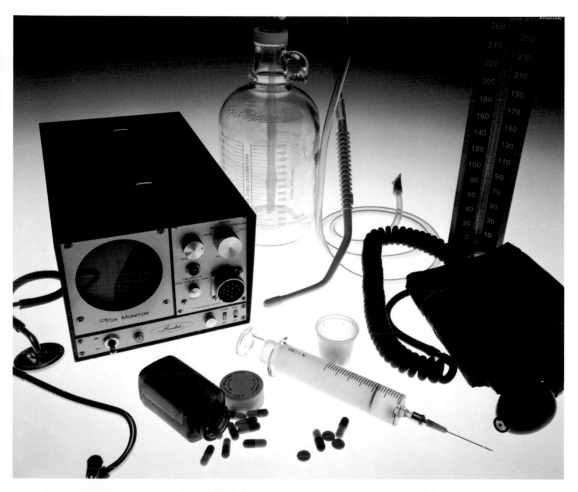

TED POLUMBAUM
Laurel Drive
Lincoln, Massachusetts 01773
(617) 259-8723
Commercial, industrial, editorial photography.
Boston / USA / Abroad

RAYCROFT/McCORMICK

175

9 East Street
Boston, Massachusetts 02111
(617) 542-7229

Advertising, corporate and industrial assignments;
studio and location.

Corning Glass Works, Badger Co., Black & Decker,
GCA Corp., Itek, American Optical, Kneissl, GTE
Sylvania, Gillette, Honeywell, Sail Magazine,
Bristol-Myers, Hilton Hotels, Oceans Magazine,
Copco, Temple-Stuart, Towle Silver, Codman.

Stock photography available.

DAVID SHARPE STUDIO
816 North Saint Asaph Street
Alexandria, Virginia 22314
(703) 683-3773

Located in the Washington D.C. area, David Sharpe
specializes in catalogue, advertising, annual report,
and interior photography with studio space to
accommodate large sets and subjects.

Clients include: AT&T; Kings Dominion; National
Geographic Society; New Republic; The Smithsonian
Catalogue; Time-Life Books; The Washington Star;
Woodward & Lothrop.

ERIK LEIGH SIMMONS
Studio: 259 A Street
Boston, Massachusetts 02110
(617) 367-6655

Advertising, annual report, editorial, industrial /corporate

Boise-Cascade, Case-Hoyt, Damon Corporation, John Deere
& Company, Grumman Aerospace, IBM, Polaroid Corporation,
Rollei of America, S.D. Warren, Scott Paper Company,
St. Regis, Time-Life.

J. MICHAEL SULLIVAN
5003 Cordell Avenue
Washington, D.C. 20014
(301) 986-0161

Represented in Washington by:
Opus Fotografiks
(301) 652-7888

"Last year we advertised in another book…"

BILL WEEMS
2030 Pierce Mill Road NW
Washington, D.C. 20010
(202) 667-2444

Agent: Katie Phelps
The Phelps Agency
32 Peachtree Street NW
Atlanta, Georgia 30343
(404) 524-1234

Annual report, advertising
and editorial illustration.
Excellent with people,
children.

"Bill is one of the
best damn location
photographers any-
where—fun to work
with as well."

All photographs below © Bill Weems 1979

THROUGH A GROUND GLASS LIGHTLY— Let the Viewer Beware

The studio photographer's goal is to make objects look natural—but those of us in the business know how much artifice must necessarily go into each photo. Consider an ad showing a bottle of premium Scotch whiskey that is flanked by a silver water pitcher and an ice-filled tumbler of the spirit.

Since a silver pitcher behaves somewhat like a spherical mirror, the set is "tented" (surrounded with white or black seamless paper) to avoid having the entire contents of the studio reflected on its surface.

A diffused light bank is placed so that the shape of its reflection on the glass and silver objects satisfies my sense of how these materials should be rendered.

An additional masked light source is directed at the label.

Tiny mirrors concealed behind the golden liquor provide backlight to emphasize its transparent color.

The ice cubes are of sculpted acrylic (at $40 each).

A mixture of glycerine and water is sprayed onto the glass to simulate condensation.

By the time the exposure is finally made, the subject lies on an artifical set surrounded by a battery of reflectors, scrims, light sources, etc., and makes sense only from the camera's viewpoint. But the amazing thing about the resulting photograph is that it will be regarded by most people as being completely "natural"—it will look right despite the fact that such a pattern of light and color never occurs in a natural setting.

Am I or any photographer being deceptive by employing these techniques? I think not. When I make studio photographs for advertising or editorial purposes, I am making illustrations. As such, I am hired to use my craft and knowledge to enhance the client's product. In the case of the Scotch ad, I know that refrigerated ice cubes are cloudy, but acrylic cubes are clear. However, if acrylic cubes help produce a more desirable rendering of the liquor, I see no reason not to employ them. Besides, we have become so accustomed to seeing plastic ice cubes in photographs that real ice cubes have begun to look phony.

Which brings me to the one great misconception about photographs that I would like to see put to rest: Namely, the belief that the photo is an authentic document representing TRUTH in and of itself.

Those who cling to this belief deceive themselves. How many photos of ghosts and flying saucers, how many humorous snapshots of buildings "sitting" on human heads like haut couture hats do we need to see before recognizing that photographs are a distortion of the real world, not an unbiased reflection of it?

The fact is that the photographer's mind is behind every image, making choices, manipulating the process to satisfy his own likes, dislikes, and prejudices. This holds true for the photojournalist as well as for the glamour photographer. I feel compassion for the poor soul who blindly believes in the reality of a pin-up model who appears to have gravity-defying breasts that are actually the result of skillfully-applied gaffer tape and retoucher's pink. I scratch my head in wonder at the person who does not recognize that fashion models are freaks who represent only a tiny fraction of the human population, creatures who possess that rare combination of physical characteristics idealized by the fashion world (and its photographers). And finally I must laugh at those who believe that those happy people gracing the picture-gossip mags are interesting, jolly, and in love all the time.

In none of these cases has the photographer deceived anyone, he has just followed his sensibilities in the same way image-makers throughout the history of art followed theirs. I am certain that the average ancient Greek looked no more like a classical sculpture than today's citizens look like our movie stars and cover girls. So, I will continue to make photos which are right for me and for my clients. And I leave it up to the viewer to decide upon the veracity of the "facts" presented in those photographs.

NORMAN SNYDER

"Diet"

Anncr: Stiller and Meara.

S: Hi Honey. What's for dinner?

M: Eight hundred calories.

S: Not again. Last week it was the Siberian Waterskier's Diet...

M: It wasn't easy finding whale meat...

S: What is it this week?

M: The Costa Rican High Jumping Team Regimen.

S: Sylvia, I don't want to win the decathlon, I just want to improve my backhand.

M: Bernard, on this you get your favorite...ribs.

S: Where are they? I'm starving.

M: There, under the pot cheese. You always like something that sticks to your ribs.

S: You call that a rib? It looks like a piece of sugarless gum. What are you having?

M: A crab leg and a brussel sprout.

S: A toast. To all the starving people in suburbia.

M: Very funny.

S: I forgot to tell you. I brought home a little Blue Nun for dinner.

M: You should have phoned ahead. I don't think I have a spare rib for her.

S: No, my sylph, Blue Nun is a wine. A delicious imported white wine.

M: We can't have white wine if you're having meat.

S: Blue Nun is the perfect wine for any meal. It goes as well with my rib as it does with your leg.

M: Does it go with spinach?

S: Of course.

M: Would it go with yogurt?

S: Sure, why?

M: Tomorrow night we're having spinach yogurt.

S: I'll get two bottles.

Anncr: Blue Nun. The delicious white wine that's correct with any dish. Another Sichel wine imported by Schieffelin & Co., New York.

"Airport"

Anncr: Stiller and Meara.

M: Excuse me sir, is this your first flight?

S: How could you tell?

M: Most passengers don't put their heads between their knees before takeoff.

S: I couldn't help it. I glanced out the window and the people below all looked like ants.

M: They probably were ants. We haven't left the ground yet.

M: Like a set of earphones for our in-flight movie, "Death Wish?"

S: I think I'll just read my book.

M: I see you're reading Fear of Flying.

S: So far it hasn't been very instructive.

M: Chapter six will make you fasten your seat belt. May I take your dinner order now, sir.

S: I'll have the Sky Club Steak.

M: And perhaps some wine with your meal?

S: Excellent.

M: We have a little Blue Nun on board.

S: Good, if we run into turbulence would you send her over?

M: No, Blue Nun is a wine. A delicious imported white wine.

S: I can't have white wine with steak.

M: Blue Nun is the perfect wine for any dish. It goes as well with meat as it does with fish.

S: Thank you stewardess. You've really made me feel more secure. There's just one thing.

M: Sir?

S: I wonder if I could have a date.

M: We don't have any dates, sir. Only pears and figs.

Anncr: Blue Nun. The delicious white wine that's correct with any dish. Another Sichel wine imported by Schieffelin & Co., New York.

Finalists
The One Show
Consumer Radio Commercial
Produced for Blue Nun/Schieffelin
  by Della Femina, Travisano &
  Partners Inc.
Copy Written by Helen Nolan and
  Mark Yustein

MICHAEL G. BORUM
623 Sixth Avenue, South
Nashville, Tennessee 37203
(615) 259-9750 (studio)
(615) 794-2758 (home)

Existing photography: The Image Bank
(212) 371-3636

Member ASMP

Advertising and editorial illustration, food and product
still lifes, annual reports, travel, people.

I love technical challenges and pride myself on making
the most of any photographic situation whether on location
or in my well-equipped studio.

FAUSTINO
P.O. Box 1252
Coral Gables, Florida 33134
(305) 854-4275

New York Representative: Noel Becker
150 West 55th Street
New York, New York 10019
(212) 757-8987

Overseas Representative: Image Bank—Worldwide

Extensive experiences in travel and resort location work, underwater, aerials, all types of outdoor location photography.
Well versed in outdoor lighting techniques for fashion and products.

Stock photography available.

Director—Cinematographer

Clients include: Jamaica Tourist Board, CBS Records, Aero Peru Corporation, American Express, Kool Cigarettes (International), Hilton Hotels, National Airlines, Pizza Hut, Hertz, CP Hotels, Holiday Inns, Pepsi-Cola Company, Shell Oil, Princess Hotels International, Eastern Air Lines, Costa Rica Board of Tourism.

BILL HYMAN STUDIOS, INC.
689 Antone Street, N.W.
Atlanta, Georgia 30318
(404) 355-8069

Studio Representative: Lisa Nan

1978 was a good year for us! 1979 was even better! And with such good friends and clients as Adams & Associates; Ad Lanta; BDA; Barclays Bank; Boise-Cascade; Bozell & Jacobs; Campbell-Mithun; Cargill; Wilson & Acree; Case Hoyt-Atlanta; Coca-Cola; Color Graphics; D'Arcy-McManus & Masius Ltd. (London), Days Inns; Dunkin' Donuts; Dymo; Eurasia Ltd.; Evans/Lowe & Stevens; Foote, Cone & Belding; Grumman American Aviation Corp.; Henderson Advertising; Homelite; IBM; J.C. Penney; J. Walter Thompson; Klein-Sieb; Lanier Business Products; Leslie Advertising; Life Insurance Company of Georgia; Liller Neal Weltin; Louis Benito Advertising; McDonald's; Oliver White Associates; Piedmont Aviation; Richway; Saunders Leasing Systems; Sheraton Hotels; STP; Sunkist; Techsonic Industries; and Trane (just to mention a few), 1980 should be incredible!

PARISH KOHANIM
10 Biltmore Place N.W.
Atlanta, Georgia 30308
(404) 892-0099

PARISH KOHANIM
10 Biltmore Place, N.W.
Atlanta, Georgia 30308
(404) 892-0099

Four years in New York and San Francisco. Six years in Atlanta. Major accounts include: IBM, Coca-Cola, Krystal Foods, Kraft, Kentucky Fried Chicken, Delta Air Lines, Monsanto, McDonald's, Max Factor, Georgia-Pacific, Janus Slacks, Fortune, Cosmopolitan, Forbes, Playboy, Time, Business Week.

Products, fashion, people, beauty, studio, and location.

NICK NICHOLSON
1503 Brooks Avenue
Raleigh, North Carolina 27607
(919) 787-6076

121 West 72nd Street, #2 E
New York, New York 10023
(212) 362-8418

Advertising & editorial illustration, travel locations,
leisure activities, industrial, and annual reports.

Existing photography available through the Image Bank:
(212) 371-3636

Member ASMP

THE IMAGE BANK

TRIAD STUDIOS, INC.
Ed Malles-Hugh Hunter
807 9th Court South
Birmingham, Alabama 35205
(205) 251-0651

Eye opening photography for annual reports,
corporate, industrial, trade and consumer ads,
product illustration, editorial, and fashion.

Members ASMP

PHILLIP VULLO PHOTOGRAPHY
565 Dutch Valley Road NE
Atlanta, Georgia 30324
(404) 874-0822
Representative: Jennifer Black

"Polish Man"

When I was a kid in Chicago, I didn't know anything about Poland but I knew everything there was to know about being Polish. My friends were Polish. My neighbors were Polish. I thought everyone in the world must be Polish. Then I started school and I realized that Chicago wasn't a city in Poland, but a city in the United States. That didn't make me like America less, it just made me want to learn something about the place all my family was from. So this year I'm doing something I've planned for 20 years. I'm going to the place I thought I lived in when I was a kid. I'm going back to Poland. For the first time.

Anncr:
There's an airline around–Pan Am–that makes trips like this pretty easy.
With frequent schedules and 747s. And fares and Pan Am tours that can save you a lot of money.
Every American has two heritages. Pan Am would like to help you discover the other one.

Finalists
The One Show
Consumer Radio Commercial
Produced for Pan Am by
    Ally & Gargano, Inc.
"Polish Man" written by Helayne Spivak
"Babe Ruth" written by Tom Messner

"Babe Ruth"

Remember in the World War II movies…in order to trap a spy, they'd ask him who was Babe Ruth.
Of course, the guy wouldn't know, and that would prove he wasn't an American.
Well, that wouldn't work today.
We'd bet there are lots of people in Tokyo or Rome, who know who the third string catcher for the Dodgers is.
If these little trivialities of American life truly are known throughout the world, Pan Am can take a good deal of the credit.
Pan Am music fades in:
Pan Am brings the rest of the world closer to America. And America closer to the rest of the world.
Pan Am goes to 92 cities in 61 countries on 6 continents.
And when we help a business traveler make a meeting somewhere on the other side of the world, we wouldn't be surprised if the conference started out something like this:
Oriental accent: "How did the Mets make out last night?"
Lyric: We're America's airline to the world. Pan Am.

ARNDT & BERTHIAUME
1008 Nicollet Mall
Minneapolis, Minnesota 55403
(612) 338-1984

JON BRUTON
Jon Bruton Studios, Inc.
3838 West Pine Street
St. Louis, Missouri 63108
(314) 533-6665

Contact Judie Drewel

RALPH COWAN
869 North Dearborn Street
Chicago, Illinois 60610
(312) 787-1316

Photographs for Abbott Laboratories, Amphenol, Armour-Dial,
American Can, American Oil, Bang & Olufsen, Chemetron,
Continental Can, Cramer Furniture, Eastman Kodak, FTD Florists,
Greyhound, Hitachi, Howard Paper Mills, S.C. Johnson,
Kellogg, Kimberly-Clark, Massey-Ferguson, Montgomery Ward,
National Sea Products, Nordberg Symons, Ralston Purina,
Sears, Skil, H.P. Smith, Spaulding, Star-Kist, Stow/Davis,
Xcor International and others.

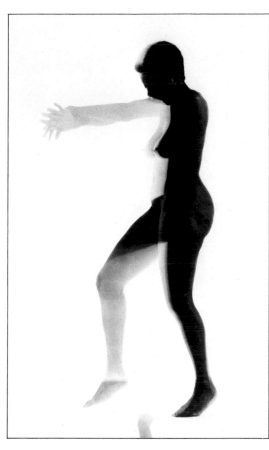

GIANNETTI/HAGEN PHOTOGRAPHY
1008 Nicollet Mall
Minneapolis, Minnesota 55401
(612) 339-3172, 375-1454

Boyd Hagen and Joe Giannetti just wanted me to tell everyone that they've photographed in the arctic and the tropics (and in between); that they have a large comfortable studio in downtown Minneapolis, complete with production staff; that they are just good friends; and that Joe is the one with the beard. Oh, and also that they've worked for:

Time, Newsweek, Business Week, The New York Times, Rolling Stone, McGraw-Hill, Minnesota Mining and Manufacturing (3M), Honeywell, IBM, American Can Corporation, Warner Brothers, Univac, Sperry Rand, Johnson & Johnson, Texas Instruments, The Guthrie Theater, Littman Medical, Beatrice Foods, FMC, Hart Ski Co., Uniroyal, National Coke, Solar Basic Industries, Atcheson Oil, Brown-Boveri, Hoffman-La Roche, WCCO-TV, Winnebago, Toro, Graber, and the St. Paul Companies.

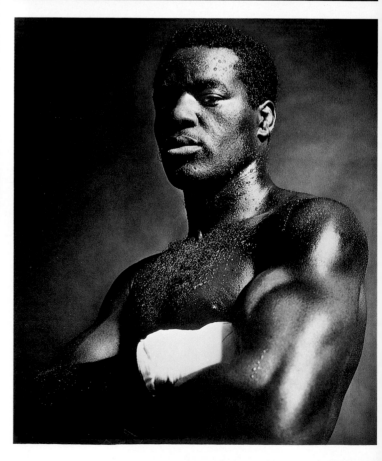

VERN HAMMARLUND
135 Park Street
Troy, Michigan 48084
(313) 588-5533

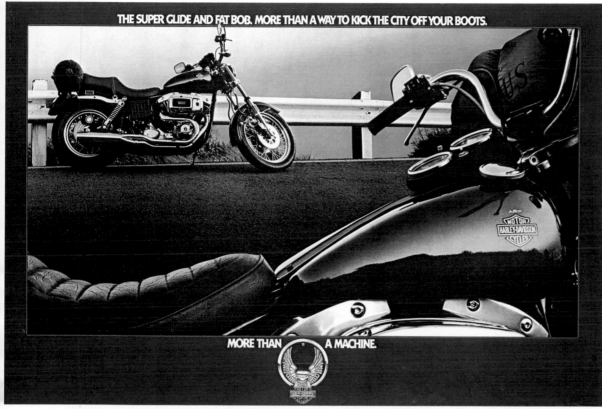

BART HARRIS
Bart Harris Photography, Inc
70 West Hubbard
Chicago, Illinois 60610
Chicago: (312) 751-2977   Los Angeles: (213) 462-1777

Represented by: Sally Murphy

Photographic illustration of people/studio and location.

(1.) G. Reiter/D. Fiesel—Art Institute of Chicago
(2.) M. Winslow—Milk Duds
(3.) R. Bonilla—Gerber Foods
(4.) D. Devary—Dial Soap
(5.) B. Murray/T. Albano—Wolf Brand Chili
(6.) J. Ward—Kellogg's
(7.) R. Deboer—Virginia Slims
(8.) D. Kristofek—Libby Foods

(1.)

(2.)

(3.)

(4.)

(5.)

(6.)

(7.)

(8.)

GEOFFREY HARTIG
Inflight Photography
3620 Pacific
Omaha, Nebraska 68105

Representative: Michael Hartig
(402) 345-2164

Advertising, illustration, editorial and slide presentation.
All the photographs on this page were shot in our studio.
We are also available on location.

RICHARD IZUI
Richard Izui Photography
315 West Walton Street
Chicago, Illinois 60610
(312) 266-8029

PLAYBOY MAGAZINE, MAY 1979

PAT MCDOWELL
Park City Photo
P.O. Box 283
Park City, Utah 84060
(801) 649-9494

Representative: Charlene Walker—Status Gallery
(801) 272-0367

Clients include: United States Olympic Committee, United States Ski Team, Utah Ski Association, Utah Travel Council, Park City Company, Park West Company, Intermountain Skier, Bay Views Publication, The Olympian, Utah Holiday, Skiing Magazine, and Powder Magazine.

RON SCOTT
2636 South Shepherd
Houston, Texas 77098
(713) 529-5868

Please write on company letterhead for
free "Color Sample Book."

Additional published work may be found
in Communication Arts magazine, Volume 19,
Number 4. (The issue with the photo of the
chicken on the cover.) Also see The Art
Annual 1976, 1977 and 1978.

© Ron Scott 1980

MARLON TAYLOR & COMPANY
225 Congress Avenue
Austin, Texas 78701
(512) 478-9301

MARLON TAYLOR SHOOTS PEOPLE. places. and things.

"As you can see, Texas doesn't look like it used to. Call it Texas mystique or Texas chic. Whatever it is, it's that 'look' that we try to capture. If you're looking for oil rigs at sunset, you're better off looking elsewhere. But, if you're looking for the borderline bizarre with a Texas twist, you've come to the right place."

The most innovative photography studio in the Southwest is nine blocks south of the Texas Capitol Building at 225 Congress Avenue in Austin.

LES WOLLAM

4307 Dickason, #217
Dallas, Texas 75219
(214) 521-8038

Having worked both coasts (L.A. & N.Y.),
I find myself in the middle with the
experience and ability to work most
anywhere. Design background and ease with
people produce quality images for corporate,
editorial, and advertising.

Accounts include: American Airlines,
Business Week, Fortune, IBM, Koehring,
Merrill Lynch, MGM, St. Regis Paper,
and Westinghouse.

"Voices"

music:	"Pomp and Circumstance" under first line.
voice:	Every day, millions of people eat their words.
1st voice:	Cheeseburger, medium rare.
2nd voice:	(British accent) A plate of fish and chips, mate.
3rd voice:	Chop suey.
4th voice:	Chopped liver.
5th voice:	Chopped steak.
6th voice:	A sausage, salami, meatball, mushroom, anchovie, pepper pizza.
	Music under V.O. and out.
voice:	Unfortunately, however, things aren't that easy for cats. After all, how many times have you seen a cat go into a restaurant and order a meow to go; or to stay? It is this unfair situation that has given rise to MEOW MIX, the cat food cats ask for by name.
cat:	MEOW.
voice:	Coming right up…now thanks to MEOW MIX cat food a cat can have his meow and eat it too.
cat:	MEOW.
voice:	Take it easy will you. What's more he gets flavors he loves, tuna, liver, and chicken in separate bite size morsels.
cat:	MEOW.
voice:	I heard you the first time…So he gets a mouthful of variety every time he opens his mouth.
cat:	MEOW.
voice:	Once more and I'm going to make you eat those words.
cat:	MEOW…through to end of commercial under V.O.
voice:	MEOW MIX tastes so good cats ask for it by name.

Finalists
The One Show
Consumer Radio Commercial
Produced for Meow Mix by
   Della Femina, Travisano &
   Partners Inc.
Copy Written by Neil Drossman
   and Mark Yustein

"Languages"

V.O.:	We asked cats all over the world what cat food they liked best.
2nd voice:	Pardonnez-moi Monsieur Chat, est ce que…
cat:	Meow.
3rd voice:	(In Chinese, asks cat what cat food he likes best)
cat:	Meow
4th voice:	(In Spanish)
cat:	Meow.
5th voice:	(In German)
cat:	Meow.
6th voice:	(In Italian)
cat:	Meow.
V.O.:	There you have it. Cats the world over ask for Meow Mix by name. Because it's got not one flavor, but three, tuna, liver, and chicken, so they get all the variety they like.
7th voice:	(In Swahili)
cat:	ROAR (African drums in background)
V.O.:	Meow Mix tastes so good most cats ask for it by name.

LARRY ALLAN
P.O. Box 99585
San Diego, California 92109
(714) 270-9549

Representative: The Image Bank
(212) 371-3636

There's a new star in animal photography on the western horizon, "Best-in-Show" winning Larry Allan. Animal portraiture by Allan has appeared in all major dog and cat publications. Allan has produced more covers for Dog Fancy and Cat Fancy magazines in the past year than any other single photographer.

Also note page 66 in "Art Directors' Index to Photographers #6".

Virtually all breeds of dogs, cats and horses on file, plus other animals.

These photographs are unretouched.

ERIK ARNESEN
11 Zoe Street
San Francisco, California 94107
(415) 495-5366

Representative: Peggy Hamik
(415) 421-3422

People, product, location and travel for advertising, annual
reports and corporate multi-media.

Alfa; AVIS, Bank of America, Bennetts, Best Foods,
Coca-Cola, Crown Zellerbach, Dole, FMC, Harrah's Hotels &
Casinos, Jeep International, Kenner Toys, Kingsford
Charcoal, Levi Strauss, Oroweat Foods, PMI, Marriott's
Great America, Seagram, Shaklee, Wells Fargo Bank, VISA.

ALAN BERGMAN
5478 Wilshire Boulevard
Suite 210
Los Angeles, California 90036
(213) 935-2744

Atlantic Richfield, BBDO, Catalina Swimwear,
CBS Records, The Fluor Corporation, Hilton Hotels,
Los Angeles Times, MCA, Merrill Lynch, Rogers &
Cowan, Time Magazine and Universal Studios are
among the satisfied clients who look to ALAN
BERGMAN for their professional photography.

Educated at UC Berkeley and the L.A. Art Center
Bergman's award winning photographs are as diverse,
humorous, sensitive and artistic as the people,
places and products his eye captures.

KEN BIGGS
1147 North Hudson Avenue
Los Angeles, California 90038
(213) 462-7739

Chicago Representative: Jim Christell
(312) 236-2396

Graphic illustration & special effects for advertising and industry.

Abbott Labs, Altec Lansing, American Express, Ameron, Astrodata, Blue Chip Stamps, Carrier Corporation, Carter Hawley Hale Stores, CBS Musical Instruments, Dayline, Flying Tiger Line, Great Western Savings, Handy Dan, Hoffman Electronics, Home Savings & Loan, Hyatt House Hotels, Kawasaki, Kilroy Industries, Morrison-Knudsen, Nikon, Norris Industries, Pan American World Airways, Pertec Corporation, Petersen Publishing, Port of Los Angeles, Singer, Teledyne, Ticor, Transcom Lines, TWA, Western Air Lines, Western Bancorporation, Whittaker, Yamaha & others.

Existing stock pictures:
Design Photographers International
Al Forsyth
521 Madison Avenue
New York, N.Y. 10022
(212) 752-3930

In Los Angeles:
After-Image
Ellen Boughn
6855 Santa Monica Blvd.
Hollywood, California 90038
(213) 467-6033

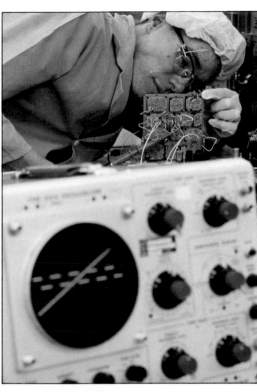

JIM BLAKELEY
520 Bryant Street
San Francisco, California 94107
(415) 495-5100

JIM BRITT
140 North La Brea
Los Angeles, California 90036
(213) 936-3131

Advertising, editorial, photographic illustration, fashion, people. Former assistant Art Director Motown Record Corporation, conceptualized, photographed and designed album covers, 1972-1975.

Head photographer American Broadcasting Companies, Inc. West Coast. Responsible for major photography advertising, public relations, personalities, glamor and sports, 1975-1978.

WOLF von dem BUSSCHE
7144 Norfolk Road
Berkeley, California 94705
(415) 845-2448

Annual reports for over seventy Fortune 500 companies.
Editorial assignments for Time-Life Books, Fortune, and
Life. Represented in permanent collections of museums in
New York, in other U.S. cities, and abroad.

Selected stock through The Image Bank.

See New York Metropolitan Area, page 62

THE IMAGE BANK

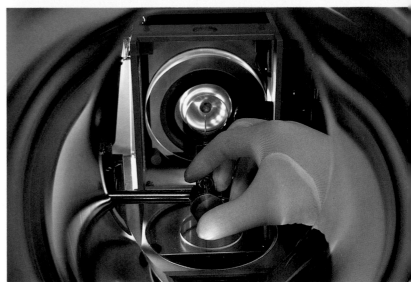

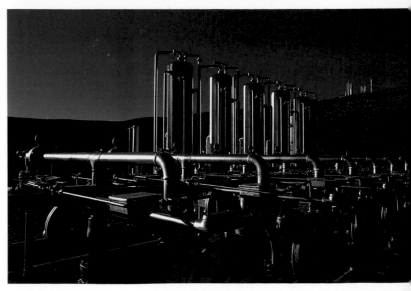

RAY CAROFANO PHOTOGRAPHY
1011¼ West 190th Street
Gardena, California 90248
(213) 515-0310

Representative: Cynthia Mattei
(213) 515-0310

Over 10 years of experience in shooting award winning
ads, brochures and annual reports.

Specializes in: Advertising, product, still life, food,
people, interiors, industrial and aerial.

Partial list of clients includes: Continental Air Lines, Toyota,
Yamaha, Mikasa Dinnerware, Emhart, Upjohn, Xerox, Ansco
Photo-Optical Products, Vivatar and Sizzler Restaurants.

R. CHANDLER STUDIO, INC.
1111 North Tamarind
Los Angeles, California 90038
(213) 469-6205

Representative: Mary Kathleen Fellows
(213) 469-6205

JAMES M. KILKELLY
837 Glenwood Avenue
Minneapolis, Minnesota 55405
(612) 374-1332

KILKELLY

a town in ireland
a photographer

BALTHAZAR KORAB, LTD.
P.O. Box 895
Troy, (Detroit) Michigan 48099
(313) 641-8881

European by birth
American by adoption
Architect by formation
Photographer by choice
Serving the arts, industry,
editorial, corporate and hotel worlds.
Fluent in five languages.

Stylist: Monica V. Korab

Associate photographer: Timothy Hursley

BUCK MILLER
8132 North 37th Street
Milwaukee, Wisconsin 53209
(414) 354-9260

I really don't have a specialty. I like to travel and take pictures. I do editorial illustration in my commercial and advertising work. Some of the people I have worked for are: Quest, Time, Sports Illustrated, Business Week, Universal Foods, Schlitz, Pabst, and Miller Brewing. If I had to describe my work to someone, I would simply say I am a photographer who likes his work.

STEVE NIEDORF
Niedorf Photography
1885 University Avenue, Suite 305
St. Paul, Minnesota 55104
(612) 644-7502

225 West Hubbard
Chicago, Illinois 60610
(312) 329-9358

Tasty. If you had to describe my work in a word, that would be it.
As a food photographer, primarily I approach every shot through the
eyes of a hungry man.

Photography is fun. My one-man campaign to refute the image of
the cantankerous Swede sets the tone at the studio. I've found
that better results and more work can be accomplished in a loose,
fun-oriented atmosphere.

I may grow up someday, but until then I'll continue to like the
people I work with. I may also stop taking $3.00 bills, but no
matter what, I'll be shooting photos that are, ultimately, tasty.

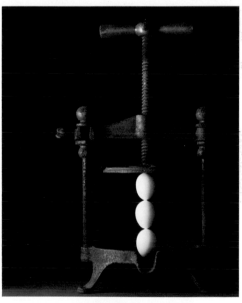

THE PICTURE PLACE
689 Craig Road
St. Louis, Missouri 63141
(314) 872-7506
Jim Clarke

Representative: Jeri Buermann

206

CHARLES SCHRIDDE
600 Ajax Drive
Madison Heights (Detroit), Michigan 48071
(313) 589-0111

One
Charlie Schridde
is worth a
thousand words.
Unfortunately, we haven't got room for a
thousand words. So we can only give
highlights of the Charlie Schridde
Legend. His childhood abduction by a
crazed film salesman. His lifelong fear of
sanity. His successful fight to have his
name changed (to Schridde). And above
all, his great eye (it's four inches across).

But his pictures say it all. See? They
speak of light and mood and tight
deadlines. They speak of everything from
movie stars to sexy cars. And they
whisper TRUTH. Listen. Closely. There!

SCOTT CAMPBELL/BUICK

GENE BUTERA-BOB FORLENZA/CHEVY

GREG HAHN-MIKE SLOAN/LA-Z-BOY

DON STERZIN/GQ

BOB FORLENZA/CHEVY

LARRY SHERIDAN/CHEVY

RICHARD TUNISON
71 East Division
Chicago, Illinois 60610
(312) 944-1188

Agent: Ina Victor
New York City
(212) 737-1722

People and products on location. Extensive site
files plus professional assistants located in various
parts of the country, as well as world-wide, who are
native to the region and assist in location shootings.

"Long Way From Home"

(Music under throughout)

A lot of people come a long way to shop at Barney's.

So when they get back from New York, they bring home more than memories.

A rancher from Nevada brought back seven Lanvin suits.

A Turkish pasha brought home two suits by Oxxford Clothes.

A San Francisco banker acquired a suit and overcoat by Hickey-Freeman.

A Japanese diplomat carried home some English tweeds by Burberry.

And for a basketball player from Bulgaria, it was one dozen Yves St. Laurent shirts.

Barney's. One convenient location at 7th Avenue and 17th Street. New York City.

You see, when you build the world's finest men's store, the word gets around.

Finalists
The One Show
Consumer Radio Commercial
Produced for Barney's by
   Ally & Gargano, Inc.
"Long Way From Home" written by
   David Altschiller and Tom Messner
"Farmers' Almanac" written by Tom Messner

"Farmers' Almanac"

Long before weather satellites even existed in somebody's mind...

Before there were television stations to make stars out of weathermen...

Americans had a very reliable source for long-range weather forecasting: the Farmers' Almanac.

And today in New York, even though few of us need to know what the best day is to plant seed or begin plowing ...the fashion conscious person can make use of the Farmer's Almanac to show him just how valuable Barney's Rainmaker Room is.

Next year, for example, the Farmers' Almanac predicts 74 days of rain...74 times to take full advantage of trench coats by Aquascutum and Burberry.

Enough opportunities to show how Christian Dior, Gleneagles, London Fog, and Giorgio Armani can make you look fashionable even on the stormiest of days.

Not to mention the 291 sunny days when the fashions in Barney's Rainmaker room also shine.

Barney's. 7th Avenue and 17th Street. Free parking. Free alterations. Open 9 am to 9:30 pm. Rain or shine.

CONSTANCE ASHLEY, INC.
2024 Farrington
Dallas, Texas 75207
(214) 747-2501
(212) 228-0900

A good client is worth a thousand words.

Fortunately, we have some very nice ones…and we want more.
Won't you join us?

Beauty, fashion, illustration, advertising, personality studies,
popular posters, retail, catalogue, editorial, video tape.'

We can do it better in Dallas.

NICHOLAS DE SCIOSE
2700 Arapahoe Street
Studio No. 2
Denver, Colorado 80205
(303) 455-6315

Chicago Representative:
Vincent J. Kamin Associates
42 East Superior Street
Chicago, Illinois 60611
(312) 787-8834

New York City Answering Service:
663 Fifth Avenue
New York, New York 10022
(212) 757-6454

From Suitcases and Ski Boots to Pepsi and Playmates. A versatile photographer in the studio and on location who is consistently able to give the highest quality and greatest refinement be it pencils or petroleum.

Clients include: Samsonite, Frontier Airlines, Playboy Enterprises,

Lange, Petro-Lewis Oil Company, Rollei of America, major Architectural Firms, IBM, J.I. Case, Pepsi, Motorola, Aqua Filter, Scott's Liquid Gold, Haugen, Land Development Corporations and Cable TV Companies.

Member ASMP: Contributing Photographer for Playboy Enterprises. Winner of over 100 Major Awards.

Beauty, Fashion, Editorial & Advertising Illustration and Audio-visual productions; experienced location photographer.

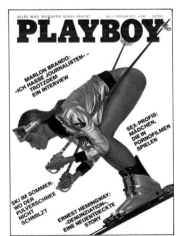

© 1979 PLAYBOY

© 1979 PLAYBOY

212

MIKE KARBELNIKOFF
Karbelnikoff Studios, Inc.
224 North Fifth Avenue
Phoenix, Arizona 85003
(602) 257-9504

Representative: Joe Callahan

Reel available.

JOHN KATZ
1821 West Alabama
Houston, Texas 77098
(713) 522-0180

DON KLUMPP
2619 Joanel
Houston, Texas 77027
(713) 627-1022

Chicago Representative: Clay Timon & Associates
(312) 527-1114

THE IMAGE BANK

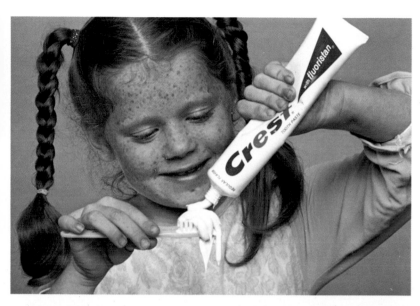

ROBERT KOROPP
1408 Wazee Street
Denver, Colorado 80202
(303) 893-0500

I specialize in fine arts photography and advertising illustration, as well as the blending thereof. If you would like to see more stock or assignment work, please send me a request on your company letterhead.

My fine arts work is all done in signed, limited editions, and any questions or requests for further information should be directed to me at my address. All images on this page, and all my limited editions, are copyrighted.

I have worked for individuals and small corporations as well as for larger ones like Kellogg's, Swift & Co., International Mineral and Chemical, Inland Steel and Pentax, and my photography has won numerous awards for them. I would be pleased to hear from you.

THE IMAGE BANK

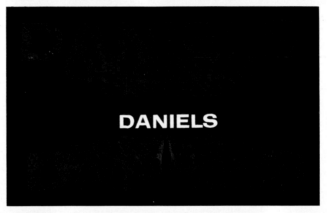

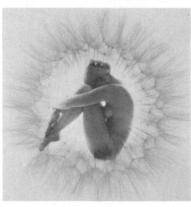

JAMES CHEN
1917 Anacapa Street
Santa Barbara, California 93101
(805) 965-5849

The mind of the interior designer and the camera of James Chen are one and the same.

"In my work, I try to climb inside the designers' minds and imagine the ultimate effect they are striving to create. I look for that special moment when light, color, space, texture and proportion are close to perfection—that is the moment I want to capture."

His clients include many of the world's leading international firms. Assignments take him through the Pacific islands and the Orient as well as the continental United States. His work regularly appears in the finest architectural and interior design magazines. James Chen's record of excellence in photographing interiors has won him a host of other corporate and commercial problem-solving assignments.

No photographer could ever be my friend.

I've been an art director for about 20 years now, and one of the first things I noticed when I started at Smith Greenland was that it was much more fun being taken to a free lunch by a photographer than by the guy who sold us art supplies, let alone a retoucher, not to mention an account executive. The reason it was more enjoyable is simple. Art directors and photographers are trained to see the world in much the same way. A great photographer would make a great art director. And vice versa.

There is no reason in the world, really, why art directors and photographers shouldn't be great friends.

Well, its never worked for me.

The trouble always starts a few weeks after the relationship has blossomed. The guy has shot a few jobs for you. They all turned out great. You looked good. He looked good. The agency looked good. Not only that, he's really a great guy and the two of you have gotten along swimmingly at every lunch and dinner you've shared over the last few weeks.

Then, over a glass of Valpolicella, you ask him if he ever heard of a guy named _____. He all but chokes on his wine and tries in a disinterested way to feign disinterest. "Yeah," he says. "Why do you ask?" "Well, I'm thinking of giving him some work on the next campaign. I wondered what you thought of him."

End of relationship.

It never fails. In a funny way, I can understand it. These guys are really insecure. They don't work for a steady paycheck. They don't know where the next job is coming from. They finally meet an art director who gives them more than one job to do, lulls them into a false sense of security, and then asks what he thinks of _____!

I'm really confused.

I'm not upset if he shoots a job for Doyle Dane. Or Y&R. Or Wells Rich. As a matter of fact I'm flattered. I'm working with a photographer who all those other guys think is terrific. I'm in really good company. Why doesn't he see it that way? It's actually insulting. He's pissed because I put him in the same category as _____.

About a month ago I got a phone call from the only person who has broken my long losing streak. A TV commerical director who has become a really close friend. After working on the first job with this guy, we discovered a similar past. Same school, same age, he used to be an art director, too.

Well, here we go again, I thought. Either I stop giving this guy work and lose a good friend, or I keep him as a friend and simply give him every commercial we ever produce.

Forever.

I opted for the latter, and we began a relationship that saw us through eight 30-second spots and a few lifts.

Well, being the fool that I am, I made a fatal mistake. On the ninth storyboard, I decided to award the job to someone else. I lost my head.

Enter the phone call I received a month ago.

It's Tuesday at 8AM. I'm just stepping out of the shower. I'm feeling great. Jackie, my girl friend, enters the bathroom with the telephone in one hand, and a disturbed look on her usually wonderful early morning face. "It's your friend, _____," she says, "and he seems really disturbed about something." There is no real necessity to get into the details of the call. Suffice to say, my pal was upset. When he got upset, I got upset.

I guess I really had my nerve. I worked with another director on a commercial. To quote my friend, "Not just a commercial," but "the best one you guys did in the last year." "Not only that, I need comedy on my reel." "Not only that, it wasn't a budget job."

Well, the expected didn't actually happen. As I said, we have a very strong friendship. We got past the anger and frustration. We talked for hours about the situation. We explained each others feelings and reasons. We kissed and made up.

We're still great friends.

Until he reads this article.

DENNIS HORLICK
Creative Director
Horlick Levin Hodges Advertising Inc.
Los Angeles

JAMES COLLISON
6950 Hayvenhurst Avenue #108a
Van Nuys, California 91406
(213) 902-0770 (Los Angeles)

Telex 66-2488

New York Representative: Malinda
(203) 227-3933

Beyond the lens and eye are the logistics of
getting things done.

It's problem solving. It's the skill and practice
of decision-making, preparation, timing, dealing
with people and unions, communications and
foreign language. These become an important
part of a track record.

The images here were made on paid assignments.

- An orphan child's trust
- The power between men and helicopter on a
  petroleum pipe project in Borneo
- The fragile Gossamer Condor
- Shiny elegance of product and company logo
- Getting ready with music
- What's going to happen next?
- Desert landsailing in So. California on a
  scorching, 106° day

- Favorite cuddlies of a child
- A Moslem mosque in remote Brunei

When a photographer creates and combines these elements with consistency and excitement, on budget,
you may have discovered an essential part of your own
success team.

All photographs and text © James Collison

Photographic illustration, food, still life.

HANK deLESPINASSE
P.O. Box 14061
Las Vegas, Nevada 89114
(702) 361-6628

New York Representative: The Image Bank
(212) 371-3636

Among the campaigns that Hank has contributed to are: TWA, Lord
Calvert Canadian Whiskey, Eastman Kodak, NBC Radio and Jeep.
His major editorial clients include Sports Illustrated, Time, Sport,
People, and Smithsonian.

"The ordinary becomes extraordinary if you blow it away with perspective and color. What's most important is to read the situation
you're in correctly. I've learned to get it right the first time."

© Hank deLespinasse 1980

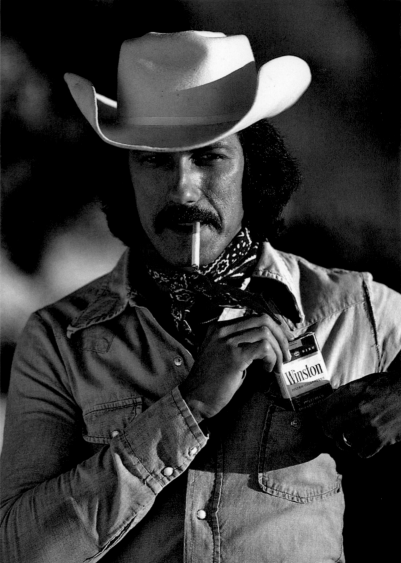

ED DULL PHOTOGRAPHY, INC.
1745 N.W. Marshall Street
Portland, Oregon 97209
(503) 224-3754

CLARK DUNBAR
922 San Leandro Avenue, Suite C
Mountain View, California 94043
(415) 964-4225

Stock Available.

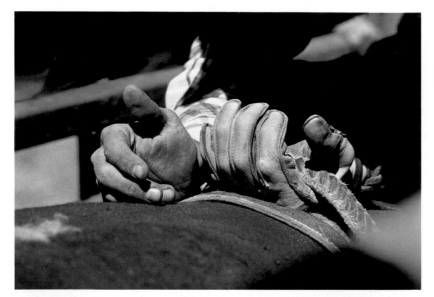

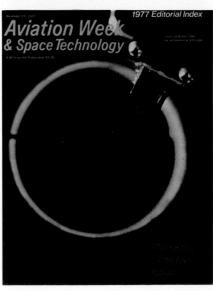

STEVE FUKUDA
2215 Filbert Street
San Francisco, California 94123
(415) 567-1325

ROBERT GARDNER
800 South Citrus Avenue
Los Angeles, California 90036
(213) 931-1108

Representative: Gail

After studying under Melvin Sokolsky, I began my career
on New York's East Side Thirteen years ago.

Presently located in Los Angeles and specializing in fashion
and beauty, still life and food illustration, I have worked
on both coasts for clients such as:

Avon, Chanel, Clairol, Jhirmack, Helena Rubenstein, Jean
Naté, Revlon, Vidal Sassoon, Viviane Woodward, Dipper's
Swimwear, Poppy Swimwear, Sandcastle, Inamori Jewels,
Rolex, Benson & Hedges, Continental Airlines, Volkswagen,
Esquire, Modern Bride, Bazaar, Seagram, Gaetano,

Canadian Lord Calvert, Boodle's, Pepsi Cola, Coca-Cola,
Olga, Vassarette, Rogers, Maidenform, Marantz,
20th Century Fox, General Foods, Nestea, Carnation,
Silverwoods, Harris, J.C. Penney, Bullock's, du Pont Qiana,
Montgomery Ward, Neiman-Marcus, Glenoit, IBM.

Stock photography available through: After-Image
(213) 467-6033

EDWARD GOLDSTEIN
660 Heliotrope Drive
Los Angeles, California 90004
(213) 663-5800

Representative: Susan Kirchmeier
New York City
(212) 758-4242

Special effects, still life, food, industrial design, annual reports.

Each photograph on this page is created by the use of special effects. There is no retouching or airbrushing. All are produced on 4x5 transparency material.

Clients include: 20th Century-Fox; Continental Airlines; McDonald's; Architectural Digest; Bon Appetit Magazine; Merrill Lynch, Pierce, Fenner & Smith, Inc.; National Semiconductor; Computer Automation; Sitmar Cruises; Rolls-Royce; 7 Up; May Co.; Broadway Department Stores, Inc.; J.W. Robinson Co.; Tahiti Tourist Board; Swedish Trade Commissions and more.

DENNIS GRAY
185 Berry Street, # 2860
San Francisco, California 94107
(415) 546-6536

Representative: Sharon Salisbury
(415) 495-4665

DANCER-FITZGERALD-SAMPLE

ROSS DESIGN

SELF-PROMOTION

DAVE HAGYARD
2349 41st Street East
Seattle, Washington 98112
(206) 322-6774

Advertising illustration, fashion,
still life, sports, travel.

Member ASMP

Alaska Airlines
Timetable
Effective January 15, 1979

Ski Eaglecrest - Juneau, Alaska

GEORGE HALL
82 Macondray Lane
San Francisco, California 94133
(415) 776-2643

Specializing in aerial and aviation photography.

Some clients: Goodyear, Pan Am, National Airlines,
Kaiser Aetna, Pacific Gas & Electric, Crocker National Bank,
Hughes Helicopters, Visa.

Over 2500 hours in the air photographing America and Europe
from the Goodyear blimps. Currently shooting all over the
U.S. from a hot-air balloon.

Representation and stock file: Woodfin Camp & Associates
(212) 355-1855.

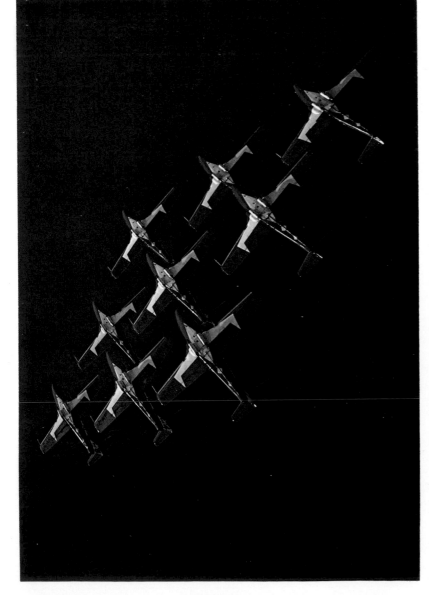

A partial list of our clients in our 35th year:
Foremost Foods Co., Shaklee Corp., E-H International, Del Monte Corp., Jacuzzi Whirlpool,
Oregon Farms, Kaiser, Safeway, Clorox, Bank of
America, Serta, General Motors Corp., Pie,
Shell Oil, Varian Associates, Hewlett-Packard,
Airco Temescal, Flecto, General Electric, Basic
American, and Prescolite.

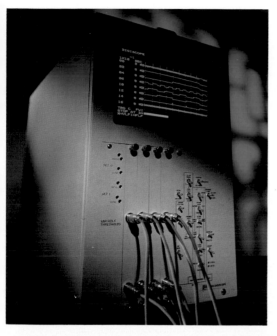

RICHARD HIXSON
333 5th Street
San Francisco, California 94107
(415) 495-0558

Specialty—advertising illustration
Serving the advertising community since 1972.
Member ASMP.

ROBT. SCOTT HOOPER
4330 West Desert Inn Road
Suite "J"
Las Vegas, Nevada 89102
(702) 873-5823

One time ad agency artist and printing company art director.
Now award winning Playboy magazine photographer with advertising, album cover and theatrical experience; specializing
in romantic couples, erotic women and productions. Seeks sensitive, creative art directors and clients for meaningful relationship.
Will travel or meet in Las Vegas.

West Coast Representative: Richard Norris (415) 928-3200

Stock Photography: The Image Bank

CHARLES KEMPER PHOTOGRAPHY
74 Tehama Street
San Francisco, California 94105
(415) 495-6468

Representative: Peggy Hamik
(415) 421-3422

Almaden Vineyards, Armour, Bank of America, Bechtel,
Blitz Beer, California Beef Council, Castle & Cooke
Foods, CBS, Charter Bank of London, Chevron, Cutter
Laboratories, Drake Willock, Jack-In-The-Box, Kim-
berly-Clark, Knudsen, Pacific Telephone, Paul Masson
Wines, Phillips, Pillsbury, Saga Foods, Seagram, Shak-
lee, Smirnoff, Straw Hat Pizza, Sunmaid, Swensen's,
Syntex, Teledyne, United Vintners.

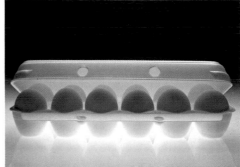

ALAN KROSNICK
215 Second Street
San Francisco, California 94105
(415) 957-1520

Working for major agencies for
the last ten years.

BON APPETIT MAGAZINE

BON APPETIT MAGAZINE

SAGA CORPORATION

CHUCK KUHN
206 Third Avenue South
Seattle, Washington 98104
(206) 624-4706

Stock photography: The Image Bank
(212) 371-4178

Specializing in advertising, corporate, editorial and fashion photography throughout the Northwest including Washington, Oregon, Alaska, British Columbia, Montana and Idaho.

Clients include: Airborne Freight, Alaska Airlines, BankAmericard, Blue Ribbon Sports /Nike, Boeing Commercial Airplane Company, Boise Cascade, Eddie Bauer, Firstbank Mastercharge, Gulf Oil, Hewlett-Packard, Homelite, Kenworth Truck Company, Komatsu, MCA Records, Nordstrom, Olympia Brewing Company, Pacific Northwest Bell Telephone, Puget Sound Power & Light, Roffe Skiwear, Safeco Insurance, the ski, Western Air Lines, Western International Hotels, Weyerhaeuser.

THE IMAGE BANK

HARRY LANGDON
8275 Beverly Boulevard
Los Angeles, California 90048
(213) 651-3212
Representative: Tricia Burlingham

254

SILKS

PERSIS KHAMBATTA

CHER

BONNIE POINTER

MARY-LAURENCE
129 Marguerita Avenue
Townhouse N
Santa Monica, California 90402
(213) 395-1169

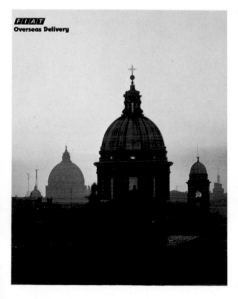

LARRY LEE
P.O. Box 4688
North Hollywood, California 91607
(213) 766-2677
(24 hour recorder)
(805) 259-1226
(Studio and home)

Industrial photography specializing in petroleum, energy,
and environmental subjects. Sharing travel expenses among
many clients keeps national and international assignment
costs to a minimum. Stock photos available.

THE IMAGE BANK

TRANSPORTATION

MANUFACTURING

SEASONS

OFFSHORE

CITIES

DRILLING

REFINERIES

PEOPLE

MINING

TRAVEL

OIL & GAS

MARSHALL LEFFERTS
1050 North Wilcox
Los Angeles, California 90038
(213) 469-6316

Agent: Tom Gilbert
420½ 32nd Street
Manhattan Beach, California 90266
(213) 469-8767

FRED LYON

Industrial Center Building
P.O. Box 836
Sausalito, California 94965
(415) 332-2056

European representative: Rapho
8, rue d'Alger
75001 Paris

Wine, food, travel-advertising, editorial, corporate.
Extensive stock archives.

KEN MARCUS
6916 Melrose Avenue
Hollywood, California 90038
(213) 937-7214

Specializing in illustrative glamour photography. Large fully equipped
Hollywood studio facilities and West Coast locations available.

Best known for his work in Playboy Magazine, Ken has also done
dozens of album covers, annual reports, billboards, magazine
covers, and hundreds of ads.

Clients include: ABC Records, Carnation, Continental Airlines, Inter-
national Industries, Max Factor, Teledyne, Sirena Swimwear, Barco
Uniforms, Basic Foods, Broadway-Hall, Olympus Cameras, Vivitar,
Caribou Records, Universal-MCA Records, Warner Brothers Records, Los
Angeles Magazine, Oui Magazine, Playboy Magazine, Penthouse Maga-
zine, Viva Magazine, Accentuate Swimwear, Ardee Sportswear, Bardon
Shirts, High Tide Swimwear, Tuaca Liqueurs, White Stag Fashions.

ROGER MARSHUTZ PHOTOGRAPHY
1649 South La Cienega Boulevard
Los Angeles, California 90035
(213) 273-1610

Awards:
One Show Gold Award 1976
A.D.L.A. (numerous)
Communication Arts Magazine 1978
Chicago '78
Creativity '78
Western Art Directors Club
    West Coast Show '78
Western Art Directors Club
    West Coast Show '77

Clients:
Allergan, American Moped, Alza, Arden Mayfair, Beckman Instruments, California
Federal Savings, Coldwell Banker, EECO, Elixir Industries, First Los Angeles Bank,
Hewlett Packard, H.F. Ahmanson, Hyland Laboratories, Jack In The Box,
Kal Kan Foods, Mattel, M.C.A., National Airlines Air Freight, National Medical
Enterprises, Neutrogena Corp., Newhall Land and Farming Co., Pro-Cision, Products
Research and Chemical Corporation, RB Industries, Revell, RTD, Santa Anita,
Sears, Roebuck & Co., Shaklee Corporation, Skyways, Smith International,
Southwest Bank, Standard Brands Paint, Taco Bell, Ticor Corporation, Trans America
Insurance, T.R.W., 20th Century Fox, Western Air Lines, Xerox Computer Services.

JIM MILLER STUDIOS, INC.
1122 North Citrus Avenue
Los Angeles, California 90038
(213) 466-9515

Hurry up. And wait.

Summer is its own time in most of the world. But here in the Napa Valley wine country summer is a fidgety, fiddling, waiting, tidying up, pregnant, getting-ready time. Before the harvest, before the crush, before Autumn.

In the vineyards, the workers tie, thin and cultivate. The work is hot, hotter, hottest.

Up behind Beringer's Rhine House-in the caves the Chinese workmen carved a hundred years ago-our '77 Chardonnay snoozes the summer away in small oak barrels. We'll let it rest there through winter and bottle it next February.

Five miles south, near Rutherford, just before you get to Beaulieu Vineyards and

Inglenook, we spend the morning walking through eighteen acres of twenty-two year old Cabernet Sauvignon vines. We have no reason for being there. Chalk it up to parenthood.

July warms up to August. The grapes draw in the heat and answer with their first hint of color. One day a morning fog stays for lunch and the winemaster smiles. Coolness brings acidity to the grapes. Acidity promises complexity. And complexity is the soul of wine.

There's a Sunday evening concert at Robert Mondavi's place. Bring your own picnic. Jazz for dessert.

Tomorrow, the pace will quicken. There are tanks to clean, gondolas to paint, machinery and people to be choreographed. (We make wine elbow to elbow here. There are more than fifty wineries in the Napa Valley.)

But tomorrow will get here without our help. Tonight we laugh and talk and eat until the moon and the crickets and the music shush us into silence.

Waiting isn't all bad.

Beringer. One hundred and two years at the same address: St. Helena, Napa Valley, California.

DAVID MUENCH
David Muench Photography, Inc.
P.O. Box 30500
Santa Barbara, California 93105
(805) 967-4488

The American Landscape...mountain, desert, coastal,
forest and prairie...its wild beauty. For advertising,
annual reports, books, editorial, prints and calendars.

Innovative seeing with 4" x 5" format camera and 35mm.
Photography collection in color and black and white.
Personally illustrated over fifteen exhibit format
nature books. David's work is sensitive to the natural
rhythms and pulse, light, spatial forms...the mysterious.

TOMAS O'BRIEN
450 South La Brea Avenue
Los Angeles, California 90036
(213) 938-2008

While food is Tom's specialty, he also takes a tasteful approach to travel, editorial, people and product assignments. Perhaps his clients will give you even more food for thought: Allergan Pharmaceuticals; AMF Voit Sporting Equipment; Asahi, Tecate and Watney's Imported Beers; Calavo Avocados; Continental Air Lines; Hughes Aircraft; Hunt-Wesson Foods; Jolly Roger Restaurants; Knudsen Corporation, Dairy Division; Love's Barbecue Restaurants; Mattel Toys; Nestle Company; Ore-Ida Foods; Pacific Southwest Airlines; Pfeiffer Foods; Pioneer Chicken; Smith International Tools; Star-Kist Foods; Western Air Lines; and Yamaha International Corporation.

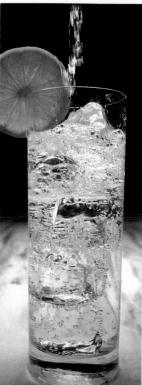

NICK PAVLOFF
Box 2339
San Francisco, California 94126
(415) 989-2664

Editorial / annual reports

Assignments completed for:
Amfac, Business Week Magazine, Crocker Bank,
Del Monte Corporation, Dillingham, Dymo
Industries, Foremost-McKesson, Fortune
Magazine, Pacific Telephone, Parcourse Ltd.,
Rand Information Systems, Saga Foods,
Smithsonian Magazine, United Airlines,
Wells Fargo Bank.

THE COMBINATION
OF THE SPIRIT, SKILLS,
TALENTS AND
DEDICATION OF THE
PEOPLE OF AFPC
FORM THE REAL
FOUNDATION UPON
WHICH THE SUCCESS
AND INTEGRITY OF
THIS COMPANY
DEPEND.

BOB PETERSON PHOTOGRAPHER
1220 42nd Avenue East
Seattle, Washington 98112
(206) EA9-2299

Photojournalistic approach to advertising,
annual reports, and corporate brochures.

THERE IS NO FINISH LINE.

Sooner or later the serious runner goes through a special, very personal experience that is unknown to most people.

Some call it euphoria. Others say it's a new kind of mystical experience that propels you into an elevated state of consciousness.

A flash of joy. A sense of floating as you run.

The experience is unique to each of us, but when it happens you break through a barrier that separates you from casual runners. Forever.

And from that point on, there is no finish line.

You run for your life. You begin to be addicted to what running gives you.

We at Nike understand that feeling. There is no finish line for us either. We will never stop trying to excel, to produce running shoes that are better and better every year.

Beating the competition is relatively easy.

But beating yourself is a never ending commitment.

Beaverton, Oregon

What a bank robbery looks like up close.

$1,000 reward.

Rat on a rat. 1-800-552-7595

Physio-Control Annual Report 1973

KEN ROGERS
P.O. Box 3187
Beverly Hills, California 90212
(213) 553-5532

Corporate, advertising and editorial.

I am a visual interpreter for my client. Often I must
take an abstract verbal idea and change it into a precise
visual solution.

I did it for Saul Bass on AT&T.
I did it for BBDO on Chrysler.
I did it for Needham, Harper & Steers on Phillips.
I did it for Time magazine on personalities.
I did it for Life magazine on action and architecture.
I did it for...
What can I do for you?

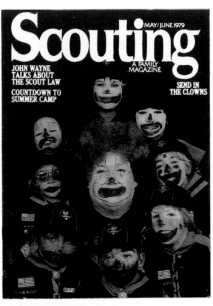

KEN ROGERS
P.O. Box 3187
Beverly Hills, California 90212
(213) 553-5532

Rogers was a big city boy with big-eyed dreams that eventually led him and his cameras to the more seductive scent of the great outdoors. He became fascinated with the evanescent spirit of adventure in an increasingly leisure-oriented society. He identified with the rugged individualists willing to go one-on-one against both their environment and themselves.

"In my photography, I'm trying to convey the physically artistic beauty of what's happening in these very personal situations, along with the excitement," he says. "I'm looking for strong design. I'm selling romance. Anyone can record a sport. I want to get the feel, the high of what a particular activity is all about."

"I photograph the terror of sound and the beauty of silence."

California Living Magazine, May 1978

Write to me on your letterhead for a free color action portfolio.

HOW A PHOTOGRAPHER GOT THE GIRL BUT NOT THE PICTURES!

Whenever I go on a location shoot for a week or more, one of the most important things I look for in a photographer is compatability. His creative talent should be a given. And, of course, I have to trust the guy to deliver, because location shoots, and reshoots, are expensive.

So let me tell you a funny experience that actually happened to an art director friend of mine. It's funny only to me, because it almost cost my friend his job.

One account this agency art director worked on was a steamship passenger line that had regular cruise service to the South Seas. The existing photographs were all out of date, so the A/D convinced the client to send him and a photographer on a cruise to Tahiti for new photographs. This would be a fun shoot.

He picked a really good photographer, a dependable straight shooter who was also a non-drinker, non-smoker, and happily married with four kids.

The first day out, they toured the ship and plotted a shooting schedule. The photographer was very organized and seemed to have things in order. The A/D felt relaxed and confident that he had chosen the right guy. They would start shooting pictures the next day.

That night after dinner, they were watching the Polynesian entertainers. Suddenly one of the dancers did the Tahitian hula right in front of the photographer's face. There was no mistaking the photographer's look of lust!

The next morning the A/D found the photographer taking hula lessons from Tamera, the lovely young thing from the night before. When asked to take pictures, the photographer said he needed to get the feel of what was happening aboard ship first!!! The A/D felt a twinge of doubt in the pit of his stomach.

At a champagne party that night, the photographer did take a few pictures of passengers being greeted by the captain. He also took a glass of champagne—the first of his life. He took another. He stopped taking pictures. Then he started dancing the hula with Tamera. The A/D had a sinking feeling when Tamera and photographer left the party arm-in-arm.

There were no more pictures taken by that photographer. Blasted by Mai Tais, he danced the cruise away with Tamera. He even flung one of his cameras into the sea.

The A/D was desperate. He needed pictures or else…He really felt his job was at stake. So he got into the photographer's stateroom, salvaged the remaining cameras and took the pictures himself.

When the ship arrived at Tahiti, the derelict photographer disappeared into the coconut trees with Tamera, never to be seen or heard from again! So much for dependable photographers…

Five years later my agency secured the account!! The pictures were old and not too good!! So a photo cruise to Tahiti was set up for me! My boss called me into his office to remind me how important it was to choose the right location photographer for this cruise.

I guess he wasn't worried about me. Tsk, Tsk!

But that's another story.

A. GIG GONELLA
Senior V.P. Creative Director
Dancer Fitzgerald Sample, Inc.
San Francisco

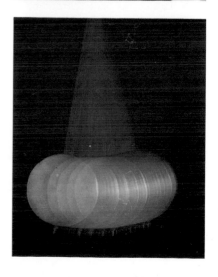

SILVERMAN STUDIOS

Jay Silverman, Inc.
1039 South Fairfax Avenue
Los Angeles, California 90019
(213) 931-1169

Representative: Laurie Lund

Advertising and editorial illustration, fashion, annual reports, still life, beauty and people.

Two superbly equipped studios, with clients like: Max Factor, M.C.A., Playboy Magazine, T.R.W., T.V. Guide, Teak, Security Pacific National Bank, Bekins, Capitol Records, Vidal Sassoon, Pentel Pen, Fisher Components, Arrowhead Puritas Waters, Inc., Dataproducts, Kahlua Liquor, Knudsen, American Savings & Loan Association, Brown Jordon, Winchell's Donut Houses, Redken Labs., Hershey, Mazda, Suzuki, Datsun, Air Micronesia, Oster Corporation, Continental Air Lines, General Mills, Sapporo Beer, Hitachi Stereo, Marantz Company, CBS & Coca-Cola...

SILVERMAN STUDIOS
Jay Silverman, Inc.
1039 South Fairfax Avenue
Los Angeles, California 90019
(213) 931-1169

Representative: Laurie Lund

Advertising and editorial illustration, fashion,
annual reports, still life, beauty and people.

SJEF'S FOTOGRAPHIE

2311 Northwest Johnson Street
Portland, Oregon 97210
(503) 223-1089

European representative: Roel Hessel Design
Langs de Baan 40
Uithoorn, N.H. The Netherlands
02975-62553

Credentials: Masters in Still Photography;
B.A. in Motion Picture/Video; B.A. in Art
Direction; Producer/Director, National T.V.
Commercials; Numerous Awards; 15 years
experience.

Specialties: Illustration, landscape, still
life, fashion, people, annual report.

Services: Styling, make-up, location scouting, motion picture
production, research in related fields, rental of antique cars for
props, sailboat chartering in northwest waters for photography
and propping, 7000 square feet of studio space.

Clients include: Alaska Airlines, Georgia-Pacific, Boise Cascade,
Freightliner Trucks, White Stag Manufacturing, Pendleton Woolen
Mills, Jantzen Inc., Estee Lauder, Tektronix Inc., Trailways,
Amsterdam Concertgebouw Orchestra, Omark Industries,
Peterbilt Trucks, Colgate-Palmolive of Europe, Blitz Weinhard Co.,
Oregon Rainbow Magazine, United Vintners, Oregon Dairy
Products Commission.

SCOTT SLOBODIAN PHOTOGRAPHY, INC.
6630 Santa Monica Boulevard
Hollywood, California 90038
(213) 464-2341

Representative: Barbara Slobodian
(213) 935-6668

A full-service West Coast studio specializing in
advertising and annual reports.

CHRISTOPHER SPRINGMANN
185 Berry Street
San Francisco, Caifornia 94107
(415) 663-8428

Corporate, annual reports, editorial illustration.

Clients include: AT&T, Avon, The Continental Group,
Crown Zellerbach, Eaton, Foremost-McKesson, IBM,
Polaroid, Shell, SOHIO, Standard Oil of California,
Union Oil, Xerox.

Consumer magazines include: Business Week, Forbes,
Fortune, GEO, Life, Money, National Geographic,
Newsweek, Smithsonian, Sports Illustrated, Medical
Economics and Medical World News.

SMITHSONIAN

VOLKSWAGEN OF AMERICA

ERNST AND ERNST

EATON/CUTLER-HAMMER

TED STRESHINSKY
50 Kenyon Avenue
Kensington, California 94708
(415) 526-1976

Mail: P.O. Box 674
Berkeley, California 94701

New York Representative: The Image Bank
(212) 371-3636

Travel, advertising, corporate
and editorial assignments.
Stock photos.

© Ted Streshinsky, 1979

RAY STRYKER
3763A Army Street
San Francisco, California 94110
(415) 285-6526

Corporate/annual reports,
advertising/editorial and
industrial illustration,
music, travel, specializing
in location photography.

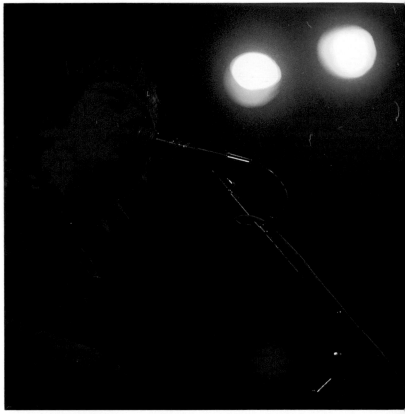

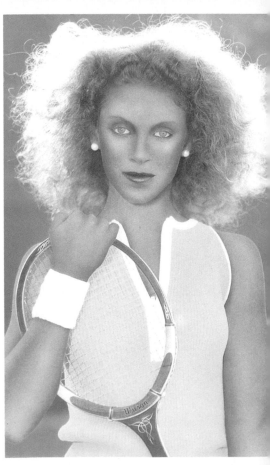

HARALD SUND
5330 39th Avenue, Southwest
Seattle, Washington 98116 USA
(206) 932-1120

Worldwide travel for corporate/industrial,
advertising and editorial photography.

Voyages dans le monde entier pour les
entreprises, l'industrie, la publicité et
les journaux.

Reisen in der ganzen Welt für
Unternehmen und Industrie, Fotos
für Werbung und Zeitungen.

© Harald Sund, 1979

WALTER SWARTHOUT STUDIOS
370 Fourth Street
San Francisco, California 94107
(415) 543-2525

San Francisco Representative: Ron Sweet
(415) 433-1222

Southern California Studio:
7207 Melrose Avenue,
Los Angeles, California 90046
(213) 934-8214

Los Angeles Representative: Patricia Stevens
(213) 934-8214

New York Representative: Jane Mautner
(212) 777-9024

The following pictures were "pulled" from a two week shooting on location for a major California wine maker.

JOHN TERENCE TURNER

173 37th Avenue East
Seattle, Washington 98112
(206) 325-9073

Occasionally located in Sun Valley, Idaho
from December through March (use Seattle
telephone number). Studio in Seattle.

Areas of specialization: industrial, annual reports,
sports (tennis, running, skiing, sailing, climbing),
fashion and editorial. Widely travelled on assignments
in the Orient, South America and the Caribbean. Formerly
fluent in Spanish. Numerous awards for annual report,
corporate brochure, sport and advertising photography.

Stock photos: The Image Bank

Clients include: AMF Head, Airborne Freight, BASF, Bayliner
Corporation, Eddie Bauer, Inc., Carnation Company, Cummins
Engine Company, Demetre Sweaters, Diet Pepsi, Dow Pharmaceutical,
Dynastar Skis, EIR Sweaters, Flying Dutchman Yachts, GUTS
(General Universal Training Supplies), Gore-Tex, Hughes Airwest,
Kenworth Trucks, K2 Corporation, KING Broadcasting Company,
Liberty Bell , Merchant du Vin, Nike Athletic Shoes, O'Brien
Water Skis, Olympia Brewing Company, The Peace Corps, Rainier
National Bank, Rossignol Ski Company, Seattle First National Bank,
SERAC, Sportcaster, Sports Illustrated, Tennis Trail, Tollycraft Corporation,
Trailwagons, Scott U.S.A., the ski company, Spademan Release Systems,
Sun Valley Company, United Air Lines, The Weekly, World Pro Skiing.

THE IMAGE BANK

SCOTT U.S.A./SUN VALLEY, IDAHO

THE WEEKLY/SEATTLE

GUTS/SEATTLE

NIKE/LAS VEGAS

CUMMINS/SNOQUALMIE, WN.

AIRBORNE/BANGKOK, THAILAND

CUMMINS/DUNLAOGHAIRE, IRELAND

WILLIAM JAMES WARREN
William James Warren & Associates
509 South Gramercy Place
Los Angeles, California 90020
(213) 383-0500

EXPERIENCE: people, products and places incisively portrayed throughout
15 years of annual report, magazine and multi-media assignments.

ATTRIBUTES: versatility, speed and improvisation combined with sensitivity,
selective vision and a faculty for self direction. Fluent in the languages
of design, business and technology. As adept with hand-held available
darkness as with large format, as deft with black and white as with color.

PERFORMANCE: tenacious and unflappable, thrives on the fullest
itinerary of flights, locations and challenging visual problems.

Black and white portfolio and resume on request. © William James Warren, 1979

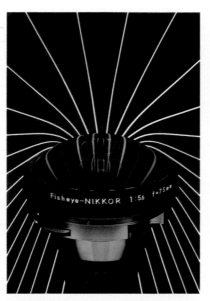

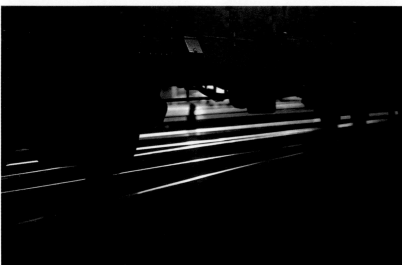
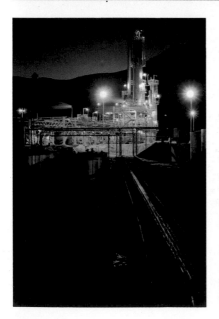

DALE WINDHAM
1008 Western Avenue
Seattle, Washington 98104
(206) 622-7474

Representative: Pat Hackett
2214 Second
Seattle, Washington 98121
(206) 623-9459

DICK ZIMMERMAN
8743 West Washington Boulevard
Los Angeles, California 90230
(213) 204-2911

Represented by: Laird Taylor Fleming
(213) 784-5814

Specializing in fashion and beauty,
character illustration and "people."

Studio and location. All format cameras.
Very large studio space. All facilities.

Stagelight
candlelight
camplight
spotlight
twilight
roomlight
carnival light
stadium light

**The Kodak
Ektramax camera
shoots just about
anything your
eye can see.**

In almost any light, the Kodak Ektramax camera can take pictures without flash! With its fast
f/1.9 lens and 400-speed film the Ektramax
camera can take pictures in light as low as candlelight. And when you want it, the Ektramax
camera has a built-in electronic flash that stops
the fastest action cold.
   In daylight, low light or any kind of light,
Ektramax is the camera for
you. Ektramax...the ultimate
"Can-Do" camera from Kodak.

DICK ZIMMERMAN
8743 West Washington Boulevard
Los Angeles, California 90230
(213) 204-2911

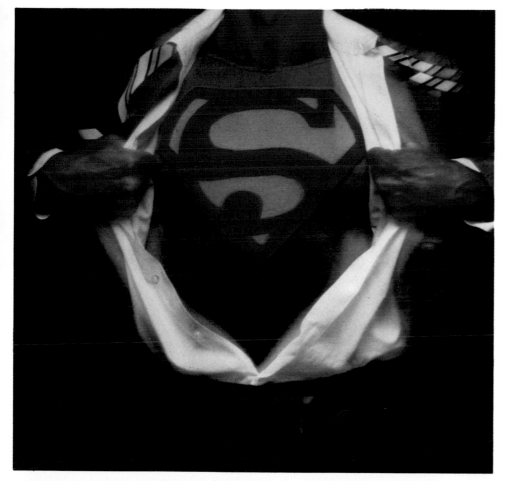

A revelation has come to me recently. I now realize that there is a vast herd of talented, gifted and/or creative people out "there." Of that herd, many are not only in competition with you and me, but they can draw better, think better and most likely tell a joke better. It's a frightening vision. You could even become insecure as hell!

However, of all these competitors, only a small group seems to get to the top and stay there. Wonder why? I think it's because the good ones, the real professionals, are mindful that there's more to solving a client's problem than creating a pretty picture or layout. They know that phone calls must be returned, appointments kept and at least a moderate level of moral and business ethics should be maintained. They get up and at the day, every day.

Most importantly, when they accept an assignment they follow it through! All assignments are not exciting, but the good guys (good persons just doesn't work) know they are part of a process and cheerfully accept it. And they deliver. They are <u>professional</u>!

The rest of the herd is just hanging on.

So that's my big revelation.

JERRY DEMONEY
Design Director
Mobil Oil Corporation
New York City

"Peru's Golden Treasure"

(Rod Serling type voice—soft but dramatic
SFX: Simple, dramatic horn/percussion music background)

You're in a room filled with gold.
Your heart beats fast.
There's no way to prepare yourself for the splendor—
all that's left of 5 great civilizations,
2000 years of wealth and power.
The gold of Peru—never made into anything as ordinary
as money—this is but a sample of gardens of gold,
golden suns and unbelievable golden temples.
Most of them lost—only the tales of their beauty remain
—and this room.

You can see crowns, swords, jewelry and golden figures
more delicate than any other in the world.
Gilded masks, a Jaguar statue and gloves of purest gold.
"Peru's Golden Treasures" will be on view at the American
Museum of Natural History, Central Park West at 79th Street,
through January 15th, open daily and Wednesdays until 9 p.m.
Whatever you've heard about it
cannot compare to what you'll see.

Gold Award Winner
The One Show
Public Service Radio—Single Commercial
Produced for American Museum of
    Natural History by Ogilvy & Mather Inc.
Copy written by Richard Pels

AFTER-IMAGE, INC.

6855 Santa Monica Boulevard, #402
Los Angeles, California 90038
(213) 467-6033

Representative in Japan: Imperial Press
Dave Jampel
Roppongi Plaza
1-1-26 Azabudai
Minato-ku, Tokyo
106 Japan
Telephone: 585-2721/2, 585-2562

Representing the files of forty-five major photographers in the areas of agriculture, fashion, sports, people, scenics, nature and industry. Our goal is to locate the photo you need—not to fit your need to our file. The photos below are presented for your pleasure by Tom & Michelle Grimm, Gus Gregory, Ken Biggs, Ken McVey, John Running, Leonard Nadel and Michael Going. Nice, aren't they?

PETER ARNOLD, INC.
The International Photo Agency
1500 Broadway
New York, New York 10036
(212) 840-6928

Cable: Arnoldfoto, New York
Telex: 428281

We represent leading nature and wildlife
photographers from the U. S. and Europe.

The photographs shown (clockwise from top left):

    hummingbird moth by Hans Pfletschinger
    walrus, Alaska by Stephen J. Krasemann
    young wood owls by Hans Pfletschinger
    dewdrops by Hans Pfletschinger
    life under the oil rig by Bob Evans

In addition we stock color and black and white
on the following subjects:

    Abstracts, anthropology, family & children,
    human interest, kinetic light designs, photo-
    micrography & scanning electron micrography,
    sports (professional & recreational), travel
    & foreign cultures, underwater....and much more.

Call us for stock or assignment.

PETER ARNOLD, INC.
The International Photo Agency
(212) 840-6928

We also represent photographers who explore new frontiers
where art and science meet:

Manfred Kage: Photomicrography (Biomedical, botany, chemistry,
electronics, geology) scanning electron micrography in color, kaleidoscope, kirlian, science fiction
and video art.

David Scharf: Scanning electron micrography in black and white
(See American Showcase, Volume I, page 173)

Call us for stock or assignment.

All photographs on this page by Manfred Kage.

HIPPURIC ACID CRYSTALLIZED 120 X

RADIOLARIAN SKELETON—SEM COLOR 1000 X

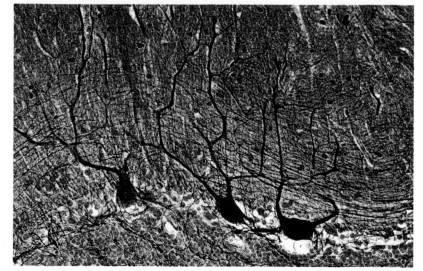

PURE ALUMINUM RECRYSTALLIZED—SEM COLOR 510 X

NERVE CELLS IN HUMAN BRAIN—250 X

Camera 5 represents 15 photographers in the following cities: New York, Boston, Washington, Miami, Chicago, St. Louis, Santa Fe, Denver, and Los Angeles. Our strong points include annual reports, editorial, sports, food, travel, advertising, fashion, people, and photojournalism. In addition to accepting both studio and location assignments, we have a stock library in excess of 1,000,000 color and black and white photos.

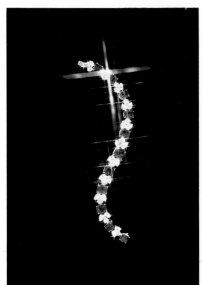

BRUCE COLEMAN INCORPORATED/NORMAN OWEN TOMALIN
381 Fifth Avenue
New York, New York 10016
(212) 683-5227

Telex: 429 093

Bruce Coleman Limited
16a Windsor Street
Uxbridge, Middlesex, England
Uxbridge 32333
Telex: 932 439

Classic stock and innovative original color
photography from a 'bevy' of talented photographers.
Every conceivable subject, in color, on file.
CONTACT US, WE STOCK THE BEST.

NO.227989© 1973 WEDIGO FERCHLAND

NO.293798© 1978 WEDIGO FERCHLAND

NO.084700© 1979 FRANK W. LANE

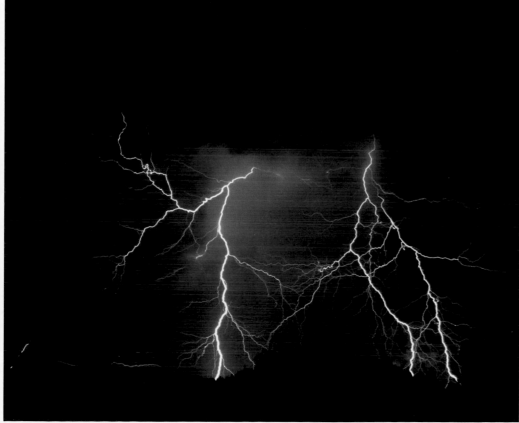

NO.308183© 1979 BARRY PARKER

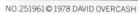

NO.251961© 1978 DAVID OVERCASH

NO.261766© 1978 FRITZ PRENZEL

222 East 46th Street
New York, New York 10017
(212) 661-6860

Stock photography and assignments covering all..
spectator…leisure…unusual sports.

You've seen our images…now you know our name.

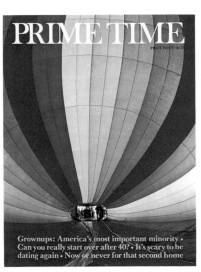

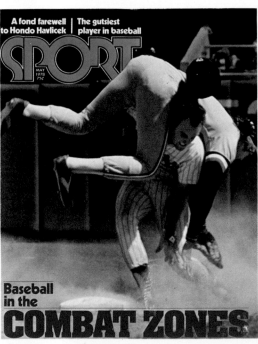

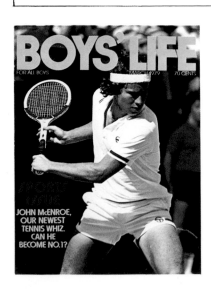

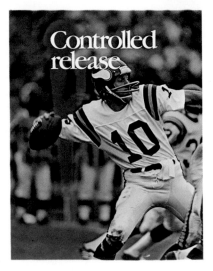

LENSMAN
1560 Wisconsin Avenue
TH No. 3246
Washington D.C. 20007
(202) 337-8014
(212) 724-6229 (local New York number)

Stock Photos—on any subject
Assignments—in any location
Archival Photos
Picture Research

H. Francis Lubbe—Director of Sales/Assignments
Vicki L. Peterson—Director of Sales/Stock Photos
Frances C. Rowsell—Photo Researcher

SISSI BRIMBERG

ROBERT MADDEN

BARRY BLACKMAN

SIMPSON/FLINT

BENSON GINSBURG

JAYBEE

BARRY BLACKMAN

COTTON COULSON

THE WONDERFUL WORLD OF "CORPORATE" PHOTOGRAPHY

They seem to be two different worlds, a few times removed by prejudice and/or envy: advertising photography and "corporate" photography.

Some ad agency art directors have already discovered that annual reports are a valuable source of ideas, and they swipe art from them often. I've occasionally recognized my photographers' creations in the layouts of art directors I am visiting. As a matter of fact, we just completed a national campaign for a major cigarette account, inspired by one of our "corporate" photographs published ten years ago.

For photographers and their representatives, on the other hand, the rush has been on for some time to get into the gold fields of big business corporate communications.

In most companies the annual report is the most important publication. Some of the brightest and most creative minds work on this project for up to six months—and often begin thinking about how to improve next year's report before this year's is on the presses. Some of these annual reports have photography budgets alone of $15,000 to $30,000. Designers may get fees exceeding $50,000.

Since 1941, publicly owned companies have been required to publish annual reports and file them with the Securities and Exchange Commission. In the beginning, the reports were only the required facts and figures. In the mid-fifties major corporations began publishing beautiful, magazine-type color brochures. By the mid-sixties, every company worth its shareholders got into the competitive act, and annual reports became more and more elaborate, full of beautiful pictures that functioned as ads for the effectiveness of the company and the desirability of its products. Annual reports were entered into competitions staged by financial magazines, paper companies, art director clubs and printers.

As there are bad ads and great ads, there are terrible annual reports and works of art. Even some of the smaller corporations are known to publish annual reports with some of the most imaginative and innovative photography.

The rates paid to top photographers for this work, $1,200 to $2,000 per day, are higher than many fees for advertising photography. Some photographers are in such high demand that clients rush to sign them up two and three months in advance. And these photographers love the work, because of its relative freedom to create (rather than to duplicate) a layout.

In corporate photography the creative process is often much simpler, more direct and usually involves the photographer much sooner: when the picture ideas are being developed. Sometimes the photographer—within a given idea, desired style and feeling—has all the freedom of expression that he or she has ever dreamed about. Far fewer executive nods are needed, because the chain of approval or rejection is much shorter as a rule.

If you want to obtain annual reports, which are always free, contact a stock broker, call a few companies for them, or respond to the newspaper ads offering them each Spring. Then you'll open the door to the world of corporate photography and see, in the best of them, some truly exciting ways to photograph products, facilities, and employees.

URSULA G. KREIS
Photographers Representative

TRW INC.

T/M 3176
23555 Euclid Avenue
Cleveland, Ohio 44117
(216) 383-3176

Gary L. Kious,
Manager of Visual Communication
Los Angeles, California
(213) 536-4880

As a public service TRW Inc. offers transparencies to magazine, newspaper, textbook and other publication editors as illustrative matter for an appropriate credit line. Advanced technology products and services covered include spacecraft, microelectronics and electronic components, computers and software, advanced energy systems concepts, automotive and aircraft parts and metalworking.

BILL JAMES

LOU ARBOLIDA

LAWRENCE MANNING

GARY KIOUS

KEN MONTGOMERY

WOODFIN CAMP AND ASSOCIATES
415 Madison Avenue
New York, New York 10017
(212) 355-1855
Cable: Campfoto, New York
Telex: 428788 Campfot

Woodfin Camp, Incorporated
925½ F Street, N.W.
Washington, D.C. 20004
(202) 638-5705
Cable: Campfoto, Washington, D.C.

Associate offices in London, Paris, Hamburg, Milan, and Tokyo.

We represent 25 major photographers around the world.
Contact us for comprehensive stock files or original assignment work.

©ROBERT AZZI 1979

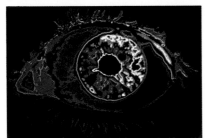

©HOWARD SOCHUREK 1979

©JONATHAN BLAIR 1979

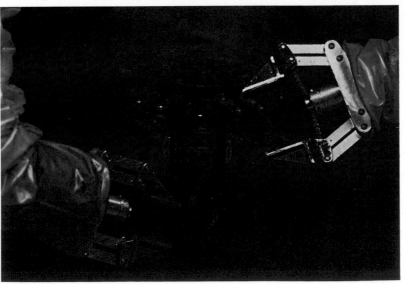

©JOHN MARMARAS 1979

©MARTIN ROGERS 1979

WOODFIN CAMP AND ASSOCIATES
415 Madison Avenue
New York, New York 10017
(212) 355-1855
Cable: Campfoto, New York
Telex: 428788 Campfot

Woodfin Camp, Incorporated
925½ F Street, N.W.
Washington, D.C. 20004
(202) 638-5705
Cable: Campfoto, Washington, D.C.

Associate offices in London, Paris, Hamburg, Milan, and Tokyo.

We represent 25 major photographers around the world.
Contact us for comprehensive stock files or original assignment work.

©CRAIG AURNESS 1979

©JAMES SUGAR 1979

©TIMOTHY EAGAN 1979

©GEORGE HERBEN 1979

©MARTIN ROGERS 1979

THE IMAGE BANK

You'll see this symbol throughout
this book.

In every case, it identifies a photographer
represented by The Image Bank.

In every case, it means that the actual
images on the page are available through
each of our offices.

We feel these photographers and their
images speak for themselves.

Quite simply, the finest stock
photography in the world . . . throughout
the world.

THE IMAGE BANK

An international network of photographic talent providing existing and assignment photography and related services to the advertising, corporate and editorial communities.

UNITED STATES

NEW YORK
The Image Bank
633 Third Avenue
New York City 10017
Telephone: 212-371-3636
Telex: 42-93-80 IMAGE

CHICAGO
The Image Bank of Chicago
510 North Dearborn
Chicago, Illinois 60610
Telephone: 312-329-1818

SAN FRANCISCO
The Image Bank West
The Icehouse/Suite 522
151 Union Street
San Francisco,
California 94111
Telephone: (415) 398-2242
Telex: 910 3727201

WASHINGTON, D.C.
The Image Bank of Washington
3203 Grace Street, N.E.
Washington, D.C. 20007
Telephone: 202-331-7733

MEXICO

The Image Bank de Mexico
Rio Sena, 70
Mexico City 5, D.F. Mexico
Telephone: 905-514-0379

CANADA

MONTREAL
The Image Bank of Canada
231 St. Jacques Street
Montreal, Quebec H2Y 1M6
Telephone: (514) 282 2438
Telex: 05 24177

TORONTO
The Image Bank of Canada
2 Carlton Street/Suite 901
Toronto, Ontario
Canada M5B 1J3
Telephone: (416) 362-1267
Telex: 06-22675

EUROPE

ENGLAND
TIB London
8 Charing Cross Road
London W.C. 2, England
Telephone: (1) 348-9685

FRANCE
The Image Bank France
130, Rue Reaumur
75002 Paris
France
Telephone: 508-8698/236-7716
Telex: 842-212687

ITALY
The Image Bank of Italy
Via Carducci, 34
20123 Milano
Italy
Telephone: 02-803-964

SPAIN
The Image Bank España
Alberto Aguilera, 22
Madrid 15, Spain
Telephone: (1) 446-7706/447-4297
Telex: 43060 RA E

WEST GERMANY
The Image Bank of Germany
Schrammsweg 25
2 Hamburg 20
West Germany
Telephone: 40-472004
Telex: 841-2174871

JAPAN

The Image Bank of Japan
55-1 Kanda-Jimbocho,
Chiyoda-ku
Tokyo, 101, Japan
Telephone: 03-2951940
Telex: 781-24447

SOUTH AMERICA

RIO DE JANEIRO
The Image Bank do Brasil
Avenida Presidente Antonio Carlos 54, 202-203
Rio de Janeiro
Brazil
Telephone: 21-232-1035
Telex: 391-2123852

SAO PAULO
The Image Bank do Brasil
Avenida Paulista 807/1602-1603
Sao Paulo
Brazil
Telephone: (11) 285-6319
Telex: 391-2123852

PORTO ALEGRE
The Image Bank do Brasil
Rua Cel Bordini 249
Porto Alegre, Brazil
Telephone: 512-22-72-66
Telex: 391-2123852

**Offices opening
in early 1980 include
the Scandinavian countries,
Finland,
the Benelux countries.**

*Representing exclusively the Gruner +Jahr Fotoservice Library
in association with G +J Images, Inc.*

**Winner of The Advertising Club of New York's
Andy Award of Merit. Winner of The International
Film and Television Festival's Gold Medal.**

INDEX

TV, FILM AND VIDEO

Brady, Mathew 11
31 West 27th Street
New York, New York 10001
(212) 683-6060

Edstan Productions 12
240 Madison Avenue
New York, New York 10016
(212) 686-3666

Gluck Durham Films 13
108 Fifth Avenue
New York, New York 10011
(212) BU 8-6394

Marco, Phil 15, 119
104 Fifth Avenue
New York, New York 10011
(212) 929-8082

Metzner Productions, Jeffrey 17
295 Fifth Avenue
New York, New York 10016
(212) 532-9670

Seawell, Harry 18
Suite 3
215 11th Street
Parkersburg, W. Virginia 26101
(304) 485-4481

Stahl Animated, Al 20
1600 Broadway
New York, New York 10019
(212) 265-2942

ILLUSTRATION AND GRAPHIC DESIGN

Fernandes, Stanislaw 23
35 East 12th Street
New York, New York 10003
(212) 533-2648

Girvin, Tim 24
Suite 418
911 Western Avenue
Seattle, Washington 98104
(206) 623-7918

Goldstein, Howard 25
7031 Aldea Avenue
Van Nuys, California 91406
(213) 987-2837

Katz, Les 26
367 Sackett Street
Brooklyn, New York 11231
(212) 625-4741

Lakich, Lili 27
8201 West 3rd
Los Angeles, California 90046
(213) 653-8669

Bernhardt Fudyma 28
133 East 36th Street
New York, New York 10016
(212) 889-9337

Besalel, Ely 30
235 East 49th Street
New York, New York 10017
(212) 759-7820

Dyer, Rod 31
5550 Wilshire Boulevard
Los Angeles, California 90004
(213) 937-4100

Follis, John & Associates 32
2124 Venice Boulevard
Los Angeles, California 90006
(213) 735-1283

The Graphic Expression 33
150 East 58th Street
New York, New York 10022
(212) 759-7788

Gribbitt! Ltd., 34
5419 Sunset Boulevard
Los Angeles, California 90027
(213) 462-7362

Heiney, John & Associates 35
200 East 33rd Street
New York, New York 10016
(212) 686-1121

Mueller & Wister 36
Suite 607
1211 Chestnut Street
Philadelphia, Pennsylvania 19107
(215) 568-7260

Overlock Howe & Co 37
915 Olive Street
St. Louis, Missouri 63101
(314) 241-8640

Ridgeway Zaklin & Associates 38
Suite 305
99 Kinderkamack Road
Westwood, New Jersey 07675
(201) 664-4543

Robertz Design Co 40
Suite 529
111 East Wacker
Chicago, Illinois 60601
(312) 861-0060

Studio Artists 41
638 South Van Ness Avenue
Los Angeles, California 90005
(213) 382-6281

Unigraphics 42
350 Pacific Street
San Francisco, California 94111
(415) 398-8232

Wardell–Berger Design 43
1450 Broadway
New York, New York 10018
(212) 398-9355

White Design, Ken 44
111 Tamarind Avenue
Los Angeles, California 90038
(213) 467-4681

PHOTOGRAPHY

Allan, Larry 223
P.O. Box 99585
San Diego, California 92109
(714) 270-9549

Amrine, Jamie 47
45 West 11th Street
New York, New York 10011
(212) 243-2178

Arakawa, Nobu 48
40 East 21st Street
New York, New York 10010
(212) 475-0206

Arndt & Berthiaume 193
1008 Nicollet Mall
Minneapolis, Minnesota 55403
(612) 338-1984

Arnesen, Erik 224
11 Zoe Street
San Francisco, California 94107
(415) 495-5366

Arnold 225
1379 Natoma Street
San Francisco, California 94103
(415) 621-6161

Ashley, Constance 211
2024 Farrington
Dallas, Texas 75207
(214) 747-2501

Avedis 49
381 Park Avenue South
New York, New York 10016
(212) 685-5888

Azzi, Robert 50
c/o Woodfin Camp
415 Madison Avenue
New York, New York 10017
(212) 355-1855

Bennett, Philip 51
1181 Broadway
New York, New York 10001
(212) 683-3906

Bergman, Alan 226
5478 Wilshire Boulevard
Los Angeles, California 90036
(213) 935-2744

Bevilacqua 52
202 East 42nd Street
New York, New York 10017
(212) 490-0355

Biggs, Ken 227
1147 North Hudson
Los Angeles, California 90038
(213) 462-7739

Blackman, Barry M. 53
(212) 686-4915

Blake, Mike 165
77 North Washington Street
Boston, Massachusetts 02114
(617) 523-3730

Blakeley, Jim 228
520 Bryant Street
San Francisco, California 94107
(415) 495-5100

Bordnick, Barbara 55
39 East 19th Street
New York, New York 10003
(212) 533-1180

Borum, Michael 183
623 Sixth Avenue South
Nashville, Tennessee 37203
(615) 259-9750

Brignolo, Joseph 56
RD #1 Box 121
Oxford Springs Road
Chester, New York 10918
(914) 496-4453

Britt, Jim 229
140 North La Brea
Los Angeles, California 90036
(213) 936-3131

Brown, Ed 58
100 West 92nd Street
New York, New York 10025
(212) 580-2483

Brown, Nancy 59
6 West 20th Street
New York, New York 10011
(212) 675-8067

Bruton, Jon 194
3838 West Pine
St. Louis, Missouri 63108
(314) 533-6665

Bryson, John 60
12 East 62nd Street
New York, New York 10021
(212) 755-1321
(213) 456-6170

von dem Bussche, Wolf 62, 230
7144 Norfolk Road
Berkeley, California 94705
(415) 845-2448

Carofano, Ray 231
1011¼ West 190th Street
Gardena, California 90248
(213) 515-0310

Carroll, Don 63
33 East 60th Street
New York, New York 10022
(212) 371-3648

Chandler, Ralph 232
1111 North Tamarind
Los Angeles, California 90038
(213) 469-6205

Chandoha, Walter 64
RD #1 P.O. Box 287
Annandale, New Jersey 08801
(201) 782-3666

Chen, James 233
1917 Anacapa Street
Santa Barbara, California 93101
(805) 965-5849

Cobb, Jan 66
381 Park Avenue South
New York, New York 10016
(212) 889-2257

Cochran, George 67
381 Park Avenue South
New York, New York 10016
(212) 689-9054

Collison, James 235
3737 Weslin Avenue
Sherman Oaks, California 91403
(213) 902-0770

Couzens, Larry 68
124 East 27th Street
New York, New York 10016
(212) 684-6585

Cowan, Ralph 195
869 North Dearborn
Chicago, Illinois 60610
(312) 787-1316

Cross/Francesca 69
502 East 88th Street
New York, New York 10028
(212) 988-8516

Davidson, Darwin K. 70
32 Bank Street
New York, New York 10014
(212) 242-0095

Day, Bob 71
29 East 19th Street
New York, New York 10003
(212) 475-7387

deGennaro, George 236
902 South Norton Avenue
Los Angeles, California 90019
(213) 935-5179

deLespinasse, Hank 238
P.O. Box 14061
Las Vegas, Nevada 89114
(702) 361-6628

De Lessio, Len 72
110 East 23rd Street
New York, New York 10010
(212) 254-4620

DeScoise, Nicholas 212
Studio #2
2700 Arapahoe Street
Denver, Colorado 80205
(303) 455-6315

DeVito, Bart 73
404 Park Avenue South
New York, New York 10016
(212) 889-9670

Doubilet, David 74
1040 Park Avenue
New York, New York 10028
(212) 348-5011

Dull, Ed 239
1745 N.W. Marshall
Portland, Oregon 97209
(503) 224-3754

Dunbar, Clark 240
Suite C
922 San Leandro Avenue
Mountainview, California 94043
(415) 964-4225

Dunn, Phoebe 75
20 Silvermine Road
New Canaan, Connecticut 06840
(203) 966-9791

Durrance II, Dick 166
Dolphin Ledge
Rockport, Maine 04856
(212) 355-1550

Eagan, Timothy 76
39 East 12th Street
New York, New York 10003
(212) 777-9210

Eisman, Jamie 167
518 South Fourth Street
Philadelphia, Pennsylvania 19147
(215) 922-7652

Everett, Michael 77
16 East 17th Street
New York, New York 10003
(212) 929-4461

Faustino 184
P.O. Box 1252
Coral Gables, Florida 33134
(305) 854-4275

Fraser, Douglas 78
45 East 34th Street
New York, New York 10016
(212) 689-8853

AMERICAN SHOWCASE
OF PHOTOGRAPHY ILLUSTRATION AND GRAPHIC DESIGN
AND TYPOGRAPHY
PASTORE DE PAMPHILIS RAMPONE

THIS ENTIRE 1980 ISSUE OF AMERICAN SHOWCASE WAS SET BY PASTORE DE PAMPHILIS RAMPONE/COMPUTER TYPOGRAPHERS 145 EAST 32ND STREET NEW YORK 10016/PHONE (212) 889-2221 PHOTOMECHANICALS/VIP/TYPOSITOR AND COLOR PROOFING

AMERICANSHOWCASE
VOLUME3

Printed in Japan

by

DAI NIPPON PRINTING CO., LTD.

you can see from this book

as recognized by quality book publishers

in the u.s. and europe as well as in japan

what these three lines mean

for

your next book

DAI NIPPON
printing co., ltd.
International Sales Division

1-12 Ichigaya Kagacho
Shinjuku-ku, Tokyo, Japan
Telephone: 03-266-3301
Telex: J22737 DNPRINT TOKYO

New York   San Francisco   Dusseldorf   London   Sydney   Hong Kong   Jakarta   Singapore

The American Edition
Subscribe
Six issues for $25
Twelve issues for $45
ZOOM USA MAGAZINE INC.
Box 2225
Grand Central Station
New York City 10017

INDEX

STOCK PHOTOGRAPHY

TO EXPAND YOUR CREATIVE MUSCLE, EXERCISE YOUR CREATIVE OPTIONS

One summer day on a beach many years ago, a bully kicked sand into the eyes of a scrawny post-pubescent. Half the size of his tormentor, this young 97-pound weakling, so the legend goes, was powerless to retaliate. But he had learned his lesson. History has failed to record the name of the beach or the bully. But years later, Charles Atlas was the strongest man in the world, pulling locomotives–if not freight trains –singlehandedly, in demonstrations of his awesome strength. How did that skinny, timorous, little kid become the world's strongest man? It was more than spinach. One can be sure he used every useful resource available.

The moral of this story is clear: to become a creative Charles Atlas, you, too, must use every resource at your disposal. Don't let other creative people kick sand in your eyes.

Have you ever dreamed of turning the world on end...expressing your visions with new depth and impact...transforming the conventional into exciting adventures in color, texture, mood?

The Nikon F2A is designed to help you realize your creative capabilities. As it does daily, for an overwhelming majority of 35mm professionals. And for reasons that are anything but abstract.

Take the fascinating world of multi-image photography. The matchless accuracy of the Nikon F2A viewfinder lets you compose with absolute confidence, aided by the reliability of Nikon center-weighted exposure control. And, the precise F2A registration assures each image appears exactly where you planned.

This confidence is yours with any of 6 interchangeable viewfinders. With any of 21 finder screens. With 2 high-performance motor drives: the new, lower-cost MD-3 that puts single shots and continuous sequences at up to 4 frames per second at your command, and the legendary MD-2 with power rewind and 5 fps speed. Even with bulk-film and large-format camera backs.

And, for the most dramatic perspectives in 35mm photography, every F2A accepts the nearly 60 Nikkor lenses from 6mm through 2000mm. Optics unrivalled in quality and variety – calculated to inspire your imagination as no others can.

There are countless reasons why creative photography acquires new meaning with the Nikon F2A. Your Nikon dealer will help you find them. Look for him in the Yellow Pages. And, be sure to inquire about the traveling Nikon School of Photography. Or write to Dept. N-38, Nikon Inc., Garden City, New York 11530. Subsidiary of Ehrenreich Photo-Optical Industries, Inc. EPOi (In Canada: Nikon Division, Anglophoto, Ltd., P.Q.)

© Nikon Inc. 1978

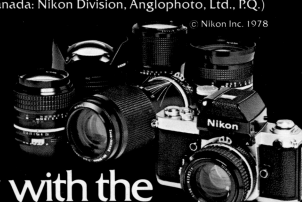

Abstract photography with the Confidence of Nikon